Michigan
ALUMNUS

MAY/JUNE 1989

UNIVERSITY OF
MICHIGAN
NATIONAL CHAMPIONSHIP

1989

University Of
Michigan
National Championship

1989

Acknowledgements ————————————

UMI Publications, Inc. is proud to present the University of Michigan National Championship 1989. This team led by Glen Rice and a new young coach, Steve Fisher, accomplished the impossible dream; winning the NCAA championship.

We would like to thank all the people who made this book possible. First of all Mr. Bo Shembechler, Mr. Jack Weidenbach, Mr. Bruce Madej, Mr. Kennan Delaney, and Mr. Mike Murray. Our thanks also go to all the rest of the people in the athletic department who made this project so enjoyable.

This book was written by three people. Mr. Steve Kornacki of the Detroit Free Press, Mr. Bob Wojnowski of the Detroit News, and Mr. Mike Murray from the University of Michigan. They were there to record all the action.

Most of the photography in this book was the work of Mr. Per Kjeldsen of the University of Michigan and the photo department of the Detroit News. We also went to Sports Illustrated and Wide World Photos to attain the best possible photos for this book.

The Detroit News and The Detroit Free Press and the Sports Information Department deserve extra special thanks for allowing Bob, Mike, and Steve to add this project to their already busy schedules.

Finally we would like to thank the most important people of all: THE TEAM. This book is for them and about them.

Please enjoy.

Photo credits: Per Kjeldson — 39, 40, 41, 42, 43, 44, 45, 46, 47, 48, 49, 51, 52, 53, 55, 57, 59, 62, 65, 67, 68, 69, 98, 99, 100, 101, 102, 103, 104, 105; Wide World Photos — 50; Jeanette Bartz (Detroit News) — 54; Jay Salvo — 56; Bob Mitchell — 58; Photographic Service, Univ. of Iowa — 60; S.R. Smith — 61; Sports Info-Indiana Univ. — 63 Michael S. Green (Detroit News) — 64; Kirthmon Dozier (Detroit News) — 66, 70, 71, 72, 73, 76, 77, 78, 79, 80, 81, 82, 83, 84, 85, 86, 87, 88, 89, 90, 91, 92, 93, 94, 95, 96, 97; Sports Illustrated — 107, 108, 109; Detroit Free Press — 110, 111, 112, 113, 114, 115; Detroit News — 116, 117; Ann Arbor News — 118, 119, 120, 121. NCAA Program Cover, reprinted by permission of the NCAA and Host Communications, Lexington, KY. Any ommission of a photo credit is unintentional. We would like to thank all the people who submitted photographs, including: Mr. Chante Brockway, Mr. Dan Grogan, Mr. Hugh Morton, and Mr. Bill Woods.

Michigan National Championship staff, Ivan Mothershead, Publisher; Charlie Keiger, Associate Publisher; Smith Barrier, Senior Editor; Merry Schoonmaker, Associate Editor; Jay Epping, Pam Reese, Scott Walden, Assistant Editors; Composition by R.J. Publishing Co., Charlotte, N.C.

Table of Contents _____

Foreword

Friends,

When you think of The University of Michigan, you think of an academic institution of great international importance and prestige. At the same time, we have always taken great pride in our equally outstanding tradition of athletic excellence. Michigan's storied past has played a significant role in the development of intercollegiate athletics in this country. The NCAA history books include the likes of Fielding H. Yost's "Point-a-Minute" teams, Fritz Crisler's many innovations, and a seemingly endless list of hockey, tennis and swimming championships.

It's time to enter a new chapter about the 1988-89 Michigan basketball team.

Under tremendous adversity, with an interim coach thrown into the helm just days before the national tournament began, this basketball team accomplished what few could have ever expected — they won it all. With their backs against the wall, this courageous group of young men and coaches discovered how dedication, desire and hard work can turn the odds in your favor.

There is a credo we live by here in Ann Arbor. It goes as follows:

"What the mind can conceive and believe, the body can achieve. And those who stay will be champions."

It was a long and sometimes very difficult season for these Wolverines. They opened the campaign with the Maui Classic championship. They slumped a bit at mid-season, then caught their stride as the year wore on. The players and staff alike agreed — this was a team on a mission. This book chronicles that mission, capturing many of the frustrations and joys of a very special season.

Read and enjoy.

Bo Schembechler
Director of Intercollegiate Athletics
The University of Michigan

Head Coach Steve Fisher

Much has been said about Steve Fisher's epic drama, "The Dream."

"The Dream" features his chance to serve as interim head coach for the Michigan Wolverines.

"The Dream" finds U-M beating Seton Hall for the National Championship.

"The Dream" continues with Bo Schembechler offering Fisher the head coaching job on a permanent basis.

"The Dream" also has a scene with Fisher in the White House shaking hands with President George Bush.

But, if you want to give Fisher nightmares, just mention Bloom High School.

Bloom High School? In his earlier days as a head coach at Rich East High School in Illinois, Fisher spent a good part of eight years trying to foil Bloom HS in the state tournament. Nothing ever worked.

"When I look back on it, I can vividly remember doing whatever we could to beat them," said Fisher. "We were always in the games, but somehow, Bloom always seemed to manage to pull out the win.

Fisher smiled. "I think our Michigan team used the same strategy."

Twenty years after accepting the assistant varsity basketball coach, head tennis coach and math teaching positions at Rich East, Steve Fisher is the head coach of the defending national champion Michigan Wolverines. Yet, despite two full decades in the profession, Fisher is still considered a rookie coach by many.

Anyone familiar with Fisher knows that he has paid his dues.

"My first coach was my dad (Howard), and I think he was the one that had the greatest influence in my wanting to become a coach," Fisher recalls. "He coached me at St. Mary's Grade School in Herrin, a small community in southern Illinois.

"My parents provided our whole family with great opportunities and were tremendously supportive," Fisher continued. "My dad had the best backyard basketball court in town and we played every day, all year long.

"I owe as much to him as to anyone for the success I've had in my career."

"By the time I got to high school, I was a pretty good player, and I had my sights set on a basketball scholarship at Missouri," continued Fisher. "But I suffered a serious knee injury in my senior year, and Missouri was out the window. So I ended up playing at Illinois State, which is a great school, on a Teacher-Education Scholarship."

Due primarily to the knee injury, Fisher saw limited playing time in his four seasons at Illinois State. "I started just two games in my career there," Fisher said, chuckling. "I think my career-high was just seven points. As you can see, that is where I first learned about life on the bench."

After earning his B.S. in 1967, Fisher joined the ISU staff as a graduate assistant while pursuing his Master's Degree. That year, Fisher served as an assistant to both the freshman basketball team and varsity tennis team.

Tennis? "I had never had any experience in tennis, but in those days, staffs were small and you had to wear a lot of hats," he explains. "Actually, I did little more than to drive the team to their meets and run errands like that."

Fisher received his Master's in '68 and was hired as an assistant coach by Les Wothke at Rich East High School. "It's funny, but because of my 'experience' at Illinois State, Rich East also made me the head tennis coach, in addition to teaching math," Fisher said. "Years later, I was also asked to teach P.E. and driver's education." (It should be noted that as tennis coach, Fisher led Rich East to two conference championships and a district title.)

After three years as assistant, Fisher assumed the role of head varsity basketball coach in 1971, a position he held for eight seasons. During his tenure, his teams compiled an impressive 141-70 record and won four conference championships. He also produced three all-state players on his way to becoming the winningest coach in the history of the school.

Fisher met his bride-to-be while teaching at Rich East, and in August of 1974, Steve and Angie were married. Four years later, the first of their two sons, Mark, was born.

In May of 1979, Wothke, then the head coach at Western Michigan, gave Fisher the opportunity to join the Broncos' staff. Fisher accepted and spent three seasons in Kalamazoo. During his second year with the team, WMU won the Mid-American Conference crown.

In 1982, Fisher moved to Ann Arbor replacing Don Sicko as assistant coach of the Wolverines. "Bill Frieder gave me a great opportunity here, and I have always been appreciative of that," said Fisher. During his seven seasons as assistant, Fisher shouldered many of the bench-coaching responsibilities, as well as running many practices and scouting upcoming opponents.

Frieder accepted the head coaching post at Arizona State just before the '89 tourney began, and that was when Athletic Director Bo Schembechler gave Fisher his once-in-a-lifetime chance.

As history will record, Fisher made the most of the opportunity, leading the Wolverines to their first National Championship and garnering the head coaching job on a permanent basis.

Fisher has adjusted nicely to his new role with the Michigan program. "There are many more demands placed on the head coach in terms of administrative duties and in dealing with the media and public," Fisher explained, "but at least it is a program I have been very familiar with, and that has helped to make a very smooth transition."

Fisher's first thoughts after winning the National Championship? "To tell you the truth, I think it's going to be some time before I realize the significance of what we've accomplished," said Fisher. "My initial concern immediately after we won it was to find my family. I wanted to share that special moment with them, so I just hoped they could make their way down to the court for the celebration."

The Fishers — Steve, Angie, Mark and Jonathan — did celebrate that victory together, joining the players and staff for one shining moment.

Bloom High School? Fisher can now put that behind him, thank you.

And back home in Herrin, Steve Fisher's first mentor watched the gathering with a smile.

Nice job, coach.

STEVE FISHER'S ADDRESS
PRESS CONFERENCE ANNOUNCING HIS APPOINTMENT AS HEAD COACH
MONDAY, APRIL 10, 1989

> *"To have an opportunity to be the head basketball coach at such a prestigious academic-athletic institution as the University of Michigan defies description."*

"I still don't want to wake up. This for Steve Fisher is the culmination of a dream come true. To have an opportunity to be the head basketball coach at such a prestigious academic-athletic institution as the University of Michigan defies description. There is no finer job in America. I know that. I think many of you know that. I'm pleased and proud to have been selected by Bo and his staff and President Duderstadt to head up this University of Michigan basketball program. I've also been around enough to know that the success that our team had in the NCAA Tournament was a significant factor in Steve Fisher being named. I went from someone who very few people knew, and even those who knew me very few knew well, to someone that everyone in America felt they knew. For that, I'm tremendously indebted to our players. You can punch all the buttons, but if you don't have a Glen Rice, or Rumeal Robinson, or Terry Mills, or a Mike Griffin, Mark Hughes, etc. to do what they did, who knows if I would have had the opportunity to be sitting in front of you right now.

"I guess the first formal announcement would be that I feel very pleased and excited to let everyone know that Mike Boyd will remain at Michigan. He will be the number one head assistant at the University of Michigan. In addition to that, Brian Dutcher will move up to a full-time position in our program. I think these two men have contributed greatly to the success we've had. Mike Boyd is highly regarded around the country not only as a recruiter but also as a teacher, quality coach, and someone who parents will relate to and want their sons to play for. I feel fortunate that he is going to remain with our staff. Brian Dutcher is a young coach who reminds me of a lot of the young coaches that have gone on 10 or 11 years after they got a chance to become exceptional head coaches. When you get to know Brian, you'll also be pleased and excited that he is part of our staff.

"I feel that I owe a lot of people a debt of gratitude. I mentioned our players. I also feel that Bo put a lot of faith in me when he said 'Fisher you are the guy who's going to run this program. I know you can do it.' "

"I know that I will give everyone, especially Bo — but everyone, the type of program that you can be proud of. We will emphasize a great many things. Winning will be one of those. We will pride ourselves on continuing to be successful on that basketball floor. I also know that national championships are few and far between for any of us. We were blessed, lucky, good, all that wrapped into one to allow that to happen this year. It may never happen again. But it won't happen from lack of effort, lack of heart, or determination from any of us from the coaching staff right down through the players. We will have that kind of a program.

"We will also have the type of program that will emphasize the student-athlete. We will continue to recruit the type of young men that not only our faculty, students, and alumni can be proud of, but that each and every person in this state and country who follows Michigan basketball will say, 'that is a class team.' The way they carry themselves both on and off the floor will be representative of the way that I would want my son to carry himself. I can commit that to all of you.

"Without further adieu, I would just like to graciously accept this new challenge. I'm going to wear this mantle proudly and continue to roll up my sleeves and go to work. Recruiting is important, so we have to be sure we continue to recruit good players, and when we get them here we have to work with them and help make them better in every regard. Above all else, when they leave here we want them to leave as Michigan men. We want them to leave proud and happy for the type of experience that they had here and they will be the best possible recruiters for this athletic program and university that we could have. We want them to go back and tell their families and friends that they made the right decision for all the right reasons and that it was a great, great experience."

Assistant Coach
Mike Boyd _____

Many see him strictly as one of the nation's premier recruiters. For the past 10 years, players such as Tim McCormick, Roy Tarpley, Gary Grant, and Glen Rice have certainly supported that assumption. During that time span, the Michigan basketball program has captured two Big Ten titles, one NIT crown and the '89 National Championship.

And sure, Boyd probably knows more tricks of the trade than nearly any other recruiter.

For example, when headed off to a long recruiting trip, Boyd packs two suitcases. "I make my travel arrangements so that I always have a quick stop in Detroit," explains the 42-year-old Boyd. "I take one bag with me and leave the other in my car at the airport parking garage. Then after about a week of living out of that suitcase, I fly back into Detroit, switch bags, and then I'm ready to go for another week or so."

Granted, it's that kind of savvy and relentless approach that has made Mike Boyd a top-notch recruiter. But what many people don't know is that Boyd is also an outstanding all-around coach. When he's off the recruiting trail, the New Castle, IN, native tutors with Michigan's big men during practice. In addition, Boyd plays a major role in implementing the Michigan offense each fall.

"Mike's an unsung hero in many regards because all people seem to know about him is that he's a great recruiter," said head coach Steve Fisher. "He is a great recruiter. But at the same time, he does many more things for this basketball program, and that is what makes him such an important member of our staff."

Boyd's interest in basketball dates back to his grade school days when he starred in hoops, football and track. Boyd was a prep standout in all three sports, but an ankle injury as a senior curbed his gridiron career, at least temporarily. Boyd bounced back in time to earn a basketball scholarship from Northern Michigan.

Boyd played for four years under former NBA coach Stan Albeck and the late Glen Brown, twice leading the team in rebounding and serving as captain his senior year. With his basketball eligibility expired, Boyd decided to play football as a fifth-year student, and established 19 receiving records in his only season with the NMU gridders. Boyd earned his B.S. from Northern Michigan in 1970.

After a stint in semi-professional football, Boyd accepted a position at General Motors Institute as Admissions Counselor and Recruiter. While in Flint, he got his first taste of national championship glory.

"I played for a team called Julie's Pawn Shop in the Flint city league," Boyd explained. "We had a great season in 1974, and at the end of the season, we traveled to Springfield (MA) and won the national amateur championship."

Shortly after winning that title, Boyd moved to Kent State where he served for five seasons as an assistant coach. During the last half of the '76 season, Boyd filled-in as interim head coach for a 16-game span. Boyd also made the most of his stay at KSU and earned his Master's Degree in 1978.

In 1979, Boyd was hired by Johnny Orr to join the Michigan basketball staff. "Orr had trouble getting in touch with me to offer the job, because I was out recruiting at the time and, well, I was spending a lot of time on the road," Boyd said.

And that's exactly why Orr wanted Boyd.

Away from the game, Boyd has many interests. "Sometimes you have to get away from it, because I like to spend a lot of time with my family," Boyd said. "I pride myself on being able to leave basketball at the court and concentrate on other things I enjoy."

One of those other things is golf, a sport Boyd has refined to the point where he is considering joining the Seniors' Tour after retirement.

Boyd also enjoys putting together model cars, a hobby that has produced some sleek replicas during the last eight years.

But his latest — and perhaps most enjoyable — pastime has been cycling. "I like it because it's a good workout, and I can share the experience with my wife, Michelle," said Boyd.

Mike and his Michelle reside in Ann Arbor with their three children, Stephani, Michael, Jr., and Matt. Mike's family has always known what few others have had the chance to discover.

There's a lot more to Mike Boyd than meets the eye.

Assistant Coach
Brian Dutcher

Fifteen years ago, the kid would hang-out at Crisler Arena with his dad. While the Michigan team practiced at one end of the court, the seventh-grader would shoot jumpers and layups at the other end, dreaming — as all kids dream — about winning the big game on a thrilling last-second shot. The fantasy would continue until, alas, the team broke into a full-court scrimmage. His dream would have to wait until tomorrow.

For Brian Dutcher, "tomorrow" came in 1989.

Dutcher, in his first season as a Michigan assistant coach, helped guide the Wolverines to the National Basketball Championship. But this was not his first experience with the U-M program. From 1972 through 1975, Brian's father, Jim, served as an assistant to Johnny Orr. That was when Brian got his first taste of Michigan and Big Ten basketball.

"I was a gym rat," says Dutcher of his younger days. "I would always come over to practice with my dad, shoot baskets, then raid the concession stands for whatever popcorn and ice cream we could find.

"For a junior high kid growing up in the Ann Arbor area, it was the best of all possible worlds."

The Dutchers moved to Minnesota in 1975 when Jim was offered the head coaching job with the Golden Gophers. Upon graduation from high school, Brian enrolled at Minnesota and joined the varsity basketball staff.

"I was officially a 'student assistant' and helped the team in any way I could," Dutcher said. "I shot game films for four years, traveled with the team, and sat in with the coaching staff while breaking down the game films. The experience was terrific. That's when I knew that I wanted to go into coaching."

After graduation, Dutcher taught and coached basketball at Apple Valley (MN) High School for one year, then joined Lou Henson's staff at the University of Illinois as a graduate assistant. His first season at Illinois was one Dutcher will never forget.

"The team capped the year by winning the Big Ten title, which was great," says Dutcher, "and I capped the year by getting married."

Brian and his new bride, Jan, had met while undergrads at Minnesota. "We were married on 8/4/84 . . . it's one of the few dates I've ever remembered," Dutcher said with a smile.

In 1985, Dutcher was hired on as a full-time assistant at South Dakota State where he served for three seasons before coming to Ann Arbor. Dutcher welcomed the chance to return to the area, this time with a wife and young daughter (Erin) alongside him.

"I've had the opportunity to learn from several top coaches," Dutcher said. "But I think I probably learned the most from my dad. I think my coaching style more closely matches his, and so I have confidence in my abilities."

When Bill Frieder left the Michigan staff prior to the '89 tournament, Dutcher assumed a much greater role in terms of game preparation. Coach Steve Fisher was the first to notice Dutcher's performance and commitment. "We were short-staffed during the tournament, so we all had to take on additional responsibilities," Fisher said. "Brian did a tremendous job of working with our kids, studying game films, and scouting the other teams.

"Brian played as great a role as anyone in the success we enjoyed in the tournament."

And to Dutcher, winning the national title has been the highlight of his brief, if promising, career.

"Most coaches go their whole lives without winning it, but I was fortunate enough to be in the right place at the right time," Dutcher said. "Winning it all was like a dream."

Indeed, the kind of dream any gym rat could appreciate.

Trainer
Dan Minert

If they had opened the team's MVP ballotting to include the entire staff, Dan Minert might have given Glen Rice a run for his money. Minert has concluded his seventh lucky season with the Wolverine cagers, and those in the basketball program feel fortunate to have Minert involved.

"Danny's a professional in everything he does," says head coach Steve Fisher. "You could use any number of words to describe him — thorough, diligent, dedicated, loyal. There is no way to measure his importance to the program."

The Wolverines were beset by a series of ailments during the championship season. From sore backs and injured knees to twisted ankles and the flu, Minert was always ready.

A native of South Haven, MI, Minert worked with the Wolverine hockey team as an undergraduate and then joined the Michigan staff full-time as the head trainer for the U-M icers for three seasons.

He earned two degrees at Michigan including his master's degree in 1977. He was athletic trainer at Brighton High School from 1972 until 1980 when he returned to Michigan.

Dan is a member of the National Athletic Trainers Association and serves on the medical staff of the Michigan State Special Olympics.

Minert is married to the former Elizabeth Hary. They have two daughters, Hilary, 14, and Lauren, 11, and reside in Brighton.

Equipment Manager
Bob Bland

The team had plenty of free time at the Maui Classic. After a heated practice each morning, coaches and players alike could be found lounging by the hot tub or strolling the white sand beaches.

For Bob Bland, however, there was work to be done. Uniforms had to be laundered, jerseys needed folding, socks needed sorting — it's the kind of unglamourous work that never makes headlines but must get done. And you could always count on Bob Bland to do it.

Bland has distinguished himself in his two seasons with the Michigan cagers. He greets every request with a smile and then tackles each task with a sense of urgency, because Bland realizes his importance to the basketball program.

The Kilgore, Ohio, native is also the assistant to head football equipment manager Jon Falk and assists with the day-to-day equipment operations of the Michigan athletic program.

Bland received his B.A. from Otterbein College in 1984 where he also served as the student manager for the Cardinals' football, basketball and baseball teams. Bland was head equipment manager at Otterbein until coming to Michigan in 1987. He is also a member of the Athletic Equipment Managers Association.

Bob lives in Ann Arbor with his wife, Mary Jane, and their children, Jennifer and Brian.

Graduate Assistant Coach
Joe Czupek

For Joe Czupek, timing was everything.

He had proven himself for four years as a student manager with the Michigan basketball team when the position of Graduate Assistant Coach became available in 1988. Czupek jumped at the opportunity and made the most of it, serving as a capable aide who made the squad's travel arrangements as well as bench coaching duties and assorted administrative responsibilities. Indeed, Czupek's eye for detail proved valuable to the Wolverines in 89.

Czupek, nicknamed 'Smoke', earned his B.A. in Sports Management and Communication through the Michigan School of Physical Education in 1988.

The Chicago, IL, native moved on to join the Arizona State basketball staff after the Wolverines won the National Championship. There he hopes to continue to pursue a Master's degree in Policy and Administration.

Administrative Personnel

Bo Schembechler
Athletic Director

Jack Weidenbach
Senior Associate Director

Don Lund
Associate Director

Phyllis Ocker
Associate Director

Fritz Seyferth
Associate Director

Will Perry
Assistant Director

Bob DeCarolis
Assistant Director

Al Renfrew
Assistant Director

Bruce Madej
Assistant Director

Gwen Cruzat
Faculty Representative

Doug Kahn
Faculty Representative

Jeff Long
Administrative Assistant

Keenan Delaney
Promotions Director

Mike Murray
Assistant Public Relations

Jody Humphries
Assistant Public Relations

Steve Lambright
Assistant Ticket Manager

Glen Rice

6-7, 215 pounds, senior, Flint, MI

To say Glen Rice had a good tournament is a lot like saying Moses took a message. Rice didn't have just a good tournament, he had the best tournament — as in, the best tournament ever.

Numbers don't lie . . .

• During Michigan's six NCAA contests, Rice scored (in order) 23, 36, 34, 32, 28 and 31 points.

• His 184 tournament points broke Bill Bradley's (Princeton, '65) mark of 177. Rice also set tourney records for total FG's (75) and 3-point FG's (27).

• Rice shot 57.3% from the field during the NCAA's and an amazing 55.1% (27-49) from three-point range.

• Rice was named Most Outstanding Player of both the Southeast Regional and the NCAA Final Four.

While it would be impossible to list all of Rice's accomplishments in this space, it would be equally difficult to describe his importance to the 1988-89 Michigan team.

"Our first option all season long was Glen Rice," said head coach Steve Fisher. "He did an incredible job for us all year long. But when the tournament rolled around, you could see this fire in his eyes. You could see that he wanted to prolong taking that #41 jersey off for the last time. In all my years of coaching, I have never seen a performance to compare with the one Glen gave us during the tournament."

Rice won his second consecutive Big Ten scoring title in 1989, averaging 24.8 points per conference contest. With 2,442 career points, Rice leaves Michigan as the all-time leading scorer in U-M and Big Ten history.

"You don't see a player of Glen Rice's stature very often," Fisher said. "He's a very special young man who has helped to give this university and the whole state something special in return.

"We will miss Glen Rice."

CAREER STATISTICS

YEAR	G-S	FG-ATT	PCT	3PT-ATT	PCT	FT-ATT	PCT	REB-AVG	PF-D	AST	TO	BK	STL	PTS	AVG	HIGH
1985-86	32-0	105-191	.550	—	—	15-25	.600	97-3.0	43-0	21	29	5	13	225	7.0	16
1986-87	32-31	226-402	.562	3-12	.250	85-108	.787	294-9.2	74-1	76	66	15	14	540	16.9	33
1987-88	33-33	308-539	.571	33-77	.429	79-98	.806	236-7.2	62-0	92	70	8	36	728	22.1	40
1988-89	37-37	363-629	.577	99-192	.516	124-149	.832	232-6.3	75-1	85	81	11	39	949	25.6	38
TOTALS	**134-101**	**1002-1761**	**.569**	**135-281**	**.480**	**303-380**	**.797**	**859-6.4**	**254-2**	**274**	**246**	**39**	**102**	**2442**	**18.2**	**40**

CAREER HIGHS

POINTS: 40 vs. Florida, 3/19/88 (NCAA Second Round Game)
REBOUNDS: 19 vs. Bradley, 11/21/86 (Pre-Season NIT First Round Game)
ASSISTS: 8 vs. Youngstown State, 12/21/88

Mark Hughes

6-8, 235 pounds, senior, Muskegon, MI

No one wanted to win the National Championship more than Mark Hughes. Hughes, the recipient of the 1989 Thad Garner Leadership Award, had toiled long and hard for four long years with the Wolverines. As a freshman, he saw limited action as Tarpley, Rellford & Co. won its second consecutive Big Ten crown. Hughes served as Michigan's young starting center as a sophomore, but the Wolverines slumped to fifth place and were eliminated by North Carolina in the NCAA's second round. A part-time starter as a junior, Michigan finished second in the conference race but was again shown the exit by Dean Smith's team.

After his first three years, Mark Hughes had a generous taste of success, but wanted more. He wanted it all.

That dream began to take shape when the Wolverines ousted the Tar Heels in the third round of the tournament. And in that game, Hughes came to the fore with six hard-earned rebounds, a blocked shot and three important free throws. He followed that performance with a seven-board effort in U-M's 102-65 Southeast Regional final win over Virginia. His ultimate goal was now well within reach. Mark Hughes decided he would not let this opportunity slip away.

Hughes battled Illinois' front-liners in the semi-finals and made four-of-five shots and grabbed six caroms to help lead Michigan into the finals against Seton Hall. Hughes played inspired defense in the title game, playing a crucial role in the Wolverine "D" that held Seton Hall's front line to just 29 total points on 44% shooting.

His dream was realized: Michigan had won the National Championship. But to Hughes, the initial euphoria was still very much dream-like. "I'm happy — real happy — but it hasn't hit me yet that we are the national champs," said Hughes during the post-game celebration.

CAREER STATISTICS

YEAR	G-S	FG-ATT	PCT	3PT-ATT	PCT	FT-ATT	PCT	REB-AVG	PF-D	AST	TO	BK	STL	PTS	AVG	HIGH
1985-86	14-0	12-24	.500	—	—	7-9	.778	18-1.3	13-0	2	5	3	2	31	2.2	8
1986-87	32-31	86-158	.544	0-0	—	22-29	.759	192-6.0	96-6	42	30	19	24	194	6.1	13
1987-88	34-16	65-123	.528	0-0	—	26-43	.605	133-3.9	80-2	33	27	17	23	156	4.6	10
1988-89	35-4	104-171	.608	1-2	.500	29-48	.604	142-4.1	58-0	40	26	7	12	238	6.8	21
TOTALS	115-51	267-476	.561	1-2	.500	84-129	.651	485-4.2	247-8	117	88	46	61	619	5.4	21

CAREER HIGHS

POINTS: 21 vs. Holy Cross, 12/29/88
REBOUNDS: 12 vs. Western Michigan, 12/10/88
ASSISTS: 5 vs. Indiana, 2/19/89

Loy Vaught

6-9, 225 pounds, senior, Grand Rapids, MI

Never play Loy Vaught one-on-one.

First, before you even begin to play, he disarms you with a smile and his soft-spoken nature. Relax, you tell yourself, so how tough can this guy be?

Plenty.

It's not enough that Vaught grabs every rebound within his reach, but he also has a very disturbing habit of making his shots — nearly all of them.

It's not easy to beat someone who doesn't miss. That's exactly what it's like to face Loy Vaught on the basketball court.

As a junior, Vaught made a Michigan-record 62.1% of his shots. This past season, he broke his own school mark and finished among the nation's leading shooters with a 66.1 field goal percentage. At the same time, Vaught paced the Wolverines with 296 rebounds — an average of 8.0 boards per contest. His 8.4 rebounding average in league play ranked Vaught second among all Big Ten players. To his credit, Vaught was also one of the team's top free throw shooters sinking nearly 78% of his tosses from the charity stripe.

In fact, his accomplishment was so outstanding that the Wolverine coaching staff honored Vaught with the establishment of the new Michigan Outstanding Rebounder Award.

"I think Loy's contributions to this championship were enormous," said head coach Steve Fisher. "Even in the tournament when he didn't have his shot falling for him, Loy worked extra hard on defense and rebounding, and to be truthful, that's where we needed him most."

Vaught enjoyed several outstanding outings during the championship season. In a pivotal early season contest against Ohio State, he drained 10-of-12 shots for 22 points and nine rebounds. At Illinois, Vaught scored 22 points on nine-of-11 shooting and pulled down eight boards. Also, in Michigan's second matchup with the Buckeyes, the Grand Rapids native missed just one shot on his way to a 15-point, 12-rebound performance.

CAREER STATISTICS

YEAR	G-S	FG-ATT	PCT	3PT-ATT	PCT	FT-ATT	PCT	REB-AVG	PF-D	AST	TO	BK	STL	PTS	AVG	HIGH
1986-87	32-1	68-122	.557	0-0	—	11-22	.500	125-3.9	73-1	12	32	31	11	147	4.6	12
1987-88	34-20	151-243	.621	0-0	—	55-76	.724	226-6.6	96-4	22	50	10	19	357	10.5	24
1988-89	37-21	201-304	.661	2-5	.400	63-81	.778	296-8.0	94-3	36	50	19	23	467	12.6	26
TOTALS	**103-42**	**420-669**	**.628**	**2-5**	**.400**	**129-179**	**.721**	**647-6.3**	**263-8**	**70**	**132**	**60**	**53**	**971**	**9.4**	**26**

CAREER HIGHS

POINTS: 26 vs. Youngstown State, 12/21/88
REBOUNDS: 16 vs. Illinois, 4/1/89 (NCAA Championship Semi-Final Game)
ASSISTS: 3 Six Times, Most recently vs. Wisconsin, 2/25/89

Mike Griffin

6-7, 215 pounds, senior, Rosemont, IL

Every team needs a Mike Griffin. Unassuming. Unselfish. Does his job the best he can. Period. He's what the experts call "a role player."

Sometimes you almost don't even know he's on the court. In fact, you can sometimes look at the box score and not even notice him, because there are some games when Griffin doesn't even take a shot. In Seattle, Griffin took just one shot. That's exactly one shot in two games as a starting guard. He never even scored!

Be assured, however, that Michigan's opponents took notice of Mike Griffin.

Without flash or fanfare, Griffin was one of the most valuable players on a team that boasted many heroes. Whereas spectators generally pay more attention to points, rebounds and assists, Griffin excels in second-effort, defensive help and charges taken.

In the championship semi-final against Illinois, for example, Griffin spearheaded a Wolverine defense that held the Illini to just 44.8% shooting and registered three assists and a pair of key steals. In the finals against Seton Hall, Griffin's tenacity and off-ball help played a major role in the 43.1% FG shooting by the Pirates. Griffin also contributed three assists and four rebounds.

"Mike is a smart ball player, and when he's out on the court, he knows exactly what we need as a team to win the game," said head coach Steve Fisher. "He's a dedicated young man whose unselfishness is admirable. He's the consumate team player."

Versatility? Griffin displayed that by starting at center, forward and guard during the course of the championship season. A former academic all-Big Ten recipient, Griffin enjoyed an outstanding outing against Grambling State when he collected eight points, six assists and four rebounds.

CAREER STATISTICS

YEAR	G-S	FG-ATT	PCT	3PT-ATT	PCT	FT-ATT	PCT	REB-AVG	PF-D	AST	TO	BK	STL	PTS	AVG	HIGH
1986-87	31-1	36-82	.439	0-1	.000	16-21	.762	71-2.3	74-5	46	36	4	17	88	2.8	12
1987-88	34-3	25-45	.556	0-0	—	25-35	.714	68-2.0	88-2	63	31	7	20	75	2.2	9
1988-89	37-31	33-65	.508	0-2	.000	33-43	.767	89-2.4	104-3	103	56	9	24	99	2.7	8
TOTALS	102-35	94-192	.490	0-3	.000	74-99	.747	228-2.2	266-10	212	123	20	61	262	2.6	12

CAREER HIGHS

POINTS: 12 vs. Michigan State, 1/15/87
REBOUNDS: 9 vs. Memphis State, 11/24/86 (Pre-Season NIT Second Round Game)
ASSISTS: 8 Twice, Most recently vs. Northern Michigan, 12/20/88

Terry Mills

6-10, 230 pounds, junior, Romulus, MI

"There are no two ways around it — the improved play of Terry Mills had a tremendous impact on the success we enjoyed in the NCAA Tournament."

That is the testimony of Steve Fisher when addressing the circumstances that turned the third-place Big Ten team into the eventual National Champions.

And Fisher was right on target. As the NCAA tourney began, Mills caught fire. With a renewed enthusiasm and determination, Mills embodied the very spirit of the 1988-89 Wolverine cagers, carrying through on their self-imposed "mission." In the team's come-from-behind win in the opener against Xavier, Mills, who collected 18 points, six rebounds and five assists in the game, assumed the center position and played that spot effectively for the remainder of the tournament. It was a move that many believe made the difference.

Mills responded with a 24-point performance versus South Alabama and tallied 16 on eight-of-11 shooting against J.R. Reid and North Carolina. When Mills' metamorphosis was complete, the Wolverines found themselves crowned as the reigning National Champions.

"It's a great feeling to win it, especially when you know it took a total team effort," Mills said. "Most people didn't give us much of a chance when the tournament started, so we knew we had to pull together even more to accomplish our goals — and we did."

The 1988-89 regular season was not without its rewards for Mills. One of just two players who started every game for the Wolverines (Glen Rice was the other), he opened the Big Ten campaign with a 20-point outburst against Northwestern. He followed that by pacing U-M to a convincing 99-73 win over Ohio State with 23 points on 10-of-13 FG shooting. In a contest at Wisconsin, Mills hit the Badgers with 15 points, grabbed nine boards and rejected three shots. As it turned out, Mills led all Big Ten players with 22 blocked shots in '89.

CAREER STATISTICS

YEAR	G-S	FG-ATT	PCT	3PT-ATT	PCT	FT-ATT	PCT	REB-AVG	PF-D	AST	TO	BK	STL	PTS	AVG	HIGH
1987-88	34-33	181-341	.531	0-2	.000	51-70	.729	216-6.4	90-1	56	67	35	21	413	12.1	23
1988-89	37-37	180-319	.564	0-2	.000	70-91	.769	218-5.9	95-3	104	77	49	20	430	11.6	24
TOTALS	**71-70**	**361-660**	**.547**	**0-4**	**.000**	**121-161**	**.752**	**434-6.1**	**185-4**	**160**	**144**	**84**	**41**	**843**	**11.9**	**24**

CAREER HIGHS

POINTS: 24 vs. South Alabama, 3/19/89 (NCAA Second Round Game)
REBOUNDS: 14 vs. Purdue, 2/7/88
ASSISTS: 7 Three times, Most recently vs. Northwestern, 3/9/89

Rumeal Robinson

6-2, 195 pounds, junior, Cambridge, MA

It was a scenario all schoolyard heroes envision. With just seconds remaining in the National Championship game, you're at the free throw line with a one-and-one situation and the chance to give your team the victory.

Coolly and calmly, you toe the line. Dribble the ball. Take a slow, deep breath. Eye the back of the rim, present the ball, release . . .

Few would argue that Rumeal Robinson truly lived a dream when he drained a pair of free throws against Seton Hall to give the Wolverines their first-ever national title. With the Wolverines trailing late in overtime, it was Robinson who took matters into his own hands.

"I didn't want to put the burden on anyone else's shoulders," explained Robinson shortly after the game. "Sure, it would have been just as easy for me to come down and throw the ball to someone else and let them handle it. But I wanted the ball. If there was any way we were going to get the shot, I wanted it to be me.

"As it turned out, they fouled me, and — thank God — they went in, and we're national champions."

Robinson, dubbed 'Mr. Clutch' by Sports Illustrated, had the Wolverines headed on the championship path the entire season, but few took notice until those final seconds. In fact, when the 1988-89 campaign began, it was Robinson who scored 20 points and held All-America guard Mookie Blaylock to just 4-of-14 shooting to give U-M a 91-80 win over favored Oklahoma in the Maui Classic title game. Later in the year, he tallied 22 points and 10 assists in a win against Iowa, and he posted 24 points and seven dishes versus Minnesota.

It was during Michigan's title drive, however, that Robinson established himself as one of the premier playmakers in college basketball.

CAREER STATISTICS

YEAR	G-S	FG-ATT	PCT	3PT-ATT	PCT	FT-ATT	PCT	REB-AVG	PF-D	AST	TO	BK	STL	PTS	AVG	HIGH
1987-88	33-32	115-208	.553	7-25	.269	84-126	.667	101-3.1	86-2	158	81	10	39	321	9.7	29
1988-89	37-36	199-357	.557	30-64	.469	122-186	.656	125-3.4	105-5	233	131	4	70	550	14.9	24
TOTALS	**70-68**	**314-565**	**.556**	**37-89**	**.416**	**206-312**	**.660**	**226-3.2**	**191-7**	**391**	**212**	**14**	**109**	**871**	**12.4**	**29**

CAREER HIGHS

POINTS: 29 vs. North Carolina 3/25/88 (NCAA West Regional Semi-Final Game)
REBOUNDS: 8 vs. Western Michigan, 12/10/88
ASSISTS: 13 vs. North Carolina, 3/23/89 (NCAA Southeast Regional Semi-Final Game)

Sean Higgins

6-9, 195 pounds, sophomore, Los Angeles, CA

The crowd, as they say, was going wild. It was certainly the most vocal crowd in Crisler Arena all season. The Michigan band couldn't play "The Victors" loud enough to suit the screaming masses.

No, this wasn't the final seconds of a classic Big Ten game. In fact, it wasn't a game at all. This was the championship pep rally to greet the Michigan team upon its arrival from Seattle. A few dignitaries were introduced first, then the basketball support staff, and then, finally, the players. And with each introduction came a thunderous ovation.

Sean Higgins couldn't wait any longer. In typical Hollywood fashion, playing it up to the Maize and Blue faithful, Higgins stepped up onto the make-shift stage, arms upraised, shades in place — before he was ever introduced.

And the crowd loved it.

Of course, there was little Higgins did during the course of the championship season that the fans didn't love. Higgins was a steady and reliable scorer for the Wolverines, and had a penchant for peaking at crunch time.

Case #1: The Wolverines fell behind early in the first overtime period at Iowa, but it was Higgins to the rescue. The sophomore from Los Angeles reached into his bag of tricks and reeled off three 3-pointers to push the game into a second OT. Higgins contributed an additional driving hoop as Michigan came from behind for a 108-107 victory.

Case #2: It was an ending right out of an old "B" movie — almost too unbelievable to believe. The underdog Wolverines squared-off against the Fighting Illini, a team that had twice soundly defeated Michigan, in the national semis. With the final seconds ticking off the clock, Terry Mills attempted a shot from the right corner. The ball caromed off the rim and Higgins rebounded, tossing the ball back through the net to give U-M an 83-81 win.

CAREER STATISTICS

YEAR	G-S	FG-ATT	PCT	3PT-ATT	PCT	FT-ATT	PCT	REB-AVG	PF-D	AST	TO	BK	STL	PTS	AVG	HIGH
1987-88	12-0	48-96	.500	10-20	.500	11-14	.786	38-3.2	24-0	13	16	0	3	117	9.8	20
1988-89	34-16	158-312	.506	51-110	.464	54-70	.771	107-3.1	76-2	51	60	11	10	421	12.4	31
TOTALS	46-16	206-408	.505	61-130	.469	65-84	.774	145-3.2	100-2	64	76	11	13	538	11.7	31

CAREER HIGHS

POINTS: 31 vs. Virginia, 3/25/89 (NCAA Southeast Regional Championship Game)
REBOUNDS: 9 Twice, Most recently vs. Seton Hall, 4/3/89 (NCAA Championship Game)
ASSISTS: 5 vs. Ohio State, 2/23/89

Demetrius Calip

6-1, 160 pounds, sophomore, Flint, MI

Few can appreciate the pressure Demetrius Calip experienced in the NCAA tournament.

During the course of the season, Calip was used sparingly. He played little until Kirk Taylor twisted a knee late in the season, but even then, though he was the only pure point guard behind Rumeal Robinson, Calip's action was limited. He scored just 40 points all season long and averaged less than five minutes per game. But when the tourney rolled around, Steve Fisher knew that the Wolverines needed Demetrius Calip.

And Calip responded. He responded with a career-high nine points in Michigan's opening round thriller against Xavier. He dished five assists and sliced through the South Alabama press in U-M's second round contest. Against North Carolina, Calip pestered Jeff Lebo for the better part of 21 minutes, then followed that performance with five assists and as many rebounds in the regional final versus Virginia.

Yes, when the Wolverines needed him most, Demetrius Calip was ready. In all, Calip averaged 15 minutes per game in the post season, usually spelling Rumeal Robinson and lending some terrific defense as well as running the Michigan offensive attack.

"There's no question about it, we needed Demetrius to play well for us to have any chance of winning that tournament," said head coach Steve Fisher. "I thought he did an outstanding job, especially in those first two very close games against Xavier and South Alabama. We had to come from behind to win both of those games, and Demetrius Calip played a very important role in each of them."

Calip also had his share of shining moments during the regular season, the highlight of which came in Michigan's thrilling 108-107 double-overtime win at Iowa. With the Wolverines trailing in the final few seconds of that contest, Calip drove the ball the length of the court to set up the winning basket.

As a result of his efforts, Calip shared the 1989 Rudy Tomjanovich Most Improved Player Award with teammate Terry Mills.

CAREER STATISTICS

YEAR	G-S	FG-ATT	PCT	3PT-ATT	PCT	FT-ATT	PCT	REB-AVG	PF-D	AST	TO	BK	STL	PTS	AVG	HIGH
1987-88	6-0	3-8	.375	0-1	.000	1-2	.500	4-0.7	0-0	4	3	0	2	7	1.2	4
1988-89	30-0	22-50	.440	2-9	.222	14-17	.824	19-0.6	19-0	25	23	0	7	60	2.0	9
TOTALS	**36-0**	**25-58**	**.431**	**2-10**	**.200**	**15-19**	**.789**	**23-0.6**	**19-0**	**29**	**26**	**0**	**9**	**67**	**1.9**	**9**

CAREER HIGHS

POINTS: 9 vs. Xavier, 3/17/89 (NCAA First Round Game)
REBOUNDS: 5 vs. Virginia, 3/25/89 (NCAA Southeast Regional Championship Game)
ASSISTS: 5 Twice, Most recently vs. Virginia, 3/25/89 (NCAA Southeast Regional Championship Game)

J. P. Oosterbaan

6-10, 240 pounds, senior, Kalamazoo, MI

Pay close attention to what John Paul Oosterbaan has to say, because more times than not, it pays.

Sure, J.P. hustled as much as anyone during practice. His job, after all, was to battle with the likes of Terry Mills and Loy Vaught during scrimmages and work-outs. Day after day, Oosterbaan learned how to give (and take) plenty of pounding under the boards. It's no picnic in the paint. In the end, his hard work and determination helped the Wolverines reap big dividends in the NCAA Tournament.

But that's nothing new for J.P. Oosterbaan. Big dividends have become almost as important to J.P. as basketball. While serving as one of the team's top center reserves, he has also been the squad's number one financial whiz.

It's a hobby for the Kalamazoo native. Though most college students may court interests chiefly in music or dance, this giant on the court puts more stock in the market.

To the Michigan coaching staff, Oosterbaan has always been a blue chip. "Day in and day out, we could always count on J.P.," said head coach Steve Fisher. "He's very, very knowledgable about basketball and very helpful especially with the younger guys.

"He's really been a good role player in our system and has done a great job in the classroom," Fisher said. "It's been almost like having another coach on the bench."

Oosterbaan saw action in 22 games during the championship season, shooting 56.4% for the year and scoring a career high 10 points in Michigan's 125-75 win over Northern Michigan.

Although he red-shirted his freshman year, Oosterbaan decided to forego his fifth year of eligibility to concentrate on graduate school and a possible law career. Consequently, Michigan's run through the NCAA tourney became J.P.'s swan song.

CAREER STATISTICS

YEAR	G-S	FG-ATT	PCT	3PT-ATT	PCT	FT-ATT	PCT	REB-AVG	PF-D	AST	TO	BK	STL	PTS	AVG	HIGH
1986-87	25-0	25-38	.658	0-0	—	11-17	.647	30-1.2	27-0	14	8	7	0	61	2.4	8
1987-88	23-1	10-27	.370	0-0	—	5-10	.500	13-0.6	13-0	7	4	1	1	25	1.1	4
1988-89	22-0	22-39	.564	0-1	.000	9-13	.692	26-1.2	15-0	11	9	3	0	53	2.4	10
TOTALS	**70-1**	**67-104**	**.644**	**0-1**	**.000**	**25-40**	**.625**	**69-1.0**	**55-0**	**32**	**21**	**11**	**1**	**139**	**2.0**	**10**

CAREER HIGHS

POINTS: 10 vs. Northern Michigan, 12/20/88
REBOUNDS: 5 vs. Illinois-Chicago, 12/6/86
ASSISTS: 3 Three times, Most recently vs. Northern Michigan, 12/20/88

Kirk Taylor

6-3, 180 pounds, sophomore, Dayton, OH

Kirk Taylor's problem was unique, but one that he really didn't mind having. You see, it's hard to carry the box containing your NCAA championship ring when you hobble along on crutches. Fortunately, Taylor somehow managed the task and joined his teammates for a victory celebration in their Kingdome locker room.

It is safe to say that no individual player's season changed more in 1988-89 than Kirk Taylor's. When the Wolverines opened the season at the Maui Classic, Taylor established himself as U-M's top backcourt sub, playing disciplined defense in the first two games and exploding for 12 points (on five-of-eight shooting) and six assists in the title game against Oklahoma.

During the course of the season, Taylor's contributions were vital to the success of the Wolverines, but the campaign literally took a turn for the worst on February 11. On that afternoon at Minnesota, Taylor twisted a knee that would later require reconstructive surgery, cutting short his sophomore season and clouding his basketball future.

Most young men might let a setback like that destroy what had otherwise been a very satisfying year. But Kirk Taylor wouldn't allow that. He continued to join his teammates on the bench at Crisler Arena, offering encouragement when possible and spurring the Wolverines on to even greater fortunes.

Perhaps Taylor knew, even back in February, that his last move to the basket would come on the Kingdome floor in April — with crutches in tow and scissors in hand.

CAREER STATISTICS

YEAR	G-S	FG-ATT	PCT	3PT-ATT	PCT	FT-ATT	PCT	REB-AVG	PF-D	AST	TO	BK	STL	PTS	AVG	HIGH
1987-88	16-0	8-27	.296	1-4	.250	0-5	.000	13-0.8	15-0	7	4	0	2	17	1.1	7
1988-89	21-2	33-69	.478	7-18	.389	22-36	.611	46-2.2	30-1	46	23	6	20	95	4.5	12
TOTALS	**37-2**	**41-96**	**.427**	**8-22**	**.364**	**22-41**	**.537**	**59-1.6**	**45-1**	**53**	**27**	**6**	**22**	**112**	**3.0**	**12**

CAREER HIGHS

POINTS: 12 vs. Oklahoma, 11/27/88 (Maui Classic Championship Game)
REBOUNDS: 6 vs. Tampa, 12/5/88
ASSISTS: 6 Twice, Most recently vs. Iowa 2/9/89

Rob Pelinka

6-5, 198 pounds, freshman, Lake Bluff, IL

Some might call him a walking good luck charm. It seems wherever Rob Pelinka goes, success is sure to follow.

Of course, it helps when you've got all the right tools — a solid 6-5 frame, great quickness and excellent hands. But add to that a tremendous work ethic and an undying will to win, and it is easy to see why Pelinka possesses the Midas touch.

Pelinka earned all-state and honorable mention All-America honors at Lake Forest High School, scoring 1,327 points in just two years with the varsity squad. He averaged 30 points and 10 rebounds per game as a senior. He shot nearly 90% from the charity stripe, and at one point sank 46 consecutive tosses.

Oh yes, in his spare time, he batted .400 as a member of the varsity baseball team.

The summer before enrolling at Michigan, Pelinka used his golden touch to lead Team Illinois to a stirring AAU win over the Soviet Union's National Junior team.

Fortunately, success has followed Pelinka all the way to Ann Arbor, where he will be just one of three sophomores to sport an NCAA Basketball Championship ring in the fall.

Pelinka opened his promising collegiate career by seeing action in 26 games in 1988-89. Though he averaged just four minutes per game as a freshman, he did earn his first-ever start against Holy Cross in the Utah Classic. True to form, Pelinka made the most of the opportunity, scoring a career-high eight points and grabbing five rebounds in Michigan's 100-63 victory.

CAREER STATISTICS

YEAR	G-S	FG-ATT	PCT	3PT-ATT	PCT	FT-ATT	PCT	REB-AVG	PF-D	AST	TO	BK	STL	PTS	AVG	HIGH
1988-89	26-1	9-25	.360	4-14	.286	7-10	.700	15-0.6	7-0	10	12	2	3	29	1.1	8
TOTALS	**26-1**	**9-25**	**.360**	**4-14**	**.286**	**7-10**	**.700**	**15-0.6**	**7-0**	**10**	**12**	**2**	**3**	**29**	**1.1**	**8**

CAREER HIGHS

POINTS: 8 vs. Holy Cross, 12/29/88
REBOUNDS: 5 vs. Holy Cross, 12/29/88
ASSISTS: 2 Twice, Most recently vs. Holy Cross, 12/29/88

Marc Koenig

6-0, 165 pounds, junior, Los Angeles, CA

He scored just two points all season — just two points — but Marc Koenig's contributions to this basketball team were exactly what the Wolverines needed. Koenig wore many hats during the course of his first season on the Michigan basketball team. He was part cheerleader, part fan, part guidance counselor, part coach.

A junior from Los Angeles, Koenig joined the Michigan squad in the fall as a walkon to help bolster U-M's scout squad. Few on the coaching staff at that time could have forseen the tremendous lift he would later provide his teammates during long practices and tough games. Always upbeat, Koenig was a favorite among the Crisler Arena crowds, often seen waving a towel and shouting encouragement to those who battled on the court.

Koenig's only two points came in December in the closing minutes against Youngstown State. His only rebound came against Northern Michigan, and he had a lone assist, that coming in U-M's win over Central Michigan. He saw playing time in just one NCAA tournament game, Michigan's 102-65 win over Virginia in the Southeast Regional finals.

But to all who closely followed the Michigan basketball team, Marc Koenig made a difference.

CAREER STATISTICS

YEAR	G-S	FG-ATT	PCT	3PT-ATT	PCT	FT-ATT	PCT	REB-AVG	PF-D	AST	TO	BK	STL	PTS	AVG	HIGH
1988-89	7-0	1-1	1.000	0-0	—	0-0	—	1-0.1	1-0	1	3	0	2	2	0.3	2
TOTALS	7-0	1-1	1.000	0-0	—	0-0	—	1-0.1	1-0	1	3	0	2	2	0.3	2

CAREER HIGHS

POINTS: 2 vs. Youngstown State, 12/21/88
REBOUNDS: 1 vs. Northern Michigan, 12/20/88
ASSISTS: 1 vs. Central Michigan, 12/7/88

Eric Riley

6-10, 200 pounds, freshman, Cleveland, Ohio

Playing time becomes increasingly scarce when you have to battle Loy Vaught, Terry Mills and Mark Hughes. So rather than be relegated to seeing strictly "mop-up" minutes in Wolverine blow-outs, Eric Riley thought it best to ride the pine in '89, saving all four years of college eligibility and, in the process, making the difficult transition from prep to collegiate hoops that much easier.

"High Rise" worked hard with assistant coach Mike Boyd, the man who tutored centers Tim McCormick and Roy Tarpley during their successful days with the Wolverines. That, along with a regimented strength and conditioning program established by coach Brad Andress, has provided Riley with a healthy outlook for the upcoming seasons.

"I have every reason to believe that Eric has an excellent future in front of him," said Boyd. "He's a dedicated athlete who, although he didn't play this year, was as supportive as anyone in helping our team to improve.

"If he can continue to work hard, Eric could be a leader of this team someday."

Riley averaged 23 points and 14 rebounds as a senior at St. Joseph High School where he earned first team all-state and honorable mention All-America honors.

With these credentials, it may not be long before Michigan's Eric Riley becomes the center of attention.

Chris Seter

6-9, 205 pounds, sophomore, Brookfield, WI

Up until the NCAA tournament, fate had not been kind to Chris Seter.

With several front line veterans on the squad, Seter, then a freshman, sat out the 1987-88 season with the Wolverines to gain valuable practice experience and preserve a fourth-year of eligibility. But before he could see his first playing time in 1988-89, Seter suffered an elbow injury which required surgery to remove bone chips. The injury never quite healed right, and Seter was sidelined for the entire championship season.

"Chris has always been a hard-working young man and is a talented basketball player," said head coach Steve Fisher. "Unfortunately, Chris has been dealt an awful blow, but he's still young, and I know that if there is any way for him to return to this team, he will work hard to get the job done."

An honorable mention All-American from Brookfield (WI) Central High School, Seter is also an accomplished baseball player and golfer. Seter has his sights set on a B.A. degree and plans to attend law school.

James Voskuil

6-7, 193 pounds, freshman, Grandville, MI

James Voskuil's promising talents were restricted to the practice court this past season as the freshman forward opted to save his first year of eligibility. It is a strategy that has paid richly in valuable tutoring and experience for Loy Vaught and Mike Griffin.

"James has a solid outside shot and is a fine ball handler for a forward," said assistant coach Brian Dutcher. "A big plus for James is that he has had the opportunity to see what it takes to be a winner this year. Hopefully he will be able to take that experience and help us continue the progress this Michigan program has enjoyed."

A former all-state honoree who led Calvin Christian High School to a 22-3 record as a senior, Voskuil is an engineering student with his sights set on an M.E. James is also an accomplished soccer and tennis player and enjoys windsurfing.

Michigan's 1988-89 Championship Season . . . ____

Who Would Have Believed It?____

> **"I couldn't be prouder to be a part of this Michigan team that just won the national championship, a moment and an event that we will all have with us forever."**
> — Steve Fisher

A pensive Steve Fisher sat quietly in his seat, staring out the airplane's small window and looking aimlessly into the clouds. He, along with the University of Michigan basketball team and staff, was headed back to Ann Arbor after a short visit to Washington, D.C. and the White House. Fisher glanced down at his hands, and perched boldly on his right was the ring, the NCAA National Championship ring, a reminder of his team's overtime win against Seton Hall in the finals. His team? Was it really his team?

Fisher had been caught up in a dream-like state for nearly a month, but an awakening pinch would have proved pointless. This was his Michigan team. He was the head coach. And they had just won the National Championship.

Who would have believed it?

Certainly no one on December 28. That was the date Alaska-Anchorage upset the heavily-favored Wolverines, 70-66, in the opening round of the Utah Classic. Michigan converted just five-of-thirteen free throws in its first defeat of the season.

Who would have believed it?

Certainly no one on January 23. The surprising Indiana Hoosiers took a commanding lead early in the Big Ten race with a 71-70 win in Ann Arbor that night. The loss marked Michigan's third defeat in four games and dropped its league record to 3-3.

Who would have believed it?

Certainly no one on February 11. Guard Kirk Taylor's season came to an abrupt halt with a knee injury that afternoon and U-M suffered an 88-80 thrashing at the hands of the upstart Minnesota Golden Gophers.

Who would have believed it?

Certainly no one on March 15. Just days after dropping the regular-season finale to Illinois and hours before departing for Michigan's first round game in Atlanta, head coach Bill Frieder accepted the head coaching post at Arizona State and Athletic Director Bo Schembechler named Steve Fisher in-terim coach. Though a #3 seed in the Southeast regional, the Wolverines were suddenly long-shots, at best, to advance to Lexington.

But just one week later, it was a very different story . . . and many began to believe.

Fisher and many others agree that the turning point was the North Carolina game. After narrow victories over Xavier and South Alabama, the Wolverines met the Tar Heels for the third consecutive year in the NCAA Tournament. But unlike past meetings, Michigan held its own, playing with confidence and great intensity, wearing down North Carolina's strong inside game. U-M prevailed, 92-87, and just as suddenly, Michigan had instilled new-found hope in its supporters.

They believed.

And so they drove, hundreds of them, to Lexington to see the Wolverines make short order of Virginia in the Southeast regional finals. There were upwards of 5,000 Maize and Blue faithful in attendance, and they helped spur U-M to a convincing 102-65 win as Michigan advanced to the Final Four for the first time since 1976.

With a strong contingent of boosters making the long journey to Seattle, the Wolverines went to work, first turning back league rival Illinois and then slipping past a tough Seton Hall squad in the title game.

When it was all over, Michigan had done what few had thought possible — they won the NCAA Championship. But before it even began there were a handful of individuals who figured the Wolverines could go all the way — even on December 28, even on January 23, even on February 11.

Why, even on March 15.

Because even while this team suffered a few setbacks, they never stopped believing in themselves. The Michigan players and staff, who had earlier proclaimed to be on a "mission," believed all along that they had the talent and desire needed to win the championship.

Mission accomplished.

The Season

1	Vanderbilt	W	91-66
2	Memphis State	W	79-75
3	Oklahoma	W	91-80
4	Grambling State	W	102-62
5	South Dakota State	W	104-66
6	Tampa	W	98-65
7	Central Michigan	W	108-62
8	Western Michigan	W	107-60
9	Eastern Michigan	W	80-57
10	Northern Michigan	W	125-75
11	Youngstown State	W	121-72
12	Alaska-Anchorage	L	66-70
13	Holy Cross	W	100-63
14	Northwestern	W	94-66
15	Minnesota	W	98-83
16	Illinois	L	84-96
17	Ohio State	W	99-73
18	Wisconsin	L	68-71
19	Indiana	L	70-71
20	Purdue	W	99-88
21	Michigan State	W	82-66
22	Iowa	W	108-107
23	Minnesota	L	80-88
24	Purdue	W	84-70
25	Indiana	L	75-76
26	Ohio State	W	89-72
27	Wisconsin	W	92-70
28	Michigan State	W	79-52
29	Iowa	W	119-96
30	Northwestern	W	88-79
31	Illinois	L	73-89
32	Xavier	W	92-87
33	South Alabama	W	91-82
34	North Carolina	W	92-87
35	Virginia	W	102-65
36	Illinois	W	83-81
37	Seton Hall	W	80-79

1 Michigan 91
Vanderbilt 66

Michigan coach Bill Frieder couldn't find much to fault in a 91-66 win over Vanderbilt in the opening round of the Maui Classic.

The Wolverines, led by 18 points from Glen Rice and 17 by Sean Higgins, went on cruise control after struggling the first 12 minutes of the game.

The Lahaina Civic Center was packed with 3,000 fans for the opening tourney games, which included Oklahoma's exciting 97-93 win over Ohio State and emerging star Jay Burson.

"We were overanxious early in the game," Frieder said. "We made foolish fouls and took quick shots. But it was not selfish. We really had them ready, and they tried too hard at first.

"We had them in bed at 10 every night, and the only thing after 5:30 was film, food or study table."

Frieder said his players weren't complaining about the early curfew. "They know we have exams in two weeks and a mission here," he said. "We got up today at six, and shot at seven."

U-M shot 63.2 percent in the game, setting the tone for what would be a hot-shooting season.

The Commodores couldn't show a replacement that even remotely resembled 7-foot center Will Perdue, last season's first-round draft choice of the Chicago Bulls. Forward Frank Kornet (17 points) and guard Barry Goheen (12 points) were their only consistent scorers.

"We just gave them too many easy shots inside," Goheen said.

Vanderbilt did not have the inside muscle or depth to stick with the Wolverines in the opener for both teams.

U-M played without starting point guard Rumeal Robinson most of the way, but it made little difference. Robinson was in serious foul trouble nearly the entire game. He would learn to avoid the silly fouls that cost him playing time in this one.

U-M thrived on strong play from its front line. Rice supplied the early cushion, while Mark Hughes (10 points), Terry Mills (12 points) and Loy Vaught (12 points) kept the lead intact. Those four players were 25-for-36 (.694).

"Rice gave us the scoring when we had to have it early," Frieder said.

The Wolverines placed six men in double figures, including forward Higgins (17 points, all in the second half) and Robinson (10 points).

U-M struggled early, but took the lead for good with 7:33 remaining in the first half. Hughes' basket made it 18-17 for the Wolverines, and began a string of 12 unanswered points.

Rice scored four of his 15 first-half points during the stretch, and center Mills banged in a pair of 15-footers.

U-M held Vanderbilt scoreless for just over five minutes late in the first half to take a 28-17 lead.

The Wolverines played the final 13:46 without point guard Robinson. He picked up his third foul at that point and was replaced by Kirk Taylor.

Starting guards Goheen and Barry Booker (2 points) were held to a combined 14 points. Vanderbilt took 19 three-point attempts in the second half in an attempt to get back in the game. The Commodores were just 5-for-22 on the night.

Robinson committed his fourth foul 41 seconds into the second half and again was replaced by Taylor. Robinson returned midway through the second half.

Michigan	FG	FT	R	A	TP
Rice	8-14	1-2	6	2	18
Mills	6-8	0-0	2	2	12
Griffin	1-3	0-0	6	3	2
Higgins	7-13	0-1	1	3	17
Robinson	5-7	0-0	2	5	10
Calip	0-1	0-0	0	1	0
Taylor	3-5	0-0	3	2	6
Pelinka	0-0	0-0	0	0	0
Vaught	6-8	0-0	5	1	12
Oosterbaan	2-3	0-0	2	0	4
Hughes	5-6	0-0	4	0	10
Totals	43-68	1-3	35	19	91

Vanderbilt	FG	FT	R	A	TP
Kornet	6-11	4-5	4	0	17
Milholland	2-7	0-0	4	0	4
Reid	4-6	2-3	3	1	10
Booker	1-5	0-0	2	2	2
Goheen	4-7	2-2	0	4	12
Wilcox	1-4	0-0	0	1	2
Grant	2-4	0-1	4	0	4
Wheat	3-9	1-1	2	1	9
Mayes	0-5	0-1	0	0	0
Ballestra	1-1	0-0	1	0	2
Benjamin	2-3	0-1	1	0	4
Totals	26-62	9-14	26	9	66

Three-point goals: Michigan 4-11 (Higgins 3-6, Rice 1-3, Robinson 0-1, Taylor 0-1); Vanderbilt 5-22 (Wheat 2-6, Goheen 2-4, Kornet 1-3, Booker 0-4, Mayes 0-3, Wilcox 0-2).

Turnovers: Michigan 10, Vanderbilt 16

2 Michigan 79
Memphis State 75

Sometimes the boxscore lies. Michigan's 79-75 win over Memphis State was one of those times.

According to the statistics, Glen Rice and Rumeal Robinson were the stars of the win that sent the Wolverines to the championship game of the Maui Classic.

Rice scored 29 on 13-for-19 outside shooting and was fabulous, but Robinson struggled at point guard. He got into foul trouble before fouling out, and had five turnovers to only one assist.

For the second straight game, reserve guard Kirk Taylor came to the front and made a difference. He only had two points, but made four assists with no turnovers and added two steals in a productive 25 minutes.

Taylor, a sophomore from Dayton, Ohio, played 48 minutes in the first two games without committing a turnover. He added eight points and was tied for the team lead with six assists and six steals.

"Taylor's got to feel good about the way he's played," coach Bill Frieder said. "Boy, he helps us out on defense. Kirk's also given us a good effort on the boards (4 rebounds), and his ball-handling is improving."

Taylor said: "I think I'm doing a great job defensively, and the team needs more defense. These games have given me the experience I've needed."

Playing the games on the Hawaiian island of Maui did cost Taylor in one way: phone bills. He has a pre-game superstition of calling his mother, Elnora, back in Dayton.

"Yes, I'm even calling her in Hawaii," Taylor said. "I need that reassurance call, that motherly love and support."

Taylor, nicknamed "Ice T" since his freshman year at Dayton Dunbar High, would have plenty of good news to report back home during early-season games.

"They called me Iceman because I was so thin," said Taylor, now 6-feet-3, 180 pounds. "Then someone threw in the T, for Taylor, and it became Ice T."

Iced tea also came in handy on the shores of Kaanapali Beach, where the team was staying at a resort hotel. Temperatures were in the 80s and practices and games proved taxing. But Michigan's opponents had to deal with the same circumstances, which made substitutions more frequent and opened the way for players such as Taylor to star off the bench.

Taylor was instrumental in holding down Elliot Perry, the quick Memphis State guard who scored 15 points with four rebounds, four assists and three steals.

Michigan didn't put away the Tigers until the end, when Terry Mills scored four points in the final 1:22 to secure victory. He finished with 12 points. Both of the 6-11 forward's buckets came on 15-footers.

"If he's squared up and has room, it's a good shot," Frieder said. "I called it."

The Wolverines were confident headed into their first truly big game of the season against Oklahoma for the title.

Michigan	FG	FT	R	A	TP
Rice	13-19	0-2	5	2	29
Mills	6-9	0-1	3	1	12
Griffin	1-1	3-4	3	1	5
Higgins	2-5	3-4	1	2	7
Robinson	6-10	3-5	1	1	15
Hughes	2-3	0-1	4	0	4
Taylor	0-1	2-2	1	4	2
Vaught	2-4	1-3	6	0	5
Totals	32-52	12-22	25	11	79

Memphis State	FG	FT	R	A	TP
Douglas	6-9	2-2	1	2	15
Ballard	5-5	3-4	10	2	13
Mundt	3-7	0-0	2	0	6
McLaughlin	0-2	2-2	2	0	2
Perry	5-9	5-8	4	4	15
Gibson	0-2	0-0	0	0	0
Madlock	1-1	2-2	0	0	4
Smith	6-13	3-4	4	2	17
Watson	0-2	0-0	0	0	0
McLain	1-3	1-2	4	0	3
Totals	27-53	18-24	29	10	75

Three-point goals: Michigan 3-8 (Rice 3-7, Taylor 0-1; Memphis State 3-10 (Smith 2-2, Douglas 1-2, Perry 0-2, Watson 0-2, Gibson 0-1, McLaughlin 0-1).

Turnovers: Michigan 15, Memphis State 15
Fouled Out: Michigan — Robinson; Memphis State — Perry

3 Michigan 91
Oklahoma 80

The unlikely heroes mugged for an ESPN cameraman after beating Oklahoma, 91-80, to win the Maui Classic. "We're No. 1!" shouted Michigan's Sean Higgins and Kirk Taylor, arms around one another. "Whoooo!"

It never was ranked No. 1 during the regular season, but would finish there when the NCAA Tournament concluded.

The Wolverines mobbed one another in celebration at the Lahaina Civic Center. After barely beating unranked Memphis State, 79-75, in the semi-finals, U-M was the consensus underdog in the championship game. But the Sooners trailed nearly the en tire way.

In the language of the islands, the final result was Michigan no ka oi. Translated: Michigan is the best.

Winning a tournament with four Top 15 teams was quite an ac complishment, and it sent U-M to No. 2 in Monday's Associated Press poll, with seven first-place votes.

Before the season, U-M coach Bill Frieder said, "If we win that tournament, I'd say we would be a team to be reckoned with."

Frieder didn't attempt to downplay the result afterward.

"I can't lie," he said, smiling. "That's a big, big victory for us. We got three important wins here. We'll be good, I know that. How good remains to be seen."

Frieder wasn't in the Kingdome when everyone found out just how good the Wolverines were. And Taylor wasn't on the court for the championship game, either. A knee injury would prematurely end his season.

The Wolverines won this championship game at rim level, outrebounding Oklahoma, 37-27. They stopped the Sooners' fast break by dominating defensive rebounding, 26-15.

"The defense stayed tough at all times," Frieder said.

Glen Rice (17 points, five rebounds) was selected the most valuable player. He averaged 21.3 points in three games. Rumeal Robinson (20 points, five assists) was all-tournament with Rodney McCray of Chaminade, Stacey Augmon of Nevada-Las Vegas, Ohio State's Jay Burson and Oklahoma's Stacey King.

U-M forward Loy Vaught deserved special mention for keep ing Oklahoma from playing its game. Vaught grabbed a team-high nine-rebounds (a game-high seven on defense) and hit five of seven shots, finishing with 13 points.

"Loy did a great job," Frieder said. "He was really tough."

Before the tournament, U-M players hoped to play the Sooners in the title game because of their high-profile players, who became nationally prominent by reaching the NCAA champi onship game against Kansas in 1988.

Robinson wanted to play Mookie Blaylock. Vaught talked of taking on King.

"King's a great player," Vaught said. "I read about him in Sports Illustrated. I'd like to see what I can hold him down to."

Blaylock, who played the entire game, totaled 11 points and five assists. Robinson won his matchup. King scored 27 points, leading all scorers, but had limited success rebounding with five.

Michigan	FG	FT	R	A	TP
Rice	7-15	2-3	5	3	17
Mills	2-6	0-0	2	3	4
Griffin	0-0	0-0	2	1	0
Higgins	7-7	4-7	6	0	19
Robinson	6-9	7-9	2	5	20
Vaught	5-7	3-4	9	0	13
Taylor	5-8	2-3	2	6	12
Hughes	3-4	0-0	5	0	6
Totals	35-56	18-26	37	18	91

Oklahoma	FG	FT	R	A	TP
Henry	1-2	0-0	0	0	2
Wiley	1-2	0-0	0	0	2
King	10-14	7-10	5	3	27
Blaylock	4-14	2-2	1	5	11
Jones	7-13	1-1	3	2	18
Mullins	2-6	0-2	5	2	4
Patterson	2-5	0-0	0	0	4
Davis	3-7	3-4	9	0	9
Martin	1-2	1-2	2	0	3
Totals	31-65	14-21	27	12	80

Three-point goals: Michigan 3-6 (Robinson 1-2, Rice 1-1, Higgins 1-1, Taylor 0-1, Mills 0-1; Oklahoma 4-16 (Blaylock 1-8, Jones 3-4, Mullins 0-2, Henry 0-1, Patterson 0-1).

Turnovers: Michigan 17, Oklahoma 14
Fouled Out: Michigan — Robinson; Oklahoma — Henry

4 Michigan 102
Grambling State 62

Aloha.

There were a lot of empty seats among the announced crowd of 12,409 Friday night as second-ranked Michigan romped past Grambling, 102-62, in its home opener.

Michigan moved to 4-0 in its first game since beating Oklahoma in the championship game of the Maui Classic Sunday night. Grambling lost its third game in as many tries.

True basketball fans began grumbling about the parade of cupcakes about to play the Wolverines at Crisler Arena. Michigan wouldn't face another ranked team until Ohio State visited six weeks later. Even athletic director-football coach Bo Schembechler mumbled about the schedule after taking on his administrative role in April.

In most cases, Michigan received stiffer competition in practice than in the December games that amounted to exhibitions. Yet, one such "who-dat" would hand the Wolverines their lone loss before the Big Ten season.

"Sometimes it's hard getting up for games like these," said senior forward Glen Rice, who had a team-high 23 points and grabbed eight rebounds. "But I'm glad we've got so much talent because if one guy isn't into it, someone else can pick up the slack."

Coach Bill Frieder had lots of time to experiment and give playing time to 6-foot-9 sophomore Sean Higgins — making the transition from forward to a starting guard spot — and key reserve Kirk Taylor, who would back up Higgins and guard Rumeal Robinson.

Taylor scored nine points in 18 minutes. Higgins had five points and five rebounds in 21 minutes, missing five of seven shots from the field against the Tigers. But shooting wasn't his only flaw.

"When he threw the ball away on a four-on-one break, I took him out to make a point," Frieder said.

Said Higgins: "I made some foolish turnovers. I'm glad we play back-to-back, so I can come back and make up for this."

This one was over about as fast as you could say Maui.

Michigan took an 8-0 lead. Grambling then scored seven straight points. The Tigers led, 13-12, with 11:15 left in the first half.

Grambling's lead lasted 10 seconds as Rice drilled a three-pointer. Those were the first points of a 12-0 run that produced a 24-13 lead on a jump shot by Robinson.

Robinson made all five of his first-half field-goal attempts and was fitting nicely into his role as backcourt leader. He was particularly impressive with 19 points on 8-for-10 shooting from the field.

"He's just like a quarterback in football," Grambling coach Bob Hopkins said. "He reads defenses well and can burn you."

Michigan's superior frontline — especially junior Terry Mills, who finished with 14 points, nine rebounds and six blocked shots — also was too much for Grambling.

U-M outrebounded the Tigers, 50-31. It was volleyball at times as Mills, Rice and Loy Vaught (nine rebounds) batted the ball at each other.

Michigan	FG	FT	R	A	TP
Rice	6-14	8-10	8	3	23
Mills	6-11	2-3	9	0	14
Griffin	3-4	2-3	4	6	8
Higgins	2-7	1-2	5	3	5
Robinson	8-10	2-4	2	3	19
Calip	2-2	1-1	0	0	5
Taylor	4-7	0-0	2	1	9
Pelinka	0-1	2-3	3	1	2
Vaught	3-3	3-3	9	3	9
Oosterbaan	1-2	0-0	2	1	2
Hughes	3-5	0-1	2	0	6
Totals	38-66	21-29	50	22	102

Grambling State	FG	FT	R	A	TP
Newell	7-16	0-0	2	1	17
Glover	5-9	0-0	4	0	10
Harris	3-11	2-4	8	1	8
Smith	2-4	0-0	1	2	4
Quinn	0-2	0-0	1	1	0
Anderson	0-3	0-0	3	1	0
Blackett	4-10	0-0	2	3	9
Rhodes	0-2	0-0	0	0	0
Dupree	1-5	1-1	3	1	4
Davis	0-2	0-0	2	0	0
Wesley	4-8	2-2	3	1	10
Tanner	0-1	0-0	0	0	0
Mack	0-0	0-0	0	0	0
Harold	0-1	0-0	0	0	0
Totals	26-74	5-7	31	11	62

Three-point goals: Michigan 5-12 (Rice 3-5, Taylor 1-2, Robinson 1-1, Higgins 0-3, Pelinka 0-1); Grambling 5-14 (Newell 3-7, Dupree 1-3, Blackett 1-1, Wesley 0-2, Davis 0-1).

Turnovers: Michigan 17, Grambling 19
Fouled Out: Grambling — Quinn, Anderson

5 Michigan 104
South Dakota State 66

Forward Loy Vaught smiled widely as he checked in at the scorer's table late in the second half. Many of the 12,511 fans at Crisler Arena were chanting his name. They wanted more.

Vaught matched his career best with 24 points, and had 11 rebounds in a 104-66 win over South Dakota State. The No. 2 Wolverines are 5-0. The Division II Jackrabbits dropped to 3-1.

"It charged me up to hear the fans," Vaught said. "I couldn't figure it out at first. But I was definitely on a roll, and the fans were a big part of that. I wanted to do more and more for them."

Vaught scored on a variety of dunks, jumpers and hook shots.

"I started working on the hook my freshman year," said Vaught, a junior. "Roy Tarpley impressed me with it. We have a period called pre-practice where I work on it with assistant coaches. I'm just now starting to use it in games. I think I shot four today."

U-M coach Bill Frieder said, "Loy Vaught, in the second half, was tremendous. The reason was that he ran so well up and down the court. That led to some easy buckets. He got some of them because he didn't run with his head down."

Vaught (11-for-16) was shooting .710 for the season.

"Sometimes I'm hesitant to run because I'm not confident I can do anything if I get it at full speed," Vaught said.

Among the starters, Glen Rice had 23 points, Rumeal Robinson 16 and Sean Higgins 15. Vaught, with 20 in the second half, exceeded a point per minute with just 20 minutes of action. He also scored 24 last season against Illinois.

U-M never trailed, pulling away for good late in the first half, Rice scored eight of the Wolverines' nine unanswered points, stretching the lead to 50-31.

South Dakota State's offense was pretty much the same thing: Ober and Ober again. Cullen Ober led the Jackrabbits with 22 points and eight rebounds. The 6-10, 240-pound junior center from Glencoe, Minn., likely is two inches taller than listed.

"He was not intimidated by (Terry) Mills," Jackrabbits coach Jim Thorson said. "Both are listed at 6-10, but there seemed to be a discrepancy in the measuring system in our state. I guess Pony Express hasn't delivered the new rulers. Actually, it's just that Ober doesn't want to be listed at 6-11 or 7-feet."

Ober made a surprising comeback last season. He fell 45 feet from a silo while repairing farm equipment on Labor Day, suffering a broken lumbar vertebra. But Ober, who is majoring in dairy production, recovered to start all 30 games in 1987-88.

"I was told I wouldn't play last year when the doctor talked to me in the emergency room," Ober said. "A specialist later told me it would be no less than three months. But on October 15, I was practicing. I started the first game.

"It was fun to play here. I was kind of surprised we played with them most of the first half. But when we messed up our execution, Michigan took advantage."

Michigan	FG	FT	R	A	TP
Rice	8-12	7-8	9	2	23
Griffin	0-0	1-2	3	2	1
Mills	2-8	5-5	6	4	9
Higgins	6-10	0-0	3	2	15
Robinson	7-10	1-2	4	7	16
Calip	0-1	0-0	1	0	0
Taylor	2-4	2-2	4	2	7
Pelinka	1-1	0-0	0	0	3
Vaught	11-16	2-2	11	0	24
Oosterbaan	3-3	0-0	3	0	3
Koenig	0-0	0-0	0	0	0
Totals	40-65	18-21	45	20	104

South Dakota St.	FG	FT	R	A	TP
Cartwright	5-13	0-1	6	0	10
Flom	4-8	0-0	1	1	8
Ober	9-22	4-4	8	0	22
Matthews	3-11	1-2	2	8	8
Nelson	2-8	4-4	2	4	8
Jacobsen	0-0	0-0	0	0	0
Neiman	0-0	0-0	1	0	0
Booher	2-5	0-0	2	0	4
Hansen	1-4	2-4	1	1	4
Flynn	0-0	0-0	0	0	0
Valentine	1-1	0-0	1	0	2
Totals	27-73	11-15	28	14	66

Three-point goals: Michigan 6-10 (Higgins 3-5, Robinson 1-2, Taylor 1-1, Pelinka 1-1, Rice 0-1); South Dakota 1-8 (Matthews 1-5, Booher 0-2, Nelson 0-1).

Turnovers: Michigan 20, South Dakota 18

6 Michigan 98
Tampa 65

Michigan was too awesome for words in this one. The Wolverine's dominating style of play caused Tampa coach Richard Schmidt to invent a verb after losing, 98-65.

"Michigan's got a lot of big guys," Schmidt said. "They can all jump, shoot and see. They studded us to death."

Studded?

Glen Rice led the Wolverines — again ranked No. 2 — with 29 points and nine rebounds. Rumeal Robinson (18 points, eight assists), Loy Vaught (17 points, eight rebounds) and Sean Higgins (16 points) added to the blowout before 11,197 at Crisler Arena.

U-M scored 50 points on lay-ups and dunks.

"Basketball is basketball," Robinson said. "All we want to do is play. Maybe they're not that talented, but we did not want to make anyone's day."

Who's coaching this team, Clint Eastwood?

The Wolverines failed to score 100 points or more for the first time in their last three games. The only time the Wolverines have hit the century mark in three consecutive games was 1965-66. They beat Purdue, 105-85; Iowa, 103-88; and Northwestern 105-92.

This season's team had the advantage of the three-point shot and an easier schedule. U-M beat Grambling State, 102-62, and South Dakota State, 104-66, last week.

Kirk Taylor's tip-in attempt of a missed shot by Demetrius Calip fell off the rim as time expired to keep the Wolverines two short of 100.

U-M took advantage of 24 turnovers, five more than any opponent had committed this season.

Robinson played pickpocket much of the game. He stole four passes for breakaway dunks, anticipating passes just beyond the perimeter for three of the steals.

"I just played the passing lane," Robinson said. "We put pressure on the ball and they didn't want the five-second count to come up, and panicked. The guy I was covering did not come to the ball, and they threw it right to me."

U-M coach Bill Frieder said: "Rumeal has really improved. He's playing more under control."

The Wolverines (6-0) led, 46-28, at halftime, and were up 61-32 when Tampa scored 10 unanswered points. The Division II Spartans (3-1) never got closer than 16 points in the second half.

Forward Bryan Williams hit four of nine three-point attempts and led Tampa with 15 points. The Spartans didn't have a player over 6-feet-7, and seldom scored along the baseline. Center Terry Rupp had 12 points and a game-high 12 rebounds.

Frieder received a box of cigars and a bag of oranges from Schmidt, who got a Division I opponent in return ... Tampa guard Kevin Starnes checked into the game in the second quarter, but forgot something: his red sweat pants. The fans razzed him, and Starnes' face turned the same color as his sweats as he pulled them off.

Michigan	FG	FT	R	A	TP
Rice	11-15	6-6	9	1	29
Griffin	1-4	0-1	0	5	2
Mills	3-8	1-1	5	3	7
Higgins	7-13	1-2	1	0	16
Robinson	8-11	2-3	4	8	18
Vaught	7-9	3-3	8	1	17
Taylor	1-3	0-0	6	0	3
Pelinka	0-0	0-0	0	0	0
Calip	0-1	0-0	0	0	0
Oosterbaan	1-3	2-2	4	2	4
Totals	39-68	17-20	37	20	98

Tampa	FG	FT	R	A	TP
Williams	5-18	1-2	1	1	15
Stiglich	0-1	0-0	4	0	0
Rupp	3-10	5-7	12	2	12
Deveaux	5-6	3-4	2	1	13
Dopwell	2-4	2-2	1	0	6
Starnes	0-2	0-0	1	5	0
Murawski	3-6	1-2	1	0	7
Henry	0-1	2-2	0	0	2
Schmidt	0-0	0-0	0	1	0
Totals	22-52	15-21	28	10	65

Three-point goals: Michigan 3-8 (Higgins 1-3, Rice 1-2, Taylor 1-2, Pelinka 0-1); Tampa 6-14 (Williams 4-9, Rupp 1-2, Brown 1-1, Starnes 0-1, Henry 0-1).

Turnovers: Michigan 14, Tampa 24
Fouled Out: Tampa — Williams, Brown, Deveaux

Going to Michigan home games in December was like watching a movie AFTER learning its ending.

All you had to do was fill in the details before witnessing the conclusion. This final at Crisler Arena was U-M 108, Central Michigan 62.

The No. 2 Wolverines (7-0) had six players in double figures for the second time in the season: Glen Rice (21), Terry Mills (19), Loy Vaught (16), Sean Higgins (13), Kirk Taylor (11) and Rumeal Robinson (10).

"They have five first-rounders," Chippewas' coach Charlie Coles said. "Or six, if you squeeze in Mark Hughes."

Coles may not have been kidding as much as some thought. Rice was the only finished product, but U-M had plenty of developing talent. They would experience many ups and downs before meshing to win the NCAA title.

Vaught shared the team rebound lead with Rice at 7.4 a game, and was third in scoring at 13.7. Yet, the redshirt junior wasn't starting.

"I just want to see more from Loy before he starts," U-M coach Bill Frieder said. "Yesterday, he did not practice due to back problems. I need to see him play like this for a longer period of time, and I need consistency from Loy in everything, not just the games."

Vaught said: "I couldn't practice. It would have been useless. The trainer told me it was back spasms. They worked on it yesterday and today. Fortunately, it almost felt normal for the game."

Central (3-2) was led by Jeff Majerle's 17 points and 16 from Carson Butler. The Chippewas were out rebounded, 50-30, and outshot, 61-29 percent.

U-M's 108 points were a season high. The Wolverines made 24 of 27 free throws, and were in the bonus 5:35 into the first half.

Mills hit a five-point play: a basket, free throw after the foul, and a two-shot technical on Coles. "That was something," Mills said . . . Rice moved into sixth place on U-M's all-time scoring list (1,653 points), passing Henry Wilmore . . . Frieder said freshman center Eric Riley and freshman forward James Voskuil have been told they will be redshirted this season . . . Many of the 12,434 at Crisler taunted Majerle to shoot every time he touched the ball in the second half, even at halfcourt. Majerle hit one of seven three-pointers in the first half. When he nailed a trey late in the game, the fans cheered.

Michigan	FG	FT	R	A	TP
Rice	9-16	1-2	10	3	21
Griffin	3-4	2-2	5	2	8
Mills	6-9	7-8	7	1	19
Higgins	4-9	5-6	6	0	13
Robinson	3-7	4-4	5	8	10
Calip	1-2	0-0	0	0	2
Taylor	3-4	2-3	5	1	11
Pelinka	1-1	0-0	0	0	2
Vaught	8-10	0-0	4	0	16
Oosterbaan	0-1	0-0	2	1	0
Hughes	2-3	2-2	5	2	6
Koenig	0-0	0-0	0	1	0
Totals	40-66	24-27	50	19	108

Central Michigan	FG	FT	R	A	TP
Wilcox	1-3	1-2	4	0	3
Briggs	1-7	0-0	4	1	2
Sanders	2-7	2-2	3	0	6
Butler	6-18	0-0	1	4	16
Majerle	6-22	2-2	2	0	17
Richmond	2-5	2-2	3	2	6
Pearson	0-3	1-2	4	1	1
Waters	0-2	0-0	1	2	0
Avery	2-4	0-1	0	2	5
Munson	1-1	4-4	0	0	6
Anglin	0-0	0-0	0	0	0
Booker	0-0	0-0	0	0	0
Totals	21-72	12-15	30	12	62

Three-point goals: Michigan 4-10 (Taylor 2-3, Rice 2-3, Higgins 0-2, Robinson 0-1); Central Michigan 8-30 (Butler 4-13, Majerle 3-13, Avery 1-2, Briggs 0-1, Waters 0-1).

Turnovers: Michigan 15, Central Michigan 15
Fouled Out: Central Michigan — Pearson

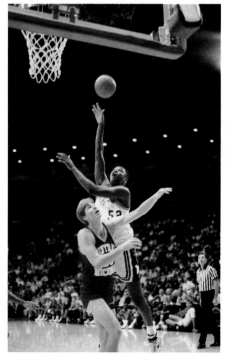

Twenty-five minutes after his team had been handed its lunch by Michigan in a 107-60 loss, Western Michigan coach Vern Payne was watching a videotape of the game in his Read Fieldhouse office with a couple of friends.

It was painful to survey in terms of his own team, but he also alluded to the greatness of his opponent.

"I think Bill (U-M coach Frieder) has done a great job of teaching a fine group of athletes how to play basketball," Payne said. "That's a very fine basketball team. I'm not sure they'd finish last in the NBA.

"They weren't necessarily playing against Western. They were playing against the game. They've learned to play well on the smallest court in the world; that court covers the distance between your two ears."

He held a finger at each side of his head.

After the No. 2 Wolverines (8-0) missed seven of their first eight shots and trailed, 10-2, they remembered what got them to this point in the season: good defense, strong inside play and hitting open shots.

What followed was 35 minutes of great basketball before a standing-room-only crowd of almost 10,000 (the fire marshal requires Western to list a sellout at 8,250).

"The first three minutes were bad, and the last two," Frieder said. In between, Western (3-3) was brought to its knees.

"We played with the same intensity we did against Oklahoma," Frieder said. "We overpowered them."

Michigan — which led at halftime, 45-24 — had eight dunks in the first half, hit its first 12 shots of the second half, and led at one point, 107-54.

For the sixth time in eight games, U-M shot better than 60 percent, hitting 42 of 68 for 61.8 percent. The Wolverines also scored 100 or more points for the fourth time in five games.

Junior point guard Rumeal Robinson tied a career high with 11 assists and had a career-high eight rebounds. Senior forward Mark Hughes had a career-best 12 rebounds.

Six Wolverines were in double figures, led by senior forward Glen Rice with 28 and Robinson with 17. U-M outrebounded smaller Western, 52-26, and blocked seven shots.

Mark Brown, a Michigan State transfer who was averaging 20 points, was held to nine.

"Our defense set the tempo," Rice said. "We didn't want Mark Brown to get loose. We're coming together real well, and I think that's because we're an unselfish basketball team."

Terry Mills (14 points) said: "We need to continue to play this way if we want to win the Big Ten and the team will appear next Sunday."

Michigan	FG	FT	R	A	TP
Rice	11-19	5-5	11	2	28
Griffin	0-0	1-2	1	1	1
Mills	6-8	2-2	6	1	14
Higgins	5-7	0-0	7	1	11
Robinson	6-9	3-4	8	11	17
Calip	1-2	0-0	0	0	2
Taylor	2-4	0-0	0	2	5
Pelinka	1-2	0-0	0	0	2
Vaught	2-5	6-9	6	0	10
Oosterbaan	3-3	0-0	1	3	6
Hughes	5-9	1-1	12	2	11
Totals	42-68	18-23	52	23	107

Western Michigan	FG	FT	R	A	TP
Holmes	5-8	5-5	4	0	16
Overstreet	7-11	3-6	6	1	17
Baumgardt	1-9	0-0	5	1	4
Stanback	1-7	2-3	1	2	4
Brown	3-10	1-2	3	1	9
Havrilla	2-2	0-0	1	0	4
Parker	1-9	0-0	3	2	2
Judge	0-1	0-0	0	0	0
Johnson	1-3	0-1	0	1	2
Warner	0-0	0-1	1	0	0
White	1-2	0-0	0	1	2
Brawley	0-0	0-0	1	0	0
Totals	21-62	15-24	26	9	60

Three-point goals: Michigan 5-9 (Robinson 2-2, Rice 1-3, Taylor 1-2, Higgins 1-1, Hughes 0-1); Western Michigan 3-11 (Brown 2-4, Holmes 1-2, Stanback 0-3, Overstreet 0-1, Parker 0-1).

Turnovers: Michigan 15, Western Michigan 21

Strategy had become a forgotten word. Michigan hadn't required much of it in December, winning its last five games by more than 40 points.

But the Wolverines had to make adjustments in beating Eastern Michigan, 80-57, before 12,208 at Crisler Arena. The Hurons (5-1) kept it close in the first half by favoring a slow-down offense over their usual running style.

No. 2 U-M (9-0) didn't pull away until switching its defensive press from the baseline to midcourt, where EMU was beginning its plays.

Sophomore guard Lorenzo Neely (Detroit Northern) was the only Huron in double figures with 18 points.

Sean Higgins led the Wolverines with 18 points against his father's alma mater. Last year, his season high of 20 points came against EMU.

"I had a dream in high school to play at Michigan," said Earle Higgins, who watched the game in a three-piece suit. "I'm glad my son has had the experience I couldn't have."

The elder Higgins was all-state at Ann Arbor Pioneer High. He attended Casper (Wyo.) Junior College before playing for the Hurons from 1967-70. Higgins ranks seventh in rebounds (577) and ninth in scoring (1,235 points) at EMU.

Higgins had a short career in the ABA with the Indiana Pacers. He lives in Southfield and is a scheduling co-ordinator for four Chrysler Corporation plants.

A signed letter of intent Sean Higgins had with UCLA was voided by the NCAA and Higgins went to U-M. An NCAA investigation released that week said that Higgins was offered $300 monthly, a car and help on his mother's house payments in Los Angeles by Kentucky assistant Dwane Casey.

"I don't know nothing about that," Higgins said. "That's no big deal now."

He never elaborated on the report during the season, and seldom was heard from until catching fire in the NCAA Tournament.

The Wolverines made their first scoring run of the game immediately after halftime, scoring 11 unanswered points for a 45-27 lead. Higgins and Rice (12 points in 19 minutes) each contributed four points.

EMU (38 percent) and U-M (57 percent) had their worst shooting nights of the season.

Rice scored a season-low 12 points, and spent the post-game in coach Bill Frieder's office studying for exams.

Michigan	FG	FT	R	A	TP
Rice	3-6	6-6	2	0	12
Mills	3-6	6-6	2	5	12
Griffin	2-2	1-2	1	2	7
Higgins	7-13	3-3	4	0	18
Robinson	2-10	2-3	7	6	6
Calip	1-1	0-0	0	0	2
Taylor	2-5	0-0	3	1	4
Pelinka	0-1	0-0	0	0	0
Vaught	6-8	0-1	8	0	12
Oosterbaan	1-3	2-2	3	0	4
Hughes	2-3	1-2	1	1	5
Totals	29-58	21-25	37	15	80

Eastern Michigan	FG	FT	R	A	TP
CH. Thomas	2-5	3-3	5	0	8
Hallas	4-10	1-2	7	0	7
Desalvo	1-2	1-1	2	0	3
Chambers	1-7	0-0	2	1	2
Neely	7-17	4-4	3	4	18
Nolan	0-0	2-2	4	1	2
CA. Thomas	3-8	2-2	5	0	9
Henderson	3-6	0-1	1	2	6
Hughes	0-0	0-0	0	0	0
Totals	21-55	13-15	30	8	57

Three-point goals: Michigan 1-4 (Higgins 1-1, Taylor 0-2, Robinson 0-1); Eastern Michigan 2-10 (CA. Thomas 1-4, CH. Thomas 1-3, Neely 0-2, Chambers 0-1).

Turnovers: Michigan 13, Eastern Michigan 16
Fouled Out: Eastern Michigan — Henderson

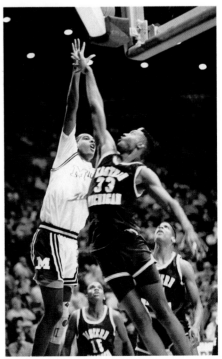

Ernestine Rice saw her sons, Glen and Kevin, compete for the second and, she hoped, last time in Michigan's 125-75 victory over Northern Michigan.

She also saw a record-setting performance.

The Wolverines (10-0) set a Crisler Arena mark with 125 points. They made 17 dunks and shot 61.5 percent. The previous record was 123 points against Illinois-Chicago in 1986.

Glen led the Wolverines with 36 points on 14-of-22 shooting. Kevin struggled after hitting two three-pointers early and finished with eight points, the same total he had in last year's 111-87 loss. The Division II Wildcats fell to 3-5.

"It's really strange for me, watching them play against each other," Ernestine said. "Glen and Kevin always played together at (Flint) Northwestern. I was hoping nobody would knock me down rooting for both Glen and Kevin."

Said Glen: "We had always talked about playing against each other. It was a lot of fun. I talked him into taking a couple of shots late in the game. He was running around and I told him to stop."

Said Kevin: "I was glad I got a chance to play against him before he turned professional. He talked me into a couple of shots. They're a great team. It seemed like he was doing most of the scoring."

U-M never stopped running, building a 58-31 halftime lead. They dominated play inside in the second half and forced 16 turnovers with its pressure defense. U-M outrebounded Northern, 50-21.

"We tried a lot of different things out there tonight," said Michigan coach Bill Frieder. "We went to a zone early and we stank. It stopped us from running. This was a good game for us."

Junior forward Loy Vaught had eight dunks and finished with 22 points on 8-of-11 shooting.

It was a learning experience for Northern coach Dean Ellis, "We appreciate that Michigan plays the state schools," he said. "It's good for us. Their pressure and size were big factors. At one time they had a lineup of 6-feet-9 and over. What do you do?"

Michigan	FG	FT	R	A	TP
Rice	14-22	8-9	8	3	36
Mills	8-11	5-6	13	1	21
Griffin	1-2	0-0	8	8	2
Higgins	4-11	3-3	4	2	13
Robinson	4-9	0-1	4	6	8
Hughes	5-6	3-3	0	1	13
Pelinka	0-2	0-0	2	2	0
Oosterbaan	4-4	2-2	1	3	10
Koenig	0-0	0-0	1	0	0
Vaught	8-11	6-6	8	1	22
Totals	48-78	27-30	50	27	125

Northern Michigan	FG	FT	R	A	TP
Vitala	4-11	0-0	1	2	10
Gray	3-4	0-0	2	4	6
Goheski	1-5	0-0	5	1	2
Rice	3-12	0-0	0	1	8
Steanstra	1-3	0-0	1	1	2
Nelson	1-4	0-0	2	0	2
Ingalls	2-3	0-0	2	2	6
Clark	2-8	1-1	0	2	5
Tidwell	8-13	4-5	5	0	20
Ledy	2-2	0-0	0	2	4
Smith	1-1	0-0	1	0	2
Koski	3-3	0-0	1	1	8
Totals	31-69	5-6	21	12	75

Three-point goals: Michigan 2-7 (Higgins 2-4, Pelinka 0-2, Rice 0-1); Northern Michigan 8-21 (Rice 2-8, Vitala 2-6, Ingalls 2-2, Koski 2-2, Steanstra 0-1).

Turnovers: Michigan 10, Northern Michigan 16

11 *Michigan* 121
Youngstown State 72

Michigan coach Bill Frieder had planted the seed earlier in December: If his players didn't put out over the cupcake portion of the schedule, he might make them practice over Christmas break.

After the Wolverines beat Youngstown State, 121-72, Frieder said he never intended to become college basketball's version of Ebenezer Scrooge. "It would take their legs away," he said.

But the hint of line drills and free-throw shooting on Christmas night made an impression.

"It was not hard to get up for these games because Coach Frieder said we had to work hard on our rebounding and higher shooting percentages," said Terry Mills, opening with the company line. "But it was especially easy to get up for these games if you didn't want to practice over Christmas. That was always a threat, always in the back of our minds. A couple of times before I was here, they say, they practiced after a couple games when he was mad. So, we never knew."

Said point guard Rumeal Robinson: "I heard it. But a lot of the guys wouldn't have gone for that."

Robinson could afford to smile. The Wolverines ate cupcakes like Paul Newman sucked down eggs in "Cool Hand Luke": often and in massive quantities. U-M (11-0) won its last eight games by an average of 40.8 points. Only Eastern Michigan (80-57) kept the Wolverines under 98 points and offered a challenge.

Glen Rice, who led all scorers with 30 points, is averaging 24.2. Loy Vaught (26 points, 10 rebounds), Sean Higgins (18), Robinson (15) and Mark Hughes (13) joined the scoring parade.

U-M hit 50 of 74 shots (.676) for its second-best shooting percentage in Crisler Arena. The record was set last December, 51-for-75 (.680) against Western Michigan.

Youngstown State (0-8) lost its 21st straight and owned what was believed to be the longest current NCAA Division I losing streak. Jim Wright of the NCAA said such marks are not researched until late in the season.

"Someday, our guys will look back and say they played in this building," said Youngstown coach Jim Cleamons, who didn't start a junior or senior. "But they'll also have to say Michigan gave us a spanking." Youngstown allowed the most points in its history.

U-M never trailed and led, 56-38, at halftime. Frieder supplied what little entertainment value existed. He read the Wolverines the riot act during a time-out. His face turned red as he pointed and shouted instructions at each player.

Less than two minutes later, Frieder received a technical from a smiling official. Save it for Indiana, coach.

"We got a little sloppy," said Frieder. "I think we got their attention."

Freshman walk-on Marc Koenig of Los Angeles scored his only points of the season and the Wolverine's last bucket of the game.

Frieder, true to a promise he made on several radio shows, signed copies of his book, "Basket Case," after the game at his home. He even supplied the address. "It's probably the stupidest thing I ever did," he said.

Michigan	FG	FT	R	A	TP
Rice	12-18	4-4	7	8	30
Mills	3-6	2-2	9	7	8
Griffin	2-3	1-1	2	3	5
Higgins	7-12	0-0	2	1	18
Robinson	6-9	2-3	5	4	15
Vaught	11-12	4-5	10	1	26
Hughes	6-8	1-3	3	2	13
Pelinka	1-3	0-1	2	1	2
Oosterbaan	1-2	0-0	1	0	2
Koenig	1-1	0-0	0	0	2
Totals	50-74	14-19	42	27	121

Youngstown St.	FG	FT	R	A	TP
Haddock	12-18	1-2	1	0	27
Kemp	3-10	3-4	4	2	9
Vasser	5-9	2-2	3	9	13
Johnson	1-6	0-0	4	1	2
Jackson	2-8	0-0	5	0	4
Marrow	3-10	0-0	2	0	6
Lark	3-5	1-2	4	2	9
Ray	1-3	0-0	0	0	2
Brown	0-2	0-0	1	0	0
Sahr	0-1	0-0	2	0	0
Hannousek	0-0	0-0	0	0	0
Totals	30-72	8-10	27	14	72

Three-point goals: Michigan 7-15 (Higgins 4-8, Rice 2-4, Robinson 1-2, Pelinka 0-1); Youngstown State 4-10 (Haddock 2-4, Vasser 1-2, Lark 1-2, Marrow 0-2).

Turnovers: Michigan 18, Youngstown State 24

12 Michigan 66
Alaska-Anchorage 70

A season of bliss was interrupted, suddenly and unbelievably, in the strangest of places by the unlikeliest of teams.

In the cold and fog of Salt Lake City, Michigan was chilled by Division II Alaska-Anchorage in one of the most shocking upsets in recent college basketball history.

The Wolverines were 11-0, ranked second in the country, averaging 101 points per game and shooting 61 percent. They had crushed their only true test, Oklahoma, 91-80 in the Hawaiian heat a month earlier.

But now, on a frigid night in Utah, they were suffering the most inglorious fate. Just as fourth-ranked Iowa had a few days earlier when it lost to California-Riverside, Michigan was upset by a Division II team in a holiday tournament.

The Seawolves controlled the game by controlling the tempo, using most of the 45-second clock nearly every possession. Their patience produced a 62.7 shooting percentage and frustration for the Wolverines.

Out of synch, and, ultimately, out of desperation, Michigan shot 47.5 percent and hit only 5-of-13 free throws.

"Coach Frieder warned us over and over, he really got on us about playing them," said forward Glen Rice, who scored 24 points but shot only 11-for-23. "Believe me, we didn't take them lightly. Anchorage just stuck to their game plan, and we didn't."

The Seawolves (11-2) were Division II runners-up the previous season, but faced incredible physical obstacles against Michigan. They had three guards under 5-10, and their starting lineup averaged 6-5.

Yet when they forced Michigan to play defense for long stretches, the Wolverines wilted. In the weeks ahead, opposing coaches would find hope in that game plan and would duplicate tempo-controlling tactics against Michigan.

"We didn't want to run and rebound with them," Seawolves coach Ron Abegglen said. "If we did, they'd beat us by a lot. Our kids stuck with the game plan very well. We've been kind of a run-and-gun outfit, but we changed things two days ago for this game. Our kids really thought they had a chance."

The Seawolves were aided by a Michigan team that, for the first time all season, couldn't shake its sluggishness. Michigan's inside defense was poor, allowing the Alaska-Anchorage tandem of 6-5 Todd Fisher and 6-8 Ron Fischer to combine for 34 points.

Loy Vaught got his first start because Sean Higgins was beginning a three-game suspension for a drinking incident. The 6-9 junior forward hardly made the most of it, with eight points and four rebounds.

"We weren't sharp," Frieder said. "I don't know if it was the (one-week) layoff or the travel, or what. That's when you need to toughen up your defense, but we just didn't get it done.

"Alaska had a good game plan. We anticipated them holding the ball, but they did a great job of it. We have to learn to play against quicker teams who slow it down."

The Seawolves trailed at the half, 36-32, but went on a 20-4 tear midway through the second half to take a 58-48 lead with nine minutes left.

Michigan cut the deficit to 63-60, but Rice missed two free throws with 3:18 left and Rumeal Robinson committed a charging foul. Alaska-Anchorage scored its last nine points from the free-throw line.

"Our guys just didn't do what they had to in crucial situations," Frieder said. "But we'll bounce back. I don't like losing but, hopefully, we'll learn from this."

Michigan	FG-A	FT-A	R	A	TP
Rice	11-23	1-5	9	2	24
Mills	7-12	0-1	9	5	14
Vaught	4-5	0-0	4	0	8
Griffin	1-3	0-0	5	5	2
Robinson	3-9	2-3	2	4	9
Calip	0-0	0-0	0	1	0
Taylor	1-6	0-1	1	3	3
Hughes	2-3	2-3	3	1	6
Totals	29-61	5-13	20	21	66

Alaska-Anchorage	FG-A	FT-A	R	A	TP
Miles	2-3	3-5	4	2	7
Fisher	9-13	0-0	4	1	18
Fischer	5-7	4-5	3	2	16
Johnson	7-12	4-7	3	3	20
Sommer	2-3	0-0	2	5	5
Carpenter	0-1	0-0	1	1	0
Brinkerhoff	0-0	0-0	1	1	0
McGee	0-0	0-0	1	0	0
McCleary	2-4	0-0	3	0	4
Myers	0-0	0-0	0	0	0
Totals	27-33	11-17	25	14	70

Three-point goals: Michigan 3-12 (Rice 1-7, Robinson 1-4, Taylor 1-1); Alaska 5-8 (Fischer 2-3, Johnson 2-3, Sommer 1-1, Carpenter 0-1).

Turnovers: Michigan 18, Alaska 18
Fouled Out: Michigan — Griffin

13 Michigan 100
Holy Cross 63

Shame in their hearts, vengeance in their eyes and a new lineup on the court, the Wolverines rebounded from a stunning upset with a methodical victory.

Already shaken by the loss to Alaska-Anchorage, Coach Bill Frieder shook up his team a little more with lineup changes, giving guards Kirk Taylor and Rob Pelinka their first career starts and forward Mark Hughes his first start of the season. To the bench went Rumeal Robinson, Mike Griffin and Loy Vaught.

"We had to shake things up," Frieder said. "I felt bad about Pelinka not playing in the last game and I wasn't satisfied with the way Rumeal, Griffin and Loy played. But I thought they responded well tonight. There are no automatic starters on this team. You have to work hard to earn a position."

Hughes responded with a career-high 21 points, but in the end, it was old standby Glen Rice leading the way with 28.

It was hardly a night for gloating, but the Wolverines did find some satisfaction in rebounding from their first loss of the season.

"I think our kids did a good job," Frieder said. "Anytime you lose your starting position, that's got to bother you a little bit. Especially when you have as much pride and character as a guy like Rumeal. I wanted to see how they'd react, and I liked what I saw."

Robinson had eight points and seven assists, as 10 Wolverines scored in the rout.

"It's no big deal who starts, it's who finishes the game," Robinson said. "The minutes are what counts. It's Coach's decision, and I have to live with it. We know what he's doing."

What they were doing the night before the Utah Classic consolation game was watching film of the Alaska-Anchorage loss — again and again and again.

"I'll tell you, our players are sick of watching that film," Frieder said. "We watched it for four hours and we told them everything they did wrong. We had a breakdown offensively and defensively. We have an All-American (Rice), and he's supposed to come through, but even he had a bad game.

"Defense was the difference tonight. When we struggled offensively a little bit, our defense picked us up."

Michigan played its second consecutive game without starting guard Sean Higgins, who was suspended three games because of a drinking incident following the Dec. 21 victory against Youngstown State.

Higgins, though, offered support from the bench, where he was the team's biggest cheerleader.

"I don't like sitting, but Coach made the decision," he said. "We established a team rule and I broke it."

Holy Cross knew quickly it had caught the Wolverines on the wrong night, and there was little the Crusaders could do.

"They were so much physically stronger than us at every position," Coach George Blaney said. "And their defense was excellent, much better than last night."

Plenty of things were much better. But an uneasiness remained as the Wolverines headed into the Big Ten season. After weeks of few worries, Frieder felt it.

"It's good that we have enough depth to change the lineup like that," he said. "But we're not where I want to be at this time, to be honest. I'm happy we bounced back, and I'm happy we're 12-1, but we've got to get better."

Michigan	FG-A	FT-A	R	A	TP
Rice	11-20	4-5	5	4	28
Mills	3-10	2-2	11	3	8
Hughes	9-14	3-4	6	1	21
Taylor	4-5	1-4	2	4	9
Pelinka	3-5	0-0	5	2	8
Calip	1-3	0-0	3	1	2
Griffin	0-2	4-4	2	4	4
Robinson	1-2	6-8	4	7	8
Vaught	2-6	2-2	8	3	6
Oosterbaan	3-5	0-2	1	0	6
Totals	37-72	22-31	48	29	100

Holy Cross	FG-A	FT-A	R	A	TP
Viviano	2-4	0-1	0	1	4
Carter	3-4	1-2	2	1	7
Evans	8-13	0-1	8	2	16
Pernell	5-13	2-2	4	2	12
Williams	1-3	1-2	1	6	3
Foley	0-0	0-0	1	0	0
Davis	3-10	0-0	3	0	8
Weedon	3-5	0-1	1	0	6
Fedina	0-3	0-0	1	1	0
Kerwin	0-1	0-0	2	0	0
Martucci	0-0	1-2	0	0	1
Dickerson	1-4	0-0	2	1	2
Martzloff	0-3	4-4	2	1	4
Totals	26-63	9-15	33	17	63

Three-point goals: Michigan 4-7 (Rice 2-3, Pelinka 2-3, Calip 0-1); Holy Cross 2-8 (Davis 2-6, Viviano 0-1, Williams 0-1).

Turnovers: Michigan 9, Holy Cross 18
Fouled Out: Michigan — Mills.

14 *Michigan* 94
Northwestern 66

If the Wolverines were awakened by their loss to Alaska-Anchorage, it didn't take them long to grow sleepy again.

Lulled by Northwestern's methodical attack, seventh-ranked Michigan trudged through its Big Ten opener like an impatient child forced to do homework. The lethargy showed, and the Crisler Arena crowd of 13,570 voiced its impatience.

With 13:51 left, the Wolverines led by only 58-48. The Wildcats, who brought a 7-4 record and an eight-game losing streak against Michigan into the contest, had success controlling the tempo and the interior with forward Walker Lambiotte (15 points) and center Evan Pedersen (13).

Glen Rice was playing with the flu; Northwestern was playing with a spark, and the rest of the Wolverines were playing with the post-holiday blahs.

Then Bill Frieder called a timeout. Animated and agitated, he slapped the Wolverines to life.

"We really got on the kids," he said. "And they responded, especially on defense."

Michigan went on a 21-8 rampage over the next 7:30 and finally subdued the Wildcats.

Said Rice, who would finish with a game-high 25 points (17 in the first half): "We realized that in the Big Ten season, you have to turn it up a notch. We realized we had to play hard each and every game."

It was a lesson the Wolverines would learn time and again. It was a lesson they would often forget, but always recall.

And on this afternoon, it was a relatively painless lesson. Frieder had experimented with his lineup again, starting Kirk Taylor at guard and Mark Hughes at center, and by game's end, the lethargy of the first 27 minutes was quickly forgotten.

Loy Vaught (18 points on 8-for-10 shooting, 11 rebounds, first collegiate three-pointer) had rallied them, but Terry Mills had sparked them with one of the finest games of his college career. His 20-point effort (on 10-for-13 shooting) was both a statement and a tease. Who could know it would also be a prophecy?

"I want to be a true center," said Mills, who played the position but was listed as a forward. "I want to run the floor like I did today. Now I have to sustain this kind of performance. If I play like this every game, I think we'll win the Big Ten."

"Terry has really been working hard, and he has a great attitude," said Frieder of his favorite whipping boy. "Terry is doing everything we've asked of him. He's playing his best basketball yet."

But Frieder spent more time apologizing for his second technical of the season than he did analyzing a lackluster game. He got nabbed with 7:25 left in the first half when he leaped to protest a call and his trademark towel flew at referee Ted Valentine.

"Before you guys rip me on the towel incident, if you watch the films you'll find it was an honest mistake," Frieder said. "I jumped up, and the towel slipped out of my hand. The ref thought I threw it at him, but I'm truly, truly sorry."

It might have been the first time Frieder had so adamantly apologized after a victory. But in the days ahead, it would become an unsettling theme.

No matter how easy the victory or how difficult the opponent, Frieder and the Wolverines would spend more time discussing their faults than extolling their feats.

Michigan	FG-A	FT-A	R	A	TP
Rice	9-16	2-5	3	1	15
Mills	10-13	0-0	5	2	20
Hughes	0-4	0-0	0	2	0
Taylor	2-2	6-10	4	3	10
Robinson	5-10	4-5	3	8	16
Griffin	2-4	0-0	4	3	4
Vaught	8-10	1-2	11	0	18
Pelinka	0-0	0-0	1	0	0
Calip	0-1	0-0	0	0	0
Oosterbaan	0-1	1-2	1	0	1
Totals	36-61	17-25	32	20	94

Northwestern	FG-A	FT-A	R	A	TP
Lambiotte	7-16	1-2	3	1	15
Schwabe	2-6	1-2	6	2	5
Pedersen	6-8	1-2	5	1	13
R. Ross	2-4	0-0	1	2	6
Styles	3-4	3-4	3	1	10
Grose	3-4	2-2	1	2	11
B. Ross	1-1	0-0	2	0	2
Holmes	0-1	0-0	0	1	0
Reece	2-4	0-2	2	0	4
Polite	0-0	0-0	0	0	0
Waters	0-1	0-0	0	0	0
Buford	0-2	0-0	0	0	0
Totals	26-51	8-14	25	10	66

Three-point goals: Michigan 5-9 (Rice 2-5, Robinson 2-2, Vaught 1-1, Calip 0-1); Northwestern 6-13 (Gross 3-4, Ross 2-3, Styles 1-1, Reece 0-2, Waters 0-1, Buford 0-1).

Turnovers: Michigan 19, Northwestern 30

15 Michigan 98
Minnesota 83

For the second straight game, the Wolverines struggled against a supposedly inferior opponent. For the second straight game, they played their best when they needed it most.

And for the second straight game, what should have been a relatively satisfying victory was smothered by enormous expectations.

This time, the Wolverines needed a bigger rally against a tougher team. They trailed, 45-41, with 16:46 remaining, only the third time they'd trailed in a second half. The Gophers were using the formula that would haunt U-M most of the season — quickness in the backcourt, physical play in the frontcourt.

Led by forward Willie Burton (19 points, 8-for-12 shooting), Minnesota rallied from a 13-point first-half deficit to take the lead. Rebounding was a key, as the quicker Gophers won the battle of the boards, 38-35.

"Their rebounding killed us," Coach Bill Frieder would say later. "They were going over the top of us and treating us like little kids."

But the Wolverines grew up in a hurry. Once again, Glen Rice and Rumeal Robinson loaded the team on their backs and sparked the comeback, establishing a pattern to be repeated all season. Michigan shot 79 percent in the second half, and a 26-9 run turned a 47-43 deficit into a 69-56 lead — and a dreary performance into a comfortable victory.

Rice scored 31 and Robinson added 24, while sparking a 9-for-14 effort from three-point range, which would prove to be Michigan's most deadly method of attack.

Sophomore Sean Higgins also made his much-awaited Big Ten debut, scoring 20 points and hitting the first of his four three-pointers just six seconds into the contest. It was an important game for Higgins, who was academically ineligible for the Big Ten season his freshman year and had missed the Northwestern game while serving a three-game suspension for a drinking incident.

He drew a start because guard Kirk Taylor was nursing a slight ankle sprain, and drew raves with his long-range bombing.

"Sean Higgins is a fine player," Minnesota Coach Clem Haskins said. "Going into the game, I knew he was a great shooter, but I had no idea he was that good."

Said Frieder: "We've got great three-point shooters, so we're going to shoot the three-pointer. When they don't go down, we may look bad, but we made nine tonight and that's what has made us successful."

A season-high 20 turnovers and 11 Minnesota steals almost made Michigan unsuccessful, as the Wolverines' lack of guard depth again proved telling. Defensive problems were especially acute when Higgins and Mike Griffin manned the backcourt.

But as quickly as this game ended, the Wolverines looked ahead to the next, the season's first big showdown at second-ranked and undefeated Illinois.

Frieder had already created a stir by jokingly offering to bet Lou Henson $500 that Illinois would beat Michigan. At times against the Gophers, it looked like a safe bet. But the Wolverines hoped a tough victory against a physical team had prepared them for the Illini.

"I hope it's a good game," Frieder said. "But if we don't play exceptional basketball, it'll be a blowout. Illinois is a great, great team."

Michigan	FG-A	FT-A	R	A	TP
Rice	11-17	6-6	7	3	31
Mills	2-5	3-7	6	7	7
Hughes	4-8	1-3	5	1	9
Higgins	8-11	0-0	3	0	20
Robinson	7-9	8-11	6	7	24
Vaught	3-5	1-1	4	1	7
Griffin	0-0	0-0	2	2	0
Taylor	0-0	0-0	0	0	0
Oosterbaan	0-0	0-0	0	0	0
Totals	35-55	19-28	35	21	98

Minnesota	FG-A	FT-A	R	A	TP
Coffey	3-6	0-0	11	5	6
Burton	8-12	3-4	5	0	19
Shikenjanski	5-8	0-0	4	0	10
Newbern	7-25	5-5	5	8	19
Lynch	7-16	0-0	4	1	15
Gaffney	3-10	0-0	3	1	9
Bond	1-1	0-0	2	3	4
Martin	1-1	0-0	2	0	2
Lewis	0-0	0-0	0	0	0
Metcalf	0-1	0-0	1	0	0
Green	0-0	0-0	0	0	0
Totals	35-80	8-9	38	18	83

Three-point goals: Michigan 9-14 (Higgins 4-6, Rice 3-5, Robinson 2-3); Minnesota 5-11 (Gaffney 3-5, Bond 1-1, Newbern 0-1).

Turnovers: Michigan 20, Minnesota 13
Fouled Out: Minnesota — Coffey, Burton

16 *Michigan* 84
Illinois 96

In a stunning display of athleticism and firepower, Illinois delivered a numbing message.

And the Wolverines, who played better than the final score indicated, heard it loud and clear.

"That might be the best team I've seen in the 16 years I've been in the Big Ten," an exasperated Bill Frieder said after the game. "Indiana's 1976 team might be the only one better. We just can't match Illinois' quickness. We knew we needed a perfect game to beat them, and we didn't get it."

For several stretches, though, the Wolverines came pretty close. Glen Rice scored 30 points, Loy Vaught added 22 on 9-for-11 shooting and Michigan battled Illinois to a 33-33 standstill on the boards.

The Wolverines even led, 44-43, late in the first half before Kendall Gill (26 points) scored five points in the final seven seconds, setting the stage for a scintillating second half. Gill's three-pointer at the halftime buzzer came after Kirk Taylor turned the ball over in the closing seconds.

"Those shots picked us up," Gill said. "I could see our mood change. And that mood carried over into the second half."

With eight minutes left, it was 78-65, and the No. 2 Illini were shredding No. 6 Michigan with quickness and a deadly fastbreak.

The Wolverines gasped once more, shaving the deficit to 78-74 with 6:03 left, but could draw no closer. Illinois hit 10 consecutive free throws down the stretch, keeping Frieder winless in Assembly Hall.

The victory was complete and efficient, and the Illini wallowed in smugness.

"Coach Henson doesn't like me saying this, but Michigan got real tired out there," said Gill, who repeatedly exploited the defensive deficiencies of guards Mike Griffin and Sean Higgins. "Rumeal and Rice were breathing heavy. When you get them down, you have to kick them."

Added Illinois guard Steve Bardo: "You could see it on their faces. We knew we had to wear them out, and we did."

The loss dropped the Wolverines from immediate contention for the No. 1 ranking in the country and the top spot in the Big Ten. But it didn't drop their spirits.

They realized they'd lost to perhaps the finest team in the country, on Illinois' homecourt, where Michigan is 0-9 under Frieder. They realized Higgins, playing his first Big Ten road game, had shot an unlikely 1-for-9.

And they realized there would be opportunities for redemption.

"I'm not that upset by the loss because it came against a great team," Frieder said. "I'm not going to jump off a bridge or anything. We played fairly well, but we had trouble with their pressure defense. Send Duke in here and they're in trouble. We aren't going to make a big thing out of this."

Said Rice: "We'll be looking forward to seeing them in Ann Arbor that last game (March 11). We'll be waiting for them."

But on this Saturday, it was a humbling, if not totally unexpected, result. Frieder had, after all, jokingly offered to bet Henson $500 that the Illini would win.

That motivational tactic had backfired, but now the Wolverines had a better one — rebounding from their second loss of the season.

"We've got a ways to go," Frieder admitted. "Right now, we're just like Iowa and Indiana and the rest of them, chasing after Illinois."

Michigan	FG-A	FT-A	R	A	TP
Rice	12-18	2-2	9	1	30
Mills	5-10	0-0	3	2	10
Griffin	0-2	0-0	3	6	0
Higgins	1-9	2-2	2	3	5
Robinson	6-13	3-6	2	8	15
Vaught	9-11	3-4	8	1	22
Taylor	0-0	0-0	0	1	0
Hughes	1-3	0-0	1	0	2
Calip	0-0	0-0	0	0	0
Totals	34-66	10-14	33	22	84

Illinois	FG-A	FT-A	R	A	TP
Anderson	6-11	3-4	7	0	16
Battle	9-16	0-1	5	4	18
Hamilton	4-9	2-2	5	0	10
Gill	8-15	8-10	4	3	26
Bardo	2-7	7-7	4	11	11
Small	1-3	1-2	3	0	3
Smith	1-2	4-4	0	0	6
Liberty	3-5	0-0	2	0	6
Bowman	0-0	0-0	0	0	0
McDonald	0-0	0-0	0	0	0
Shapland	0-0	0-0	0	0	0
Totals	34-68	25-30	33	18	96

Three-point goals: Michigan 6-18 (Rice 4-7, Higgins 1-6, Vaught 1-2, Robinson 0-3); Illinois 3-10 (Gill 2-6, Anderson 1-3, Bardo 0-1).

Turnovers: Michigan 17, Illinois 18

17 Michigan 99
Ohio State 73

On a night when Terry Mills finally showed up in Michigan's offense, Jay Burson disappeared from Ohio State's. The timing couldn't have been more fortuitous for the Wolverines, who easily rebounded from the Illinois loss with a nationally televised romp.

As important as Michigan's shackling of Burson (12 points on 6-for-18 shooting) was the long-awaited arrival of Mills. The 6-11 junior center finally fulfilled his enormous potential, while helping Michigan's frontline do the same.

Always bigger and stronger than their opposition, the Wolverines finally took advantage of it. Mills scored a career-high 23 points, Glen Rice added 23 and Loy Vaught had 22. That trio combined to shoot 28-for-36 and helped dominate the boards, 39-30.

Rumeal Robinson (14 points) chipped in with a superb defensive effort on Burson, the star guard who was averaging 24 ppg.

But at the heart of the turnaround was Mills, who stopped wandering to the perimeter and started attacking the low post.

"I think it was my best game," he said. "I worked harder in the post. There was definitely some carry-over from the Illinois game. They did a great job of denying me the ball, and I kind of gave up and stopped working. I made up my mind I wasn't going to give up at all in this game."

The relief of burying the memory of the Illinois loss was evident. Coach Bill Frieder interrupted Mills' post-game press conference by quipping, "OK, Mills, that's enough. You've only given us one good game in three years. You give us another and maybe I'll let you talk some more."

Although only a joke, it was a pointed one. Because Rice is more of a perimeter player and Vaught plays best facing the basket, Mills' low-post development was critical to Michigan's offense.

He showed why on this Monday night, as the Wolverines slaughtered a good Ohio State team.

"Some of us had a talk before the game," Mills said. "We basically said we hadn't been playing hard enough. We just made up our minds we were going to work harder and not stop."

Almost as significant as Mills' play was that of Vaught, a 6-9 junior forward who made his second start of the season. He replaced Mike Griffin in the lineup and responded with another superb shooting performance (10-for-12).

It was Frieder's seventh lineup change in as many games, and possibly his best.

"It meant a great deal for me to start, although I've been saying all along that what really matters is getting the number of minutes I deserve," Vaught said. "Now with the starting role, I'm going to get those minutes.

"It has been frustrating. It makes you think that if you'd gone somewhere else, you could play more. But Coach Frieder told me we were going to put all that stuff behind us. He and I had a big communcations gap, and that led to problems for me."

But the Wolverines proved they could address their problems quickly, even after a devastating loss like the one to Illinois.

"Having to travel back after that game and play the way we did is a credit to my players," Frieder said. "We were reacting to Illinois, rather than being the aggressor. Tonight, we were the aggressor."

And Mills, finally, was the most aggressive of the aggressors.

"I feel good now," he said. "This game gave me a lot of confidence. I feel now that I can play inside in the Big Ten. But you have to keep it in perspective. This is just one game, and it's over with. I have to come out and do it again, every time."

Michigan	FG-A	FT-A	R	A	TP
Rice	8-11	2-4	4	2	23
Mills	10-13	3-4	5	4	23
Vaught	10-12	2-2	9	3	22
Higgins	4-8	0-0	7	3	10
Robinson	6-11	1-3	0	5	14
Hughes	3-4	0-2	10	1	6
Taylor	0-1	0-0	0	0	0
Pelinka	0-0	0-0	0	1	0
Calip	0-1	1-2	1	0	1
Oosterbaan	2-3	0-0	2	0	4
Griffin	0-1	0-0	0	2	0
Totals	41-64	9-17	39	21	99

Ohio State	FG-A	FT-A	R	A	TP
Francis	2-8	2-2	2	1	6
White	3-8	1-2	3	0	7
Carter	8-14	1-1	8	1	17
Burson	6-18	0-0	4	2	12
Brown	1-4	2-2	1	1	5
Mateen	3-3	2-3	2	0	8
Lee	2-5	2-2	3	1	6
Bradley	1-3	0-0	0	0	3
Brewster	3-5	0-0	1	2	7
Jent	1-3	0-0	2	1	2
Robinson	0-0	0-2	0	0	0
Dumas	0-0	0-0	0	0	0
Totals	30-71	10-14	30	9	73

Three-point goals: Michigan 8-12 (Rice 5-7, Higgins 2-3, Robinson 1-2); Ohio State 3-10 (Bradley 1-1, Brewster 1-2, Brown 1-2, Francis 0-1, Burson 0-2, Jent 0-2).

Turnovers: Michigan 17, Ohio State 14

18 Michigan 68
Wisconsin 71

Ligaments in his right thumb freshly sprained, Rumeal Robinson stood at the free throw line before a raucous Wisconsin Fieldhouse crowd of 11,174 and eyed a basket that had been so cruel to the Wolverines.

Heavily favored but modestly inspired, Michigan had let a 10-point lead slip away, and now the game threatened to do the same.

The Badgers led, 69-68. Nine seconds remained. Robinson had been fouled by Trent Jackson at the end of a full-court drive.

The crowd roared. Robinson missed once, barely hitting the rim. The crowd roared louder. Robinson missed again, barely hitting the rim.

Terry Mills grabbed the rebound but lost the ball, and Michigan lost the game. In nine fateful seconds on a Saturday afternoon in Madison, Wisc., the seeds of discontent would be sown as the Wolverines would lose for the second time in three games and fall to 3-2 in the Big Ten.

Who could know that those same seeds would sprout Robinson's drive for redemption, which would bloom in Seattle's Kingdome on a Monday night in April?

Who could know that the last-second misses would inspire Robinson to shoot 100 free throws a day for two weeks, and vow never to repeat his failure?

Time eventually soothed the shock of this loss to a perennial doormat. The Badgers later became one of the conference's surprises, regularly upsetting favored teams.

But the Wolverines didn't have the luxury of hindsight this day. Instead they faced increasingly pointed questions.

In 18 games, they'd yet to win a pivotal road test. Robinson's thumb was ailing, a problem that would plague him the rest of the season. And now his psyche ached as well.

"What can I say?" said Robinson, who scored eight points. "I didn't capitalize on it. I feel I let the team down. If I hit the shots, we'd have been up by one, and the game probably would have been over."

It appeared to be over much earlier, when Michigan sprinted to a 10-point first-half lead. But Sean Higgins' technical foul started a 9-0 Wisconsin run and put the Badgers in the game for good.

Glen Rice had 25 points and Mills added 15, but the Wolverines were outscrapped when it counted.

"This is just a preview of coming attractions for a lot of teams," said Coach Bill Frieder, who had warned of the Big Ten's parity. "I'm used to this type of thing; you people will have to get used to it too. They outplayed us and we didn't make the plays down the stretch. Give all the credit to Wisconsin."

The Badgers, who had lost nine in a row to Michigan, gladly accepted it.

"I think Michigan was probably preparing for its ESPN game (Monday night against Indiana)," said Jackson, who scored 21. "They took us a little bit lightly."

Jackson's free throw with 30 seconds left had broken a 68-68 tie and provided the winning margin. But the Wolverines squandered three chances to win it. They had a turnover, Robinson's misses, then Mills' turnover with four seconds left.

"Mills was definitely fouled," Frieder said. "They grabbed him and pushed him and everything else. But when you rely on officiating down the stretch, you're in trouble."

"I don't think it's panic time. It was just one of those things where it's tough to win on the road."

Michigan	FG-A	FT-A	R	A	TP
Rice	9-16	2-2	5	1	25
Mills	5-10	5-6	9	1	15
Vaught	3-5	0-0	7	2	6
Higgins	4-5	2-2	1	2	12
Robinson	2-5	4-7	2	5	8
Hughes	1-5	0-0	4	2	2
Griffin	0-0	0-0	1	1	0
Taylor	0-0	0-0	1	0	0
Oosterbaan	0-0	0-0	0	0	0
Totals	24-46	13-17	31	14	68

Wisconsin	FG-A	FT-A	R	A	TP
Jones	7-13	5-5	4	3	19
Schubring	0-0	0-0	2	1	0
Portman	6-8	0-0	9	5	12
Simms	4-8	0-2	7	3	8
Jackson	7-15	5-8	1	3	21
Locum	1-5	8-9	0	2	11
Tompkins	0-2	0-0	0	0	0
Molaski	0-0	0-0	0	0	0
Totals	25-51	18-25	24	17	71

Three-point goals: Michigan 7-11 (Rice 5-9, Higgins 2-2); Wisconsin 3-10 (Jackson 2-5, Locum 1-5).

Turnovers: Michigan 15, Wisconsin 7
Fouled Out: Michigan — Higgins

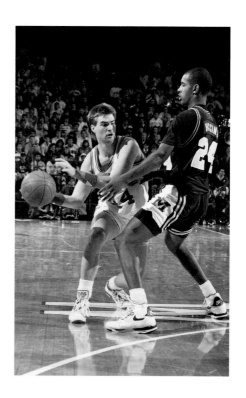

19 Michigan 70
Indiana 71

A banner unfurled early in Crisler Arena proved an ugly portent of what would transpire during Michigan's nationally televised meeting with Indiana.

"Fire Frieder" it read, as much a commentary on Michigan's losses to Illinois and Wisconsin as it was an omen.

By game's end, the feelings of impatient fans had intensified. Early in the season, the Wolverines could do no wrong. Now early in the Big Ten season, they could do no right.

And on a Monday night in January, they dipped as low as they could go. On the surface, it was a hard-fought game between two of the league's best teams. But beneath the surface churned harsh thoughts and growing concerns.

Fans and critics called it a masterful coaching job by Indiana's Bob Knight, and another indication of Bill Frieder's shortcomings.

Indiana won its 13th straight, moved to 6-0 in the Big Ten and seized command of a race it would ultimately win. Michigan lost its third in four games, dropped to 15-4 and 3-3 in the conference and saw its place as a national power suddenly questioned.

"It's especially hard losing a close game at home," said guard Sean Higgins, who scored only 10 points. "There's a lot of heartache and everyone's down. But we're Michigan, and we're going to bounce back."

Their words and their history suggested they would. Their faces hinted otherwise.

Frieder entered his post-game press conference with head down, tie askew, voice a low rasp. He had simultaneously endured a gut-wrenching defeat and a mind-boggling batch of boos. He wore a brave face, but the criticism clearly was wearing.

"Kansas won the national championship last year with double-digit losses, so I'm not worried about that," he offered, hopefully. "We have to worry about bouncing back and getting ready to play Purdue. We just have to get a win, and the rest will take care of itself."

This was to be the game the Wolverines shucked their woes and exposed the upstart Hoosiers as frauds. This was to be the game they finally got their running game in gear, finally fulfilled their potential, finally dazzled.

Instead, this was the game that exposed all their weaknesses, and left Frieder bare to receive the most severe criticism of his nine years as head coach.

Indiana had won with guile and poise. Its three-guard offense of Jay Edwards (28 points), Joe Hillman and Lyndon Jones had combined for 52 points. Using an array of screens, the Hoosiers had run their patient offense to perfection, and run the Wolverines ragged.

Glen Rice had 19 points, but for only the second time all year, Michigan shot less than 50 percent (49.1). The other time was against Alaska-Anchorage, which also controlled the tempo.

Against Indiana, the Wolverines didn't have the backcourt quickness to handle three good guards. And when Rumeal Robinson fouled out with 7:38 remaining, they had no one to run the offense.

Still, they had their chances. Trailing most of the second half, Mark Hughes' free throws with 2:09 left made it 71-70. Michigan turned the ball over but withstood two Indiana misses, then took possession with 47 seconds left.

After a timeout, Terry Mills missed a three-pointer from the corner and Hughes missed a short follow. When the clock expired, the boos cascaded.

Michigan	FG-A	FT-A	R	A	TP
Rice	8-16	2-2	6	2	19
Mills	3-9	4-6	1	4	10
Vaught	3-5	3-4	14	1	9
Higgins	4-8	0-0	1	2	10
Robinson	5-8	0-2	2	1	12
Hughes	4-8	0-0	4	2	8
Griffin	0-0	0-0	1	5	0
Calip	0-0	0-0	0	0	0
Taylor	1-3	0-1	1	1	2
Totals	28-57	9-15	31	18	70

Indiana	FG-A	FT-A	R	A	TP
Anderson	4-9	0-0	4	1	8
Hillman	5-8	0-0	1	8	12
Sloan	3-6	0-0	8	3	6
Edwards	9-15	8-10	4	2	28
Jones	4-7	4-4	4	2	12
Meeks	1-1	0-0	0	0	2
Robinson	0-2	0-0	0	0	0
Jadlow	1-1	1-2	1	0	3
White	0-0	0-0	0	0	0
Totals	27-49	13-16	23	16	71

Three-point goals: Michigan 5-10 (Robinson 2-3, Rice 1-3, Higgins 2-2, Taylor 0-1, Mills 0-1); Indiana 4-5 (Edwards 2-3, Hillman 2-2).

Turnovers: Michigan 14, Indiana 14
Fouled out: Michigan — Robinson; Indiana — Sloan.

20 Michigan 99
Purdue 88

In a stunning display of how good they can be, the Wolverines erased, for a day, the memory of how bad they had been.

Michigan entered sold-out Mackey Arena with guard problems, intensity woes and a two-game losing streak. It exited with renewed confidence and a new lease on the Big Ten race, while handing Purdue its worst home loss since an 81-65 beating by Michigan in 1985.

"I guess it was out of desperation, but we worked harder and were more aggressive on offense and defense," said forward Glen Rice, who scored 34 points on 11-for-15 shooting. "We were kind of in the dumps, but this lifts our spirits back up."

Because they had lost three of four and inspired unprecedented ire in their fans, this might have been the Wolverines' biggest victory of the season. It also might have been their most impressive.

Playing in one of the country's most hostile arenas, they completely dominated the defending conference champions, shooting 69 percent in the first half while building a 48-33 lead.

Once again, Michigan was most effective when its frontline was most effective. Loy Vaught was 7-for-7, and backup forward Mark Hughes was 7-for-11, while guard Rumeal Robinson pitched in with 15 points and nine assists.

"It seems like we always catch teams at the wrong times," Purdue coach Gene Keady said. "They were hopping mad after losing two in a row. They have extremely good athletes and they were hungry. They're probably as good as they want to be. They can either go a long way (in the NCAA tournament) or get upset in the first round."

The victory had both a soothing and stabilizing effect. It proved the Wolverines could win a tough road game, plugged the panic that started after the one-point loss to Indiana and, finally, gave Coach Bill Frieder a set lineup.

The losses to Indiana and Wisconsin convinced Frieder he couldn't play Mike Griffin and Sean Higgins in the backcourt together because of ball-handling and defensive deficiencies. So he started Griffin alongside Robinson, with Rice, Vaught and Terry Mills on the frontline, Higgins as the sixth man and reserve guard Kirk Taylor quicker off the bench. That lineup wouldn't change the rest of the season.

With the return of the Wolverines' shooting touch came their inside strength. They outrebounded Purdue, 31-18, which was necessary because the Boilermakers shot 58 percent.

"If we had played Michigan State today, we wouldn't have lost," Purdue forward Kip Jones said. "Michigan just had an outstanding game."

Rice, as usual, was the key. The Wolverines, admittedly inspired by Indiana's screening offense, set numerous screens to free him on the perimeter, perhaps for the first time acknowledging him as their primary weapon.

Said Keady: "I think Rice is the best shooter in America, from anywhere on the floor."

The victory gave Frieder ample opportunity to gloat, but he resisted. It had been a rough week, with the "Fire Frieder" signs receiving much publicity, and on Sunday, the scars were evident.

"I guess you're a good coach when the shots go in," he said. "I think it's front-runners and know-it-alls, people like that, who quit on a team. I still can't believe they booed my team at Crisler Arena. You didn't hear Purdue get booed today, did you?"

No. At least for a day, the boos had faded.

"That losing streak was one of those fluke things," said Vaught, leading the nation with a 74.2 field-goal percentage. "We just might wind up with rings on our fingers at the end of the season."

Michigan	FG-A	FT-A	R	A	TP
Rice	11-15	9-9	7	2	34
Mills	0-2	2-2	3	4	2
Vaught	7-7	0-0	5	3	14
Robinson	6-8	2-7	2	9	15
Griffin	2-4	2-2	4	1	6
Higgins	2-5	0-0	2	2	4
Hughes	7-11	3-3	2	1	17
Taylor	3-5	1-2	4	4	7
Oosterbaan	0-0	0-0	0	0	0
Totals	38-57	19-25	32	26	99

Purdue	FG-A	FT-A	R	A	TP
K. Jones	5-7	0-0	0	3	10
McCants	3-4	2-3	4	0	8
Scheffler	7-9	5-5	4	3	19
Stewart	3-7	0-0	0	4	7
T. Jones	7-12	0-0	0	6	17
Brugos	5-7	0-0	1	1	10
Clyburn	0-4	1-2	3	2	1
Berning	0-1	0-0	1	0	0
Oliver	5-8	0-2	1	3	14
Riley	0-0	0-0	0	0	0
Barrett	0-0	2-2	0	0	2
Rea	0-0	0-0	0	0	0
Austin	0-1	0-0	1	0	0
Totals	35-60	10-14	18	22	88

Three-point goals: Michigan 4-6 (Rice 3-4, Robinson 1-1, Taylor 0-1); Purdue 8-13 (Oliver 4-6, Jones 3-5, Stewart 1-1, Berning 0-1).

Turnovers: Michigan 19, Purdue 15
Fouled Out: Michigan — Vaught

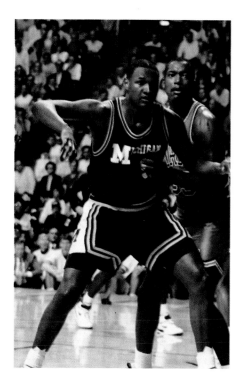

Loy Vaught repeated the numbers to make sure they were accurate.

"Oh man, it was 23-2?" said Michigan's junior center, when told of the Wolverines' second-half rebound edge. "You sure it was 23-2? I knew we got all over them, but I didn't realize it was that bad."

It was that bad for Michigan State in the second half — and that good for Michigan. In 20 incomprehensible minutes, the Wolverines buried the woes of the past two weeks while burying the Spartans.

At halftime, Michigan State had the lead (31-25), the tempo and the confidence. Taking a page from Alaska-Anchorage's playbook, the Spartans slowed the pace by milking the clock, and the Wolverines reacted as expected — with impatience.

"Michigan State did exactly what they wanted to do in the first half, and we did exactly what they wanted us to do," Coach Bill Frieder said. "We were impatient and rushed our shots. So we adjusted at halftime."

Did they ever. In outscoring (57-35), outshooting (74-42 percent) and outrebounding (23-2) Michigan State in the second half, the Wolverines offered a 40-minute microcosm of their season — when they're bad, they're very bad; when they're good, they're . . .

"Awesome," Michigan State coach Jud Heathcote said. "They came out in the second half and gave us a lesson in strength and shooting. They just overwhelmed us. Sometimes it takes giants a little time to awaken."

Forward Glen Rice awoke the quickest. He had 18 of his 29 points and seven of his 10 rebounds in the second half.

Terry Mills added 17 points and eight rebounds, helping the Wolverines control the game's most precious territory — the boards. When they started getting the rebounds, they got the fastbreaks, which forced MSU to increase the tempo, which created bad shots, which produced more rebounds . . . which led to a rout.

"We were too pumped up in the first half," Vaught said. "Then we coaxed them into our game, got the ball off rebounds and started running. Naturally, they had to run with us."

Michigan controlled the boards only after it controlled its emotions. The Spartans disdained the customary handshakes during pre-game introductions, riling the Wolverines and the sold-out Crisler Arena crowd beyond the point of clear thinking.

When MSU's lead reached 10, visions of Michigan's fourth loss in five games stirred. But Rice, who became the fourth U-M player to reach the 2,000-point plateau, erased those thoughts in a hurry.

In the process, he offered another glimpse at the senior leadership he only occasionally flashed.

"If Glen Rice isn't the best forward in the country, then (Arizona's) Sean Elliott is, and it's a coin flip," Heathcote said.

"If the game is one second old and Glen shoots a 75-footer, I don't care," Frieder said. "He can shoot and we want him to shoot. I ought to put a sign on his locker that says, 'Shoot, Glen, shoot.' "

Once again, the Wolverines were at their best when Rice was at his best. They scored on 19 of their first 21 second-half possessions, and when they closed it out by hitting their last 19 free throws, the second half became as shockingly efficient as the first half was remarkably dull.

"I don't know if that was the best we can play, but it was close," Rice said. "No one knows how well this team can play."

It would be weeks before anyone found out.

Michigan	FG-A	FT-A	R	A	TP
Rice	10-16	4-4	10	1	29
Mills	7-8	3-3	8	1	17
Vaught	4-7	3-4	3	1	11
Griffin	1-1	2-2	1	3	4
Robinson	3-5	2-2	2	6	8
Hughes	0-2	0-0	2	0	0
Higgins	2-5	4-4	2	0	8
Taylor	0-1	3-4	3	5	3
Pelinka	0-0	2-2	0	0	2
Calip	0-0	0-0	0	0	0
Oosterbaan	0-1	0-0	0	0	0
Totals	27-46	23-25	32	17	82

Michigan State	FG-A	FT-A	R	A	TP
Redfield	8-14	1-2	5	3	17
Steigenga	1-1	3-5	3	0	5
Hickman	1-2	2-2	4	1	4
Smith	3-9	7-8	0	2	13
Montgomery	5-10	2-3	3	5	14
Manns	4-8	0-0	0	2	10
Sekal	0-2	1-2	0	0	1
Mueller	0-0	0-0	0	0	0
Casler	0-0	0-0	0	0	0
Hall	0-1	2-2	0	0	2
Totals	22-47	18-24	15	13	66

Three-point goals: Michigan 5-8 (Rice 5-6, Robinson 0-2); Michigan State 4-11 (Montgomery 2-4, Manns 2-2, Sekal 0-2, Redfield 0-1, Smith 0-1, Hall 0-1).

Turnovers: Michigan 10, Michigan State 8

22 Michigan 108
Iowa 107 (double overtime)

In a scintillating double-overtime thriller, the Wolverines officially became jersey-clad advertisements for schizophrenia.

For 30 minutes, they were unstoppable. They led the eighth-ranked Hawkeyes, 67-49, with 9:23 left, stunning a sell-out crowd at Carver-Hawkeye Arena, where Iowa hadn't lost all season.

The rout was complete and confounding. Both teams brought 17-4 overall records, 5-3 Big Ten marks and flickering title hopes into the contest. Both teams preferred fast-paced styles and relied heavily on their board work.

By all indications, the game was to be a classic. But with less than 10 minutes left, it was a rout.

And then it happened. The Iowa press, pesky all game, suddenly became deadly. Guard Roy Marble, who scored a career-high 32 points, hit 14 of 18 shots after intermission. The Hawkeyes surged ahead, 83-81, late in the game, before the Wolverines caught their balance.

Terry Mills' rebound basket with two seconds left forced overtime. Then, with Iowa ahead 91-85, Sean Higgins (22 points) drilled three consecutive three-pointers, forcing another overtime.

And then, the Wolverines found the strength to regain their footing one more time.

Matt Bullard's three-point play with 2:19 left gave Iowa a 105-100 lead.

"I thought we had it won," said Bullard, who scored 13. "It was right there. I didn't think there was any way they'd come back again."

Remarkably, with Rumeal Robinson and backup guard Kirk Taylor fouled out, they did.

Loy Vaught (18 points, 14 rebounds) scored six points in the final minute, the last two on a layup with two seconds left. The game-winner came on a pass from Higgins, who had taken a pass from seldom-used Demetrius Calip, who had fallen to his knees but kept his dribble.

"That's something I've always dreamed of doing, making the game-winning shot," Vaught said.

Heroes had become goats and then heroes again in a game as emotionally draining as Michigan would play all season. Glen Rice scored 24 points, Robinson had 20 despite respraining his right thumb and Mills had 10 rebounds.

And Michigan, 18-4 and 6-3, was back in the Big Ten race, at least for the moment.

"Just a great basketball game," Coach Bill Frieder exulted. "It's too bad someone had to lose it."

But even in victory, Frieder would have worries. Robinson's sprained thumb was worsening, forcing him to sit out the first overtime. And in two days, the Wolverines, still on the brink of extinction from the race, would face another critical road test against Minnesota.

"It's a big victory, a great victory, but it's only one victory — period," Frieder said. "It doesn't mean a thing if we don't go up to Minnesota and win."

Frieder would take to Minnesota a confident team, a three-game winning streak and a cloud of suddenly swirling rumors. The day before the Iowa game, his name had surfaced as a candidate for the Arizona State job.

Carefully and ominously, he declined to comment, raising more questions for a team with still plenty to answer.

Michigan	FG-A	FT-A	R	A	TP
Rice	7-20	7-8	7	1	24
Mills	5-14	2-2	10	0	12
Vaught	8-15	2-2	14	2	18
Griffin	0-2	5-7	4	5	5
Robinson	7-13	6-9	2	7	20
Hughes	2-5	1-3	6	0	5
Higgins	9-17	1-2	6	4	22
Taylor	0-5	2-4	3	6	2
Pelinka	0-0	0-0	0	0	0
Calip	0-0	0-0	0	0	0
Totals	38-91	26-37	56	25	108

Iowa	FG-A	FT-A	R	A	TP
Horton	8-16	3-8	14	1	19
Thompson	7-15	1-3	4	0	15
Bullard	4-9	4-5	8	3	13
Armstrong	5-11	7-9	5	8	19
Marble	15-25	1-1	10	1	32
Moses	1-3	0-0	2	0	2
Lookingbill	0-0	0-0	1	1	0
Jepsen	1-1	2-3	3	0	4
Skinner	0-0	0-1	0	0	0
Totals	42-82	19-34	54	20	107

Three-point goals: Michigan 6-11 (Higgins 3-4, Rice 3-7); Iowa 4-12 (Armstrong 2-3, Marble 1-1, Bullard 1-3, Moses 0-2, Thompson 0-3).

Turnovers: Michigan 17, Iowa 23
Fouled Out: Michigan — Mills, Robinson, Taylor; Iowa — Jepsen.

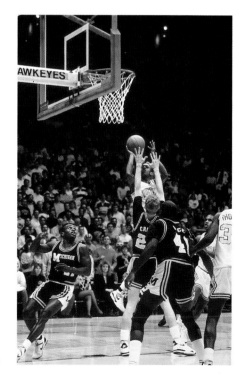

23 Michigan 80
Minnesota 88

When Minnesota left Ann Arbor a 15-point loser in January, Coach Clem Haskins vowed revenge.

In an emotional, inspired performance that rocked ancient Williams Arena, the Gophers exacted it by pounding 10th-ranked Michigan.

The Wolverines had scrapped back into the Big Ten race by winning three straight, but they were outscrapped by a Minnesota team suddenly flexing its muscles. Michigan joined Iowa, Illinois and Ohio State as Williams Arena victims as the Gophers stretched their home winning streak to 12.

"We've been waiting on them to come on up here," said center Willie Burton, a Detroit native who led the Gophers with 27 points and 11 rebounds. "That was no 15-point game at Michigan (a 98-83 loss January 12). We knew we could play with them. They have power and brute strength, but we have quickness."

Smaller and less touted, Minnesota proved it wasn't too proud to clean windows, outrebounding Michigan by an incredible 41-21 margin, including 18-4 off the offensive glass.

"Minnesota certainly didn't surprise us," Coach Bill Frieder said. "Their quickness was just too much. They're an excellent team, an NCAA tournament team, I guarantee you that. They've already proven they belong."

If the Wolverines didn't get the message in their first meeting, they received it quickly this game. The Gophers controlled the tempo from the start, slowing the pace, pounding the boards and contesting nearly every Michigan pass.

And Minnesota inflicted pain more places than the scoreboard. The Wolverines' Big Ten title hopes were severely damaged and they lost backup guard Kirk Taylor for the season with a knee injury.

Taylor, who had been providing quickness and defense off the bench and was about to displace Mike Griffin as a starter, tore knee ligaments with 13:11 left in the first half.

With that blow, Michigan's biggest weakness got weaker. Sophomores Sean Higgins (14 points) and Demetrius Calip tried to compensate, but the Wolverines were hampered defensively against Minnesota's quick guards, Ray Gaffney (career-high 24 points) and Melvin Newbern (14).

"I don't want to make excuses, but with Kirk out, we weren't able to give Rumeal (Robinson) as much rest," Frieder said. "And he didn't have it defensively down the stretch."

Still, the Wolverines had chances to seize command. When Glen Rice (29 points) converted a three-point play with 8:07 remaining, they had their first lead, 61-60, since early in the game.

But Burton's quickness inside and Gaffney's outside proved too much. Michigan shot 59 percent but its interior defense and rebounding were nonexistent.

Although several players tried to blame the loss on Taylor's injury, fatigue from the Iowa game and the road factor, at least one refused to alibi.

"We didn't come in with the instinct to eliminate a team that couldn't play with us," said Robinson, who had 14 points, five assists and five turnovers. "They played their regular game. We just didn't play ours."

Now three games behind first-place Indiana, Frieder was realistic about his team's title chances.

"We're not giving up on anything because you never know what's going to happen in the Big Ten," he said. "But realistically, this hurts our chances. The main thing we have to do now is just take them one at a time and try to grow as a basketball team."

Michigan	FG-A	FT-A	R	A	TP
Rice	12-19	1-1	1	1	29
Mills	4-6	0-0	2	1	8
Vaught	3-6	1-2	7	1	7
Griffin	0-0	2-3	2	3	2
Robinson	5-8	3-6	5	5	14
Taylor	0-0	0-0	0	0	0
Higgins	4-10	4-4	0	0	14
Hughes	2-2	2-3	0	2	6
Calip	0-0	0-0	0	0	0
Pelinka	0-0	0-0	0	0	0
Totals	30-51	13-19	21	13	80

Minnesota	FG-A	FT-A	R	A	TP
Coffey	1-2	1-3	10	1	3
Bond	6-10	0-1	8	3	12
Burton	7-14	13-14	11	4	27
Lynch	3-11	0-0	3	2	6
Newbern	7-11	0-0	4	2	14
Gaffney	8-9	5-8	3	1	24
Shikenjanski	1-5	0-0	1	0	2
Williams	0-0	0-0	0	0	0
Metcalf	0-0	0-0	0	0	0
Totals	33-62	19-26	41	13	88

Three-point goals: Michigan 7-16 (Rice 4-9, Higgins 2-5, Robinson 1-2); Minnesota 3-5 (Gaffney 3-3, Lynch 0-1, Burton 0-1).

Turnovers: Michigan 18, Minnesota 11
Fouled Out: Michigan — Rice, Griffin

24 Michigan 84
Purdue 70

Battling injuries and illness, Michigan rose from its sickbed long enough to avoid the Big Ten deathbed.

With six players suffering from ailments ranging from hamstring pulls to bronchitis, the Wolverines needed a little R&R. Instead of rest and relaxation, they settled for a quicker remedy — Rice and Robinson.

A sure tonic for most basketball ills, Glen Rice and Rumeal Robinson slapped the Wolverines from another bout of first-half lethargy and rallied them to victory.

Michigan led eighth-place Purdue by only one at halftime, before the two leaders erupted. Rice scored 15 of his 21 points and Robinson 13 of his 19 in the second half, as the Wolverines shot 69 percent after intermission.

Michigan hardly appeared eager to play five days after losing to Minnesota and losing Kirk Taylor for the season with a knee injury and only a few days after a flu and bronchitis epidemic ravaged the team.

Coach Bill Frieder called it the worst health situation his team had encountered "in 5-6 years," so he hardly complained about the ugly victory.

"This was a guts win," he said. "After a loss like that (to Minnesota) and the poor health, you can't complain. I'm happy with it, but I'm not happy with the state of my team. We've got to get healthier, more concentration and more mentally intense."

Rice had the gutsiest performance, playing with the team's most severe bout of bronchitis. He admitted the illness had everything to do with his — and the team's — sluggishness.

"I tried to run the floor but I couldn't catch my breath a lot of times," he said. "We just dug deep, hung in there and did what we had to do. There are going to be times like these."

Perhaps the only significant development to emerge was the play of guards Sean Higgins (15 points) and Demetrius Calip, who received more court time because of Taylor's injury. The Wolverines had largely conceded Indiana the conference crown, so experimentation and preparation for the NCAA tournament were under way.

Higgins was 6-for-10 from the field and Calip kick-started Michigan's slumbering fastbreak with three assists and no turnovers in 17 minutes.

"The key was picking it up defensively," Calip said. "That helped us push the ball up a little quicker. We just weathered the storm."

There would be more ahead, but on this night, surviving, rather than excelling, was the goal. There were 10 lead changes and neither team led by four in the first half alone, as the clubs matched their strengths — bruising inside games.

Reserve forward Kip Jones (career-high 25 points) and center Stephen Scheffler (18) repeatedly beat the lethargic Wolverines inside.

"We were winded and tired, but it was time to play," said guard Mike Griffin, who contributed eight key points. "We can't use the illnesses as an excuse; we had to put that aside. It sure wasn't pretty, but it was a W."

Perhaps because of its ugliness, more likely because Indiana was next on the schedule, Frieder quickly dismissed the victory and looked ahead.

"The difference between this year and last (when Michigan swept Indiana) is that we're not nearly as ready to play them," he said. "But at least all our guys who were sick are headed in the right direction."

So, hopefully, was Michigan.

Michigan	FG-A	FT-A	R	A	TP
Rice	9-16	1-1	7	2	21
Mills	1-2	0-0	3	5	2
Vaught	3-6	2-2	8	1	8
Griffin	3-4	2-2	6	3	8
Robinson	5-8	8-12	3	2	19
Hughes	4-6	1-1	4	2	9
Higgins	6-10	2-2	0	2	15
Calip	1-2	0-0	1	3	2
Pelinka	0-0	0-1	0	0	0
Totals	32-54	16-21	33	20	84

Purdue	FG-A	FT-A	R	A	TP
Oliver	1-5	0-0	4	4	3
McCants	3-9	2-2	5	0	8
Scheffler	7-12	4-6	5	0	18
Stewart	1-3	0-0	1	0	2
T. Jones	4-13	1-2	0	4	10
K. Jones	10-13	5-9	5	2	25
Clyburn	1-3	2-4	5	0	4
Austin	0-1	0-0	0	0	0
Riley	0-0	0-0	0	0	0
Barrett	0-1	0-0	0	0	0
Totals	27-60	14-23	26	10	70

Three-point goals: Michigan 4-10 (Rice 2-4, Robinson 1-1, Higgins 1-4, Calip 0-1); Purdue 2-10 (T. Jones 1-6, Oliver 1-2, Clyburn 0-1, Barrett 0-1).

Turnovers: Michigan 14, Purdue 12
Fouled Out: Michigan — Vaught

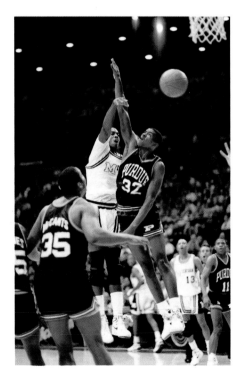

25 Michigan 75
Indiana 76

Everything was riding on Jay Edwards' shot. The game and Michigan's chances for Big Ten contention were literally up in the air.

And when the rainbow shot came down, so had the Wolverines. On both counts. The controversial three-pointer made Indiana a 76-75 winner. The No. 9 Hoosiers (21-5, 11-1) moved four games ahead of 13th-ranked Michigan (19-6, 7-5) with six remaining.

But while Indiana celebrated in its locker room, the Wolverines had the seed of future triumphs placed on their minds. Glen Rice broke the silence of disappointment by issuing a challenge to his teammates: Win the next 12 games — six in the Big Ten and six in the NCAA Tournament — for the championship.

"We're on a mission to shock the world," Rice told them.

Nobody snickered, either. This was their quiet captain speaking from the heart. Speak softly and carry a big jump shot was his way. So when he said it, the Wolverines knew he meant it. And they believed, even if few gave them a chance after the loss to Indiana at Assembly Hall.

Whether or not Edwards' 23-foot game-winner indeed beat the buzzer was debated, but the Wolverines could have put an end to any Hoosiers' hopes seconds earlier.

U-M had a 75-73 lead and the ball with 54 seconds left. They pushed the 45-second clock to the limit, and Rice worked against Brian Sloan for a clear five-footer that swirled off the front of the rim. Eric Anderson grabbed the rebound with seven seconds left, but his delayed pass upcourt to Lyndon Jones cut Indiana's transition time. With the crowd screaming, "Shoot! Shoot!" Jones passed to Edwards.

Edwards fired and fell backward to the court. "I didn't see it go in and couldn't believe it," Edwards said. "I was screaming and I didn't think he would hear me. But I knew Lyndon would get me the ball. I had to go back or he (Sean Higgins) was going to block it."

Higgins had come out to the three-point arc, but was surprised to see Edwards firing from a yard behind it. He got a hand up, but couldn't use his five-inch height advantage for a block.

The shot swished, and playing "Beat the Clock" became popular. Did it or didn't it count? The officials became the focus, as they have been much of the season.

Said Michigan coach Bill Frieder: "(Phil) Bova started to wave it off, but I guess he wasn't quick enough. (Gary) Muncy, with a smile on his face, counted it. But I'm not going to comment on it. If I say it's good, I'll be ripped for saying I'm not for my team. If I say it's not, they'll say I'm using it as an excuse."

Rice and Edwards both were held to four points in the first half. But Edwards, who scored 10 of his team's last 11 points, ended with 23. Rice's 26-game double-figures streak was broken; he finished with seven.

Said Frieder: "I'm really proud of my kids. They played their butts off . . . We did everything we had to do.

With three weeks remaining in the regular season, gaining a berth in the NCAA tournament was the Wolverines' only realistic goal.

"We've just got to bounce back and get ready for the tournament," Higgins said. "That's our objective now."

Michigan	FG	FT	R	A	TP
Rice	2-10	3-4	1	1	7
Mills	6-12	0-0	2	1	12
Vaught	8-9	0-0	10	0	16
Griffin	0-1	2-2	2	3	2
Robinson	9-15	3-3	4	2	24
Hughes	1-2	1-2	4	5	3
Higgins	5-8	0-0	4	0	11
Calip	0-1	0-0	0	0	0
Pelinka	0-0	0-0	0	0	0
Totals	31-58	9-11	30	12	75

Indiana	FG	FT	R	A	TP
Anderson	4-7	2-4	8	0	10
Hillman	5-9	2-2	3	2	13
Jadlow	3-5	1-3	6	0	7
Edwards	8-15	6-7	3	4	23
Jones	6-14	3-6	2	3	15
Sloan	0-2	1-2	2	0	1
Meeks	1-1	0-0	0	2	2
Oliphant	2-2	0-0	3	0	5
Totals	29-55	15-24	32	11	76

Three-point goals: Michigan 4-6 (Robinson 3-3, Higgins 1-2, Rice 0-1); Indiana 3-5 (Edwards 1-3, Hillman 1-1, Oliphant 1-1).

Turnovers: Michigan 9, Indiana 11
Fouled Out: Michigan — Griffin

26 Michigan 89
Ohio State 72

Reaching the 20-win mark in a season isn't particularly noteworthy. Doing so in six straight seasons is special.

Michigan improved its record to 20-6, 8-5 in the Big Ten, with an 89-72 win over Ohio State (17-9, 6-7) Thursday night before 13,276 at St. John Arena.

Only Illinois, with seven straight, has a longer 20-win streak among conference teams.

"It's a great thing to win 20," U-M coach Bill Frieder said. "Someday somebody will look at that and say that Michigan is doing a better job than we get credit for."

Glen Rice recovered from a seven-point game at Indiana to score a game-high 30 — his sixth 30-plus game this season. However, he had not yet recovered from bronchitis.

"I'm not out of it yet," Rice said. "But I feel a whole lot better. I just kept working hard, and the guys set good screens for me."

Frieder said: "Glen ran the floor much better than he had been."

The Buckeyes, whose 13-game home winning streak was broken, played without injured guard Jay Burson for the first time at St. John. His substitute at point guard, Eli Brewster, scored eight points. Burson averaged 22.1.

"They played a subpar game without Burson," Frieder said. "He's about 33 percent of their team. We couldn't even afford to lose Kirk Taylor (knee surgery) off the bench at guard."

Center Perry Carter led Ohio State with 23 points and 10 rebounds.

Michigan, which led at the half, 45-26, led by as many as 24 points in the second half.

Loy Vaught (15 points, 12 rebounds) said Burson's absence cost Ohio State in many ways.

"When he penetrates, we have to leave our man sometimes," Vaught said. "He would then drop it off to the open man. We were able to focus more."

The Wolverines had a 32-19 edge in defensive rebounding.

"We played like we were on a mission to get to the defensive boards," Frieder said.

Frieder said it was his team's best performance since a 99-88 win at Purdue — which, like this game, followed a one-point loss to Indiana.

"We were angry we lost to Indiana and wanted to beat Ohio State here," said Rumeal Robinson, who had 16 points, nine assists and five rebounds. "We'll never get that game out of our minds."

Frieder said: "We want to meet that other team in the (NCAA) tournament."

That team was the Hoosiers.

"I don't like to go out and brag," Rice said. "But if we play them again . . . I predict a different outcome. That ain't over with yet, and I would love to see Indiana in the tournament."

Michigan	FG	FT	R	A	TP
Rice	11-21	6-6	6	1	30
Mills	6-10	0-0	7	1	12
Vaught	6-7	3-3	12	1	15
Griffin	2-4	0-0	2	0	4
Robinson	5-9	5-7	5	9	16
Calip	0-0	4-4	0	0	4
Higgins	2-8	0-0	2	5	4
Pelinka	0-0	0-0	0	0	0
Oosterbaan	0-0	0-0	0	0	0
Hughes	2-3	0-1	2	1	4
Totals	34-62	18-21	40	18	89

Ohio State	FG	FT	R	A	TP
White	0-4	3-4	4	0	3
Francis	1-9	0-0	2	3	2
Carter	10-17	3-3	10	3	23
Brewster	3-7	0-0	1	4	8
Brown	0-3	4-4	2	2	4
Bradley	3-9	3-4	3	1	10
Jent	0-3	3-4	2	1	3
Lee	2-9	0-0	6	4	6
Mateen	5-9	1-3	3	0	11
Robinson	1-1	0-0	0	0	2
Totals	25-71	17-22	35	18	72

Three-point goals: Michigan 3-12 (Rice 2-6, Robinson 1-2, Higgins 0-41); Ohio State 5-16 (Brewster 2-4, Lee 2-5, Bradley 1-3, Jent 0-1, Brown 0-3).

Turnovers: Michigan 20, Ohio State 15
Fouled Out: Michigan — Mills

Some teams put on a clinic. Michigan put on a highlight film during a 92-70 win over Wisconsin.

The Wolverines had an 11-minute spurt late in the first half that featured five dunks and five three-pointers. Glen Rice scored 13 of his season-high 38 points during that sequence.

When the high-fives had subsided, U-M had outscored the Badgers, 31-11. The 13,504 in Crisler Arena didn't get much drama, but they got an eyeful early.

No. 13 U-M (21-6, 9-5) put away Wisconsin (16-8, 7-7) quickly and efficiently.

"They literally slaughtered us," said Badgers guard Trent Jackson. Forward Danny Jones had 31 points and Jackson 28, but the rest of the team managed just 11.

"Do you realize Michigan may have been the best team in the country today," said Wisconsin coach Steve Yoder. "People think Arizona and Oklahoma are. But they were just great."

Yoder, it turned out, wasn't just blowing smoke to obscure his team's sound defeat.

Terry Mills blocked three shots and Loy Vaught made eight of his 11 rebounds on defense to set the Wolverines' running game in motion.

"When we get like that," Vaught said, "we're one of the most unbeatable teams in the country. Everything clicked. If we could capture that, bottle that and have access to that before every game, we would be unbeatable. The defense sparks that. It was showtime."

Rumeal Robinson (11 points, 10 assists) had a reverse, two-handed, backward slam — a definite 10 on degree of difficulty. Rice nailed a trio of treys during the highlight film stretch and set a school record for three-point accuracy by hitting all seven shots from that range.

How big did the rim look?

"Pretty big," said Rice, who hit 13 of 15 shots and didn't miss until the second half. "I have never had a day like this, and I thank God for it. I was pretty hot and the guys were setting good screens."

U-M coach Bill Frieder said the movement Vaught and Mark Hughes displayed after setting screens produced many of the easy shots.

"When you get five guys like that clicking at the same time, they can be pretty good," Frieder said. "Glen was really stroking it, boy. And I wanted to get him even more shots. He's my No. 1 priority and he was sensational today."

Rice moved into sixth place on the Big Ten's career scoring list, and third on the Michigan list with 2,176 points. The Wolverines have four of the top seven scorers in conference history.

It was his third-highest game, behind 40 against Minnesota and 39 versus Florida last season.

His three-point shooting led a 10-for-13 (.769) team effort that was second only to the 7-for-8 (.875) here against Iowa last year. U-M led the nation with a .484 mark on treys.

Top scorers in Big Ten history after 1988-89 season:

PLAYER	TEAM	YEARS	PTS
Glen Rice	U-M	'85-89	2,442
Mike McGee	U-M	'77-81	2,439
Steve Alford	IND	'84-87	2,438
Rick Mount	PUR	'68-70	2,323
Gary Grant	U-M	'84-88	2,222
Don Schlundt	IND	'52-55	2,192
Cazzie Russell	U-M	'64-66	2,164

Michigan	FG	FT	R	A	TP
Rice	13-15	5-7	3	3	38
Mills	1-4	2-2	3	2	4
Vaught	6-10	0-2	11	3	12
Griffin	0-0	2-2	4	2	2
Robinson	5-11	1-2	3	10	11
Higgins	4-7	4-6	4	1	14
Hughes	2-2	2-2	1	1	6
Calip	2-3	0-0	3	2	5
Oosterbaan	0-0	0-0	0	0	0
Pelinka	0-0	0-0	0	0	0
Totals	33-52	16-23	33	24	92

Wisconsin	FG	FT	R	A	TP
Jones	12-21	7-7	2	1	31
Locum	2-5	0-0	0	3	5
Portmann	1-2	0-0	2	3	2
Molaski	0-2	0-0	2	2	0
Jackson	10-21	3-3	6	3	28
Simms	0-1	0-1	3	1	0
Schubring	1-3	0-0	5	1	2
Ellenson	0-1	0-0	0	0	0
Robinson	0-1	0-0	1	0	0
Robertson	0-3	2-2	2	0	2
Douglas	0-0	0-1	1	0	0
Totals	26-60	12-14	27	15	70

Three-point goals: Michigan 10-13 (Rice 7-7, Higgins 2-2, Calip 1-2, Robinson 0-2); Wisconsin 6-12 (Jackson 5-8, Locum 1-3, Molaski 0-1).

Turnovers: Michigan 12, Wisconsin 9
Fouled Out: Wisconsin — Portmann

28 Michigan 79
Michigan State 52

Plenty of heart and a bundle of good intentions were not enough for Michigan State. Seasoned talent is a much-needed commodity, too.

Michigan had too much of the latter in this one.

Coach Jud Heathcote's team was no match for Michigan's shooting or rebounding, and the Wolverines bid a fond farewell to Jenison Field House by thumping the Spartans, 79-52.

Not even the ol' Jenison magic could help the Spartans, who had won seven of the last 10 games against U-M in the 50-year-old barn.

Not this time. Loy Vaught softened up MSU from the outside, then moved inside and finished the job as Michigan continued to position itself for a strong NCAA tournament seeding.

The 10th-ranked Wolverines got 16 points from Vaught on 8-of-10 shooting and points from 10 players as they increased their record to 22-6, 10-5 in the Big Ten.

"Loy was one of the guys who found the open seams when they double-covered Glen (Rice)," U-M coach Bill Frieder said.

MSU, which had lost seven of eight, fell to 13-12, 4-11.

There could be no quarreling with the MSU preparation. The Spartans came out smoking, taking a 6-0 lead in the first minute.

But Rice's three-pointer cooled the euphoria. It disappeared for good in the last 3½ minutes of the half and just about the same amount of time at the start of the second.

The Wolverines, trailing 32-27, scored the last 11 points of the first half, then seven more to start the second, turning a close game into a 45-32 spread.

"We let it slip away and did not play well at all in the second half," Heathcote said. "We embarrassed ourselves in the second half."

Michigan didn't get — or need — much contribution from Rice, the Big Ten's leading scorer this season, who was coming off a 38-point game Saturday against Wisconsin.

Rice hit only three of seven shots, finishing with nine points, his second-lowest output of the season.

Vaught had loads of support as U-M shot 63.5 percent. Rumeal Robinson and Sean Higgins scored 11 apiece, and Terry Mills paced U-M's 36-22 rebounding lesson with eight.

The Spartans got 13 points each from Steve Smith and Kirk Manns.

Rice was announced among 10 finalists for the Associated Press player of the year award that day. He joined Stacey King and Mookie Blaylock of Oklahoma, Danny Ferry of Duke, Sean Elliott of Arizona, Pervis Ellison of Louisville, Todd Lichti of Stanford, Jay Edwards of Indiana, Sherman Douglas of Syracuse and Chris Jackson of LSU.

Michigan	FG	FT	R	A	TP
Mills	3-4	0-0	8	1	6
Rice	3-7	2-3	5	3	9
Vaught	8-10	0-0	5	1	16
Robinson	4-7	3-6	4	3	11
Griffin	2-2	1-2	3	4	5
Higgins	4-8	0-1	0	1	11
Hughes	4-5	1-1	6	3	9
Calip	2-5	0-0	0	1	4
Pelinka	2-2	1-1	1	0	6
Oosterbaan	1-2	0-0	0	0	2
Koenig	0-0	0-0	0	0	0
Totals	33-52	8-14	36	17	79

Michigan State	FG	FT	R	A	TP
Redfield	3-13	4-5	6	2	10
Hall	0-2	0-0	0	2	0
Steigenga	2-5	0-0	0	0	4
Smith	6-13	1-2	8	2	13
Manns	5-10	0-0	0	0	13
Montgomery	1-2	0-0	0	1	2
Hickman	5-11	0-0	6	2	10
Casler	0-1	0-0	6	2	10
Sekal	0-0	0-0	0	0	0
Mueller	0-0	0-1	1	0	0
Sarkine	0-0	0-0	0	0	0
Totals	22-57	5-8	22	9	52

Three-point goals: Michigan 5-11 (Higgins 3-4, Rice 1-4, Pelinka 1-1, Robinson 0-1, Calip 0-1); Michigan State 3-10 (Manns 3-6, Smith 0-2, Montgomery 0-1, Casler 0-1).

Turnovers: Michigan 11, Michigan State 12
Fouled Out: Michigan — Higgins

29 Michigan 119
Iowa 96

Click became the buzzword for the buzz saw that the Michigan basketball team had become. It was clicking on all cylinders, and clicking off wins.

The No. 10 Wolverines beat No. 11 Iowa, 119-96, at Crisler Arena for their fourth straight win, all by at least 17 points.

"Michigan is really clicking," said Iowa's Roy Marble, who scored 30 points but could have had 50 and still lost. "Their top weapon? Glen Rice, no doubt. He's definitely the main ingredient. But they have so many great players, and that makes him even more difficult to play against."

Rice scored 29 of his game-high 33 points in the second half. Rumeal Robinson had 22 points with 10 assists, and Loy Vaught and Terry Mills scored 18 each. U-M reached 100 for a school-record ninth time.

The Wolverines led by 15 at the half despite Rice's slow start.

"They held Glen in check and yet we still had a 48-33 lead," coach Bill Frieder said. "We did a much better job of reading defenses, and Rumeal set that up."

Michigan (23-6, 11-5 Big Ten) didn't allow Iowa (21-8, 9-7) to get closer than 15 points in the second half. The Wolverines reached 100 points against the Hawkeyes for the fourth time in their last six meetings.

"Hey Frieder, call off your dogs!" Iowa's Ed Horton was heard to say near the end.

"Michigan has a tough, NBA-type team," Horton said. "They're like a young pro team. And, hey, they're ready. I'd say we looked like a Final Four team today, and we lost. Michigan's ready to have a good stretch this month."

Horton's crystal ball was never so clear.

The Hawkeyes, playing without injured point guard B.J. Armstrong (strained hamstring), got a combined six points and three assists from substitutes Brian Garner and Troy Skinner. Forwards Horton (20 points) and Ray Thompson (19) surpassed their scoring averages, but it was hardly enough.

Iowa coach Tom Davis said, "It was going to take a perfect game to beat them, as well as they're playing. They got a couple of streaks early that put us in a hole we couldn't get out of."

U-M took a 30-18 lead with 10 unanswered points, and didn't have to check the scoreboard again. The Hawkeyes missed Armstrong's leadership and matched a season high with 24 turnovers. Seven Wolverines totaled 11 steals, U-M's most this season in a regulation game.

"Rumeal played great," Davis said. "He's the key to this ballclub, but they definitely have many dimensions. If Indiana is the champion of this league, how far behind is Michigan? Two points? And maybe they're better. They've kept improving."

Another prophet.

Frieder said: "This team still has room to grow, but is playing very well together."

Rice (Flint Northwestern) and Marble (Flint Beecher) hugged after the game. It was their last meeting in college, but both are projected as NBA first-round draft picks. "We're good friends and we joked around at the end," Marble said. Rice added: "I wished him the best of luck and he did the same to me. We'll definitely get together this summer."

Frieder celebrated his 47th birthday the day before. "I went recruiting," he said. "We didn't go out and do anything special. Everyone has a birthday each year, and so it's really no big deal."

Michigan	FG	FT	R	A	TP
Rice	12-19	5-8	7	7	33
Mills	8-10	2-2	7	3	18
Vaught	6-10	6-6	4	2	18
Griffin	1-1	0-0	0	0	2
Robinson	6-12	9-10	4	10	22
Higgins	5-10	0-2	3	2	11
Hughes	3-4	0-0	1	2	7
Calip	2-2	0-0	0	3	4
Pelinka	0-1	0-0	0	0	0
Oosterbaan	1-1	2-2	2	0	4
Totals	44-70	24-30	30	29	119

Iowa	FG	FT	R	A	TP
Horton	7-15	5-6	13	3	20
Thompson	8-12	3-4	4	1	19
Jepsen	2-2	0-0	7	1	4
Marble	10-23	7-14	7	4	30
Garner	1-2	1-4	2	1	3
Bullard	3-7	0-1	4	2	7
Moses	2-7	2-2	2	0	8
Skinner	1-1	0-0	0	2	3
Lookingbill	1-1	0-0	1	0	2
Totals	35-70	18-31	43	14	96

Three-point goals: Michigan 7-15 (Rice 4-7, Higgins 1-4, Robinson 1-2, Hughes 1-1, Pelinka 0-1); Iowa 8-21 (Marble 3-7, Bullard 1-5, Moses 2-4, Horton 1-2, Skinner 1-1, Thompson 0-2).

Turnovers: Michigan 13, Iowa 24

After beating Northwestern, coach Bill Frieder told reporters in confidence that his name shouldn't be connected to the Arizona State rumors. He believed Purdue coach Gene Keady was headed for the Sun Devils. What Frieder didn't add was that he'd met Arizona State athletic director Charles Harris in Chicago four days prior.

When Keady backed out five days later, the meeting proved to be no small detail. But for that night, nobody doubted Frieder. He seemed relaxed even though the Wolverines' flaws at guard were exposed by a second-division opponent.

The superior team spots points to the ready challengers to enhance competition in playground games. Michigan unintentionally did the same thing before pulling out an 88-79 win over Northwestern before 7,624 at Welsh-Ryan Arena.

But the No. 8 Wolverines (24-6, 12-5) went beyond spotting the Wildcats an early eight-point lead. They also played without starting point guard Rumeal Robinson for much of the second half.

Robinson (eight points, two assists) committed his fourth foul with 17:14 remaining and sat out nearly nine minutes. He fouled out reaching for a loose ball with 4:38 to play.

Demetrius Calip checked in and could not establish a tempo. U-M went into a slowdown game with three minutes left and its 19-point lead was whittled to six, 82-76.

Rob Ross missed a one-and-one free throw and the chance to cut it to four with 1:33 left. That was the beginning of the end of the Wildcats' upset hopes.

Glen Rice scored 26 points and moved into second place on the school's career scoring list. Few expected he would score another 198 points to become No. 1 on the U-M and Big Ten list ahead of Mike McGee.

Loy Vaught added 17 points, but Michigan's most impressive numbers belonged to 6-foot-10 Terry Mills: nine points, seven assists, five blocked shots and five rebounds. He dreams of being a guard, and all but got his wish with Calip ineffective on the point.

"I got into the flow," Mills said. "I like playing the wide-open game, getting out on the wing and running. But I told Rumeal, 'I can't have you fouling out,' When he's gone, we have trouble beating the press."

Calip had three turnovers, two points and one assist in 16 minutes.

"It's a game that I have to learn from," Calip said. "They switched their press and confused me. But I'm glad it happened here rather than in the NCAA tournament. This game should benefit me."

Amen.

Frieder said: "He will learn from it. He did not play well, and neither did Rumeal. The big thing is that we came away with a win."

"We came out slow and the guys were not really psyched up," Robinson said. "We wanted a win, and we wanted to get out. But a lot of guys are excited about Illinois Saturday."

The Wolverines won their fifth straight and finished 9-1 against the Big Ten's second division teams.

Michigan	FG	FT	R	A	TP
Rice	11-19	2-2	9	3	26
Mills	4-7	1-4	5	7	9
Vaught	8-10	1-3	8	0	17
Griffin	2-3	0-1	1	1	4
Robinson	2-5	3-3	2	2	8
Calip	1-3	0-1	0	1	2
Higgins	6-13	2-2	6	2	14
Pelinka	0-1	0-0	1	1	0
Hughes	4-6	0-0	5	0	8
Totals	38-67	9-16	43	17	88

Northwestern	FG	FT	R	A	TP
Schwabe	9-15	4-5	8	1	22
Lambiotte	5-9	3-8	3	3	13
Pedersen	4-7	2-3	2	2	10
Styles	1-4	3-4	2	1	5
Holmes	2-5	3-4	1	1	7
Buford	0-0	0-0	0	0	0
R. Ross	1-2	0-1	0	1	3
Walters	0-1	0-0	1	0	0
B. Ross	1-1	2-2	2	0	4
Reece	1-5	0-2	1	0	2
Grose	4-7	2-3	1	0	13
Polite	0-0	0-0	1	0	0
Totals	28-56	19-32	29	9	79

Three-point goals: Michigan 3-11 (Rice 2-6, Robinson 1-2, Vaught 0-1, Calip 0-1, Higgins 0-1); Northwestern 4-9 (Grose 3-5, R. Ross 1-1, Styles 0-1, Walters 0-1, Reece 0-1).

Turnovers: Michigan 15, Northwestern 13
Fouled Out: Michigan — Robinson

Tune-up? How about an overhaul?

Michigan's 89-73 loss to Illinois displayed some glaring weaknesses that threatened to haunt the Wolverines in the upcoming NCAA Tournament.

The No. 4 Fighting Illini played themselves into a No. 1 tournament seed by dominating No. 8 Michigan before 13,609 at Crisler Arena in Ann Arbor.

The final post-season tune-up produced doubt rather than confidence for U-M. It was the Wolverines' worst home defeat since an 87-62 loss to Indiana in the 1984-85 season.

"We got our butts kicked," coach Bill Frieder said. "We have to bring them back mentally. But we will get their attention in practice now."

Frieder, it turned out, would conduct only two more practices in Michigan.

Illinois (27-4, 14-4) finished one game behind first-place Indiana, a team it beat twice, and set a school record for wins in a season. The Wolverines (24-7, 12-6) finished third.

Kenny Battle (22 points) and Kendall Gill (19) led the Illini.

Michigan shot 42 percent, its second-worst percentage of the season. Rumeal Robinson was the only starter over 50 percent; he scored 22 points. Loy Vaught (15) and Glen Rice (14) hit a combined 12 of 30 shots. Rice never got to the free throw line.

"They did a great job on Glen," Frieder said. "They boxed him up. We have to get more people involved when teams do that."

U-M lost all four games to the Illini and Hoosiers, and did not beat another Top 10 team in the regular season after defeating Oklahoma in the Maui Classic title game in November.

"That was easily the best team we played," Robinson said. "They do it all at every position."

Frieder said: "They're better than Oklahoma because they have everything you need in a player at every position. They leap, they're quick and they shoot."

The game changed when Kendall Gill entered with the score tied at 17. The Fighting Illini soon made an 18-4 run.

"With Kendall in there, we're much quicker," Illinois coach Lou Henson said.

The Illini were 19-0 with Gill and 8-4 without him.

Illinois shot 61 percent, but beat U-M most significantly in defensive rebounding — where they had a 26-15 advantage, igniting an offense that featured eight dunks and 11 lay-ups. That produced 38 uncontested points.

Vaught said: "They're such quick, explosive jumpers. All five of them go to the boards. And when we did get a rebound, they cut off our angles and got a hand on the ball."

Illinois center Lowell Hamilton said the five-men-to-the-boards theory is an illusion.

"It may look like that," Hamilton said. "What we do is send four to the boards. If a guard comes in, a forward rotates out. Then we press if they get the ball."

When did the Illini feel in control?

"At the beginning of the game," Hamilton said.

That early?

"That early."

Gill said: "Our attitude is that nothing is going to stop us."

Check the final score on April 1, Kendall.

Michigan	FG	FT	R	A	TP
Rice	6-14	0-0	2	2	14
Mills	2-7	3-4	4	2	7
Vaught	6-16	3-3	12	1	15
Griffin	1-3	0-0	0	4	2
Robinson	9-17	2-5	7	3	22
Hughes	3-6	0-1	4	2	6
Higgins	1-5	0-0	2	0	2
Calip	2-3	0-0	1	0	5
Oosterbaan	0-0	0-0	0	0	0
Pelinka	0-0	0-0	0	1	0
Totals	30-71	8-13	35	15	73

Illinois	FG	FT	R	A	TP
Anderson	5-7	0-2	10	0	10
Battle	10-15	1-2	5	3	22
Hamilton	6-10	0-0	8	1	12
Bardo	2-6	3-4	3	4	7
Liberty	4-8	3-4	2	0	11
Smith	3-4	2-3	3	6	8
Small	0-0	0-0	3	0	0
Gill	7-11	3-3	1	3	19
Bowman	0-0	0-0	0	0	0
MacDonald	0-0	0-0	0	0	0
Shapland	0-0	0-0	1	0	0
Manzke	0-0	0-0	0	0	0
Totals	37-61	12-18	37	17	89

Three-point goals: Michigan 5-17 (Rice 2-6, Robinson 2-5, Higgins 0-3, Calip 1-1, Vaught 0-1, Griffin 0-1); Illinois 3-4 (Gill 2-3, Battle 1-1).

Turnovers: Michigan 18, Illinois 17

32 Michigan 92
Xavier 87

The game was most important, but the sideshow took top billing. Everyone assumed Michigan would beat Xavier in the Southeast Regional opener. But what about the coaching situation?

How would the players respond with Bill Frieder gone to Arizona State?

Did Steve Fisher, the interim coach named by athletic director Bo Schembechler just two days prior, have the toughness to get the most out of the Wolverines?

Those were the hot topics. Loy Vaught was upset that the first question regarding the Musketeers was asked 17 minutes into a press conference the day before the game at the Omni.

Fisher said he felt butterflies walking onto the court. All eyes were on him for the first time in his life. But by the second half, the matter at hand took over and Fisher felt the flow of the game.

It didn't look good for Michigan at that point.

Xavier proved exasperating much of the game. The Musketeers powered the ball inside and frustrated the Wolverines with their quick guards.

The Wolverines needed more than 23 points apiece from Glen Rice and Rumeal Robinson to put away a 15-point underdog. They got it from Terry Mills and Demetrius Calip in a 92-87 win.

Mills played with purpose found, and Calip played on a memory. Together, they were the difference. Mills (18 points, six rebounds and five assists) and Calip (career-high nine points) credited Fisher for getting them ready.

He had a successful debut as Frieder's replacement. Frieder, the new Arizona State coach, watched from the stands with his wife and daughter. He left at halftime. The emotions became too much to share in public and Frieder watched the rest of the tournament on television. He went to Seattle but never to the Kingdome. It was too hard.

Fisher yanked Calip in the first half after he threw away one ball and lost another in a brief appearance.

Calip said: "Coach Fisher put his hands on each side of my head and said, 'Give us some of the way you played at Flint Northern. I'm counting on you.' That made me feel good, and I thank God for the chance to respond."

Fisher decided to play Robinson and Calip in the same backcourt to offset Xavier guards Jamal Walker, Michael Davenport and Stan Kimbrough. They totaled 44 points.

Michigan trailed, 71-68, when Robinson joined Calip with 8:14 remaining. Robinson, Mills and Loy Vaught all had four fouls, and the switch to a zone at that time served two purposes. It cut down the possibility of defensive fouls and hindered guard penetration by the Musketeers.

The Wolverines took their first lead of the second half on a three-pointer by Rice with 4:36 left. He secured the lead for good with another trey one minute later.

"I felt it was time to hit some shots," said Rice, who played the full 40 minutes.

U-M led by one with 2:02 remaining, but Mills pushed it to three with a jump hook. Tyrone Hill (21 points) missed a 13-footer and Kimbrough missed a trey that could have tied it.

Robinson and Calip pushed the lead to seven by hitting a pair of free throws each, and the game was over.

SOUTHEAST REGIONAL

Michigan	FG-A	FT-A	R	A	TP
Rice	9-22	0-0	3	2	23
Mills	8-12	2-2	6	5	18
Vaught	2-4	0-0	3	0	4
Griffin	0-0	0-0	0	2	0
Robinson	8-13	6-9	4	8	23
Hughes	4-5	0-1	10	0	8
Higgins	3-6	1-1	3	0	7
Calip	3-5	3-3	2	1	9
Totals	37-67	12-16	33	18	92

Xavier	FG-A	FT-A	R	A	TP
Parker	0-1	0-0	0	2	0
Hill	7-12	7-7	6	2	21
Strong	8-12	2-3	10	0	18
Kimbrough	5-16	1-2	5	6	13
Davenport	6-13	3-4	2	1	15
Walker	6-9	3-5	2	9	16
Minor	2-2	0-0	1	1	4
Raeford	0-0	0-0	0	0	0
Totals	34-65	16-21	30	21	87

Three-point goals: Michigan 6-12 (Rice 5-9, Robinson 1-2, Higgins 0-1); Xavier 3-9 (Kimbrough 2-4, Walker 1-1, Davenport 0-4).

Turnovers: Michigan 17, Xavier 19.

33 Michigan 91
South Alabama 82

You've seen the commercials for movies. The ones where wide-eyed people attempt to break the world record for using the word "terrific" in one reply.

After Michigan forward Glen Rice poured in 36 points and grabbed eight rebounds in a 91-82 win over South Alabama, it was something like that.

Announcer: "Larry Brown, coach of the San Antonio Spurs, you just watched Rice advance the Wolverines in the NCAA Tournament. Give us your thoughts."

Brown: "Rice was terrific. That he played that well in a game that really means something said a lot. He'll definitely be among the top five or six players drafted. We don't have that kind of shooting on our club, and we've really got to talk about him as a possibility."

Announcer: "Steve Fisher. You're 2-0 as Michigan's interim coach. Rice has been your leading scorer in both wins. What's it like to coach him?"

Fisher: "He really keeps an ulcer from perking up, knowing you've got him in a tight ballgame. You saw Glen Rice at his best today."

Announcer: Ronnie Arrow, coach of the South Alabama Jaguars. Give us your opinion."

Arrow: "That Rice kid is unbelievable. He's going to make some coach better in the NBA. He's a very, very great player."

Rice made 16 of 25 shots, season highs in both departments. The senior forward's highest point total of the season was 38 against Wisconsin in Ann Arbor.

Terry Mills scored a career-high 24 points and grabbed seven rebounds. The 6-10 forward had 42 points, 13 rebounds and 10 assists in U-M's NCAA wins at the Omni over Xavier and South Alabama.

Fisher said: "Rice is our first and foremost option. And maybe we've convinced Terry that he is the second option."

The Jaguars (23-9) made U-M sweat it. Guard Junie (Peanut Butter) Lewis scored 25 points to lead South Alabama's four-man scoring attack. The quartet also included Jeff (Jelly) Hodge, Gabe Estaba and Neil Smith. They scored 70 of their team's 82 points.

South Alabama had a 47-44 halftime lead.

The score was tied at 80 with 2:40 remaining. Mills scored on a turnaround jumper, was fouled and completed a three-point play at that point. It enabled the Wolverines to take the lead for good with 2:17 left.

Rice followed a Jaguars' turnover with a three-point shot, and ran downcourt in a hurry. He stood in the paint, raising both arms and encouraging his teammates to play defense with an 86-80 lead at 2:05.

Not surprisingly, Rice grabbed the defensive rebound on that possession. That let the air out of South Alabama for good.

"You can put that right up there with my best games," Rice said. "I think I did a much better job defensively."

That's the closest Rice gets to taking a bow.

Michigan	FG-A	FT-A	R	A	TP
Rice	16-25	1-1	8	5	36
Hughes	2-4	0-0	4	0	4
Mills	9-13	6-8	7	5	24
Griffin	2-2	0-0	1	0	4
Robinson	5-8	1-2	1	5	12
Vaught	1-5	0-0	7	0	2
Calip	0-1	3-4	1	5	3
Higgins	2-4	2-2	2	2	6
Pelinka	0-0	0-0	0	0	0
Totals	37-62	13-17	32	22	91

South Alabama	FG-A	FT-A	R	A	TP
Estaba	7-15	1-3	9	2	15
Jimmerson	3-5	1-2	4	5	7
Barden	0-0	0-0	3	0	0
Hodge	6-14	1-1	3	2	16
Lewis	9-17	7-10	9	3	25
Smith	4-8	6-7	7	0	14
Brodnick	1-7	2-2	2	6	5
Turner	0-4	0-0	1	0	0
Nelson	0-0	0-0	0	0	0
Totals	30-70	18-25	39	18	82

Three-point goals: Michigan 4-10 (Rice 3-7, Robinson 1-2, Higgins 0-1); South Alabama 4-19 (Hodge 3-9, Brodnick 1-4, Estaba 0-1, Lewis 0-2, Turner 0-3).

Turnovers: Michigan 15, South Alabama 15

SOUTHEAST REGIONAL

34 Michigan 92
North Carolina 87

Michigan decided to run the stop sign this year. The Wolverines beat North Carolina 92-87, to break a two-year NCAA Tournament losing streak against the Tar Heels.

"It's kind of like we got a Tar Heel off our back, and thank God it's gone," Rumeal Robinson said.

The Wolverines were one game away from the Final Four for the first time in 13 years, when Johnny Orr was their coach. Coach Steve Fisher turned 44 minutes after the late night win.

"It's his birthday," Sean Higgins said. "And this is our present." Higgins would help blow out the candles on Fisher's birthday cake at a press conference the next day.

Fisher beat Dean Smith, the North Carolina legend whose 667 career wins are tied for sixth all-time with John Wooden. Smith has his name on the basketball arena at Chapel Hill and on a souvenir program somewhere in Fisher's attic.

"I remember sneaking up to get his autograph at a coaching clinic," Fisher said. "He's a legend. But, like my baseball cards, Mickey Mantle and the rest, I don't know where it is. I got it on a program. I told him it was for my boy, but it was as much for myself."

Glen Rice, who scored 34 points, and super sub Higgins clamped together for a hug of relief in the final seconds, knowing the jinx was over.

"It sent chills down my spine," Rice said. "We were pumped from the start. There was no way we were going to lose three straight to them."

Higgins, an unlikely hero with 14 points, said, "You dream about a moment like that. It just takes over your body. I've dreamed of beating North Carolina in a game like this since I was a little kid."

Michigan fans have been dreaming about such a win forever. It was U-M's first win in its three games against the Tar Heels.

Robinson (17 points, career-high 13 assists) and Terry Mills (16 points) also made significant contributions.

Michigan (27-7) is going to a regional final for the first time since 1977, when it lost the Mideast Regional final to North Carolina-Charlotte in the same Rupp Arena.

The Tar Heels (29-8) got 26 points from J.R. Reid and 19 from Jeff Lebo.

"There comes a time when you just have to congratulate the other team," North Carolina coach Dean Smith said.

Fisher jumped for joy at the final buzzer, only five minutes before turning 44 as Thursday night became Friday morning.

Higgins hit two free throws with 27 seconds left to make it 92-87 and all but seal the win. Mills rebounded the second of Kevin Madden's two missed three-pointers in the final seconds to end any threat.

Michigan took a 71-64 lead midway through the second half with a true team effort. Six players combined to score the Wolverines' first 14 points of the half. Higgins, playing more than starter Mike Griffin at the No. 2 guard spot, came off the bench and came to life for the first time in the tournament.

Michigan	FG-A	FT-A	R	A	TP
Rice	13-19	0-0	6	2	34
Mills	8-11	0-2	6	1	16
Vaught	1-3	2-2	6	0	4
Griffin	0-1	0-0	1	1	0
Robinson	7-15	0-2	5	13	17
Higgins	5-11	2-2	2	3	14
Calip	1-4	0-0	1	0	2
Hughes	1-2	2-4	6	0	5
Totals	36-66	7-12	34	20	92

North Carolina	FG-A	FT-A	R	A	TP
Bucknall	2-7	4-4	7	10	10
Madden	5-12	0-0	1	0	10
Williams	4-9	0-0	5	0	8
Lebo	6-10	2-2	1	7	19
Rice	1-3	2-2	1	4	4
Reid	12-18	2-7	6	0	2
Fox	4-5	0-0	2	3	8
Chilcutt	1-2	0-0	4	0	2
Totals	35-66	10-15	31	24	87

Three-point goals: Michigan 13-24 (Rice 8-12, Robinson 3-6, Higgins 2-5, Calip 0-1); North Carolina 7-16 (Lebo 5-9, Bucknall 2-4, Rice 0-1, Madden 0-2)

SOUTHEAST REGIONAL

35 Michigan 102
Virginia 65

It almost seemed too easy. Like a title fight that ended in the first round. Like receiving an Academy Award nomination at the first screening of your new movie.

Michigan beat Virginia, 102-65, to win the Southeast Regional and advance to the Final Four for the first time since 1976.

Glen Rice dug the Cavaliers (22-11) a big hole by scoring 21 of his 32 points in the first half. Sean Higgins buried them with 18 of his career-high 31 after the half.

Higgins hadn't lived up to the All-America billing he brought from Los Angeles Fairfax High until the regionals. Prior to leaving for Lexington, Bo Schembechler told him there were no free trips. If he wasn't going to bust his butt, he could leave it home.

"Coach Schembechler is a motivator, I'll tell you that," Higgins said. "I can see how our football team plays like it does. With all our talent, maybe all we needed was to get yelled at. It pumped me up."

Michigan had a 34-17 lead when Higgins began waving a blue towel on the bench and creating a one-man wave with his hands. The school band was playing "The Victors" with extra gusto, and you expected the ticker tape parade to start any minute at Rupp Arena.

And there were four minutes left in the first half.

"I thought it was over seven minutes before the half," Rumeal Robinson said. "I could see them forcing shots already. They were on the ropes right then."

And ready for that early knockout.

Virginia's leading scorer Richard Morgan (15 points on 5-for-18 shooting) missed his first seven shots, while Rice made his first six. Michigan's lead was never under 10 points in the game's final 26 minutes.

Rice hit a shot at the first-half buzzer that kissed the glass, swirled the rim twice and dropped. While trotting to the locker room, he winked at the fans and pointed to them.

"I felt that if we kept playing the way we were playing, I knew we would come out on top," Rice said.

Forward Terry Mills said: "I was ready to put on a party hat and get out a kazoo. But coach (Steve) Fisher told us, 'Don't think it's over.' "

Fisher reminded them how Iowa had overcome a 20-point deficit, and forced the Wolverines to double-overtime before U-M won, 108-107.

Virginia didn't have a chance, though. The Cavs shot 38 percent from the field and 41 percent from the line. They barely outscored Rice and Higgins, 65-63.

Loy Vaught (eight points, nine rebounds) flashed four fingers to the fans when he hit an open jumper to make it 54-31. "That was my way of showing everyone what I felt," Vaught said. "I could feel it right then. We were going to Seattle."

Rice said, "This means a lot. But not as much as winning the national title. That's when we can really celebrate. This will last an hour or two and it will be time to move on."

After losing at Indiana on Jay Edwards' buzzer shot five weeks prior, Rice broke the silence in the locker room by placing the team on a "mission to shock the world."

Michigan	FG-A	FT-A	R	A	TP
Rice	13-16	2-2	6	2	32
Mills	4-9	0-0	5	2	8
Vaught	4-6	0-1	9	2	8
Griffin	0-1	0-0	0	3	0
Robinson	5-9	3-3	3	7	13
Calip	2-3	2-2	5	5	6
Higgins	11-15	2-3	3	0	31
Hughes	1-4	0-0	7	2	2
Oosterbaan	1-3	0-1	3	0	2
Pelinka	0-4	0-0	0	0	0
Koenig	0-0	0-0	0	0	0
TOTALS	41-70	9-12	43	23	102

Virginia	FG-A	FT-A	R	A	TP
Stith	3-6	2-4	3	1	9
Blundin	1-1	0-0	4	2	2
Dabbs	5-10	2-4	12	0	12
Morgan	5-18	2-2	1	0	15
Crotty	5-13	2-4	3	7	14
Katstra	3-9	0-0	2	1	7
Daniel	0-1	0-2	3	1	0
Turner	1-1	0-1	1	0	2
Williams	0-1	0-3	0	0	0
Oliver	0-0	1-2	2	0	1
Cooke	1-3	0-0	1	0	3
TOTALS	24-63	9-22	33	12	65

Three-point goals: Michigan 11-20 (Higgins 7-10, Rice 4-5, Robinson 0-1, Oosterbaan 0-1, Pelinka 0-3); Virginia 8-22 (Morgan 3-9, Crotty 2-3, Stith 1-1, Cooke 1-3, Katstra 1-6).

Turnovers: Michigan 11, Virginia 15

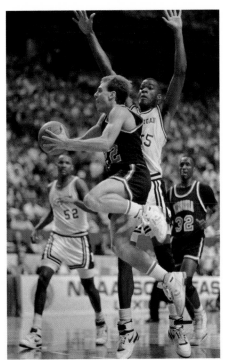

SOUTHEAST REGIONAL

NCAA

1989
NCAA
FINAL FOUR

NATIONAL COLLEGIATE
CHAMPIONSHIP

1988 NCAA DIVISION I

MEN'S BASKETBALL
CHAMPIONSHIP

CHAMPIONSHIP TEAM

51st DIVISION I MEN'S BASKETBALL CHAMPIONSHIP

The Kingdome   •   Seattle, Washington   •   April 1 & 3, 1989

The
Final Four

THE FINAL FOUR

Flashing the news for the world to see.

We've got good news and bad news. Which do you want first?

The good news: Michigan was in the Final Four at Seattle with a chance to win its first ever national basketball title.

The bad news: The Wolverines had to get by Illinois in the first game. The Fighting Illini had beaten them, 96-84 and 89-73, in the regular season. Michigan shot out of character in both games, combining for .467 from the field and .314 on three-pointers. It was .580 on field goals and .489 on treys against all others at that point.

It had been a simple case of Michigan's, playing Wile E. Coyote, being out-quicked and out-jumped and out-hustled by Illinois, in the role of the Roadrunner. Beep-beep!

But that was then, and this was now. "Michigan is playing sharper and with more emotion," Illini coach Lou Henson said before the game. "In the games I saw, they were awesome, I didn't know if they could handle a team like North Carolina and they did."

Ditto for handling the Flyin' Illini. The Wolverines stayed with them to the final play, and then triumphed.

The game ended in a most unlikely manner. But, then, wasn't this an unconventional Michigan team that was headed to the NCAA championship game?

The Wolverines beat Illinois, 83-81, to avenge two earlier losses.

And they did it with their top scorer setting a screen on the final play. They did it with a guy known for rainbows popping in a bunny shot.

With the game on the line, 81-81, Glen Rice set a pick for Terry Mills. His shot from the right baseline missed, but Sean Higgins had the angle from the left for the rebound. He grabbed it and wasted no time depositing the winning shot with two seconds left.

"I looked across court and saw him (Mills) open and threw it to him," said Rumeal Robinson. "We knew they would key on Rice, so we needed patience to find other people." After a time-out, Rice, who finished with a team-high 28 points, caught Stephen Bardo's desperation, court-length pass and the buzzer sounded.

The Wolverines (29-7) set a school record for wins in one season, and broke Illinois' streak of 10 straight wins. Michigan has not been to the NCAA final since losing to Indiana in 1976.

When it was over, there was a mob scene on the court. One by one, the players drifted away and looked to the top of the Kingdome in disbelief.

Higgins, who scored 14, lifted both hands and shouted, "Yeah, man, we're going!"

"I just want to thank God for Sean Higgins," said Loy Vaught.

As the Wolverines mugged for CBS cameras and interviews, Robinson was in the stands hugging his mother. Mark Hughes was shouting, "Coach of the year," for Steve Fisher, the interim coach who is living a dream.

Rice had his arms around Fisher and Higgins, and the joyful scene carried to the locker room after the cameras went off.

Rumeal Robinson's free throws against Seton Hall were the difference.

Versus Big Ten rival Illinois, Terry Mills leaps for inside goal against Lowell Hamilton.

The nail-biter was over, but Michigan's season wasn't.

Mills nearly made a sideline steal with under a minute left that would have given Michigan the ball and a two-point lead. But Illinois regained the ball on his attempt to save it from going out of bounds.

Hughes gave Michigan an 81-79 lead with 1:09 left. He rebounded Mills' short miss, put it in and was fouled by Lowell Hamilton. Hamilton was out of the game with his fifth foul.

Robinson, after struggling as a playmaker in the first half, set up the consecutive baskets that gave Michigan a 78-74 lead.

Robinson allowed the defense to collapse on him underneath and fed Hughes, cutting from the left, for an open slam. He stole a perimeter pass on the ensuing possession and, after drawing defender Larry Smith in tight, dropped the ball back to Rice on the break for another dunk.

Kenny Battle (29 points) answered with a three-pointer from the right baseline and Hamilton put Illinois up, 79-78. Michigan called a time-out with 1:36 remaining.

Neither team could put the other away in the second half. There were 33 lead changes and seven ties in the game.

Loy Vaught goes highest in battle for rebound against Illini.

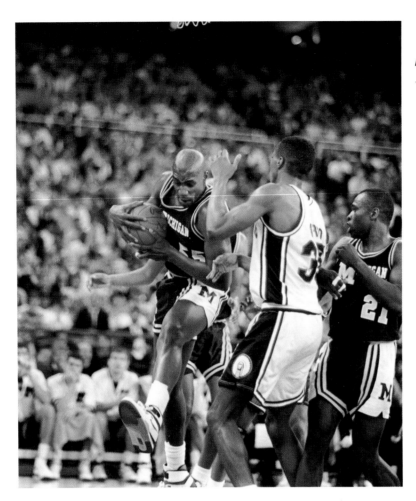

Mark Hughes takes possession on scramble in Final Four's second game with Illinois.

The Wolverines had their largest lead of the game, 53-46, early in the half. By the midway point, Illinois had caught up and set the stage for a tight game down the stretch.

Michigan led at the half, 39-38, despite shooting only 43.6 percent. In their two regular-season games, the Wolverines trailed the Illini at the half.

Rumeal Robinson takes off on fast break against Illini.

Loy Vaught grabbed 12 first-half rebounds to deny Illinois second shots and its usual array of dunks. Vaught, who had a career-high 15 rebounds last year against Florida in the NCAA Tournament, finished with 16.

"See, I told you rebounding would be the difference," Vaught said.

U-M had a 45-39 edge on the boards. The Illini shot a dismal 37.5 percent in the half, forced to rely more on outside shooting, and finished at 44.8 percent. Hamilton, playing on a slightly sprained ankle, missed all seven shots in the first half.

Vaught, the unsung hero of the Final Four, also made a big difference in the championship game with Seton Hall.

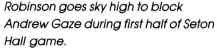

Robinson goes sky high to block Andrew Gaze during first half of Seton Hall game.

The Pirates (picked seventh in a poll of Big East coaches) were unranked in the Associated Press writers' poll on the day Michigan rose to No. 2 by beating Oklahoma to win the Maui Classic. The United Press International coaches' poll also had the Wolverines second, and Seton Hall eeked in at No. 20.

After that, the Wolverines rode a roller-coaster and the Pirates took steady steps up the respect ladder. But theirs was an unlikely title game. Where were Georgetown and Arizona? Or Illinois and Oklahoma? The top seeds in the regionals had all bit the dust.

"This is like a soap opera," Vaught said. "If you told me on October 15 that it would come down to these two teams, well . . ."

He wouldn't have believed it. He wasn't alone.

But in the end, the championship would be decided by a player standing all alone at the foul line. Rumeal Robinson had it all before him. Win, lose or another overtime — it depended on his free throws with three seconds left.

Sean Higgins drives for layup through Pirate defense.

The first tied the game at 79, and a smiling Robinson thrust a fist high. The second also hit nothing but net, 80-79 — and Michigan became college basketball's national champion at the Kingdome.

Robinson had been fouled by Seton Hall's Gerald Greene on a drive to the basket.

"I made up my mind to put it on my shoulders, and take that last shot," Robinson said. "I didn't want to pass off. I got fouled, and thank God I made those."

Robinson had a flashback to the game at Wisconsin, where with nine seconds left he missed two free throws that could have given Michigan a one-point lead. "I didn't capitalize," Robinson said at that time. "I hit those and we're up by one. I felt I let the team down."

Loy Vaught rebounds in traffic, one of seven rebounds in championship game.

Coach Fisher has a word with Mark Hughes on sidelines: Hughes played 24 minutes in championship game.

The Wolverines lost, and Robinson took free throws seriously. He stayed after practice each day for over two weeks to shoot 100 from the free throw line. Fisher was there to rebound and encourage. It was funny how things worked out.

The Wolverines (30-7) beat the Pirates (31-7) in the first overtime title game since 1963. It was the first NCAA Tournament title for Michigan, which lost its two previous trips to the championship game. It was the Big Ten's second title in three years.

"If any of you want to be my ghostwriter," said Fisher, the first interim coach to ever win the NCAA title, "I'm going to retire unbeaten, untied . . . No, good things will happen."

And who was to doubt Fisher when it came to fate? In the huddle before the overtime, Fisher told his team that a psychic friend in San Francisco, Dan Morris, had predicted an overtime win. The players later doubted the story, but Fisher maintained its validity a month later.

After accepting their NCAA rings on a podium, putting on pre-made championship T-shirts and cutting down the net, the Wolverines finally made it to the locker room.

That's where they let out a group cheer: "One, two, three — mission accomplished!"

Robinson goes after loose ball in traffic.

Glen Rice, the tournament's Most Outstanding Player, placed them on the "mission to shock the world" after U-M lost at Indiana, 76-75, February 19. Michigan then won 11 of its last 12 games.

"I told them, 'Now we're on a mission,' " said Rice, the victory net around his neck. "That got them motivated. Everyone seems to like that word, mission."

Rice and Robinson were named to the all-tournament team with Green and Seton Hall's John Morton and Danny Ferry of Duke.

Green and the Pirates had one last chance to steal Michigan's glory. A chance was all, though.

Glen Rice's jumping defense forces Darryll Walker to alter his moves.

Daryll Walker's 20-foot shot off the glass followed a three-quarter-court pass from Ramon Ramos. The shot never hit the rim, and Walker walked off the court, eyes welling in tears. Teammate Andrew Gaze patted him on the head.

At the same time, Sean Higgins was pounding the hardwood for joy in a prone position. Everyone was hugging everyone.

Cheerleaders also point to the championship.

"I had tears in my eyes," Higgins said. "I had to drop down so not to let anyone see me. The emotion just took over."

Higgins scored 10 points and hit crucial free throws near the end of regulation to keep the hopes alive.

Robinson finished with 21 points. Rice scored 31, giving him 2,442 points and making him the Big Ten's career scoring leader.

Rice had a chance to fulfill his lifelong dream of hitting a winning shot at the buzzer in college. But his jumper from the top of the key swirled off the rim, and Walker rebounded for Seton Hall as the buzzer ended regulation.

"I was shocked I missed," Rice said.

Rice gave Michigan a 69-68 lead with 58 seconds left. It was a stunning shot from the left of the key, and silenced a Seton Hall run. He finished with a tournament-record 27 treys.

Rice set an NCAA Tournament record with 182 points and 75 field goals, breaking records set by Bill Bradley (177 points for Princeton in 1965) and Elvin Hayes (70 field goals for Houston in 1968).

Higgins put the Wolverines up, 71-68, with two free throws with 34 seconds to go in regulation.

Terry Mills hits jumper.

Rice and Mills put pressure on Seton Hall shooter.

Morton (35 points) answered with a no-hesitation three-pointer 10 seconds later to tie the score at 71. It wasn't nip and tuck earlier in the half.

Seton Hall had the Wolverines right where they wanted them midway through the second half. U-M had a 51-39 lead, but quickly began playing not to lose. The Pirates had a way of doing that to teams. Their previous tournament foes shot .333 (51-for-153) in the second halves, falling prey to coach P.J. Carlesimo's defensive dragons.

Morton scored six straight in the Pirates' run of eight unanswered points. Two of the buckets came off fast breaks. Seton Hall cut it to two points twice.

Michigan pulled away again, 66-61, but Morton jerked them right back. He hit two fast-break baskets off turnovers to cut it to one, and penetrated for the short shot that gave the Pirates a 67-66 lead with 2:31 remaining.

The Wolverines opened the second half with a 14-6 run. Robinson's reverse, two-hand slam off a baseline buzz through the big trees dazzled the crowd of 39,187 at the Kingdome.

Rumeal Robinson goes the extra height for Wolverines' goal in second half.

Reverse layup in
traffic gives
Rumeal Robinson
extra charge.

But the Wolverines did as much with highlight-film footage as with teamwork.

Early in the second half, Rice saved a ball going out of bounds along the Pirates' baseline with a backward flip. Robinson caught it and shouted, "Here we go, Lo!" He dribbled upcourt and fired to Vaught near the lane. Vaught dropped it off to Terry Mills for an easy slam.

They had come together in a big way and accomplished the ultimate. The following week, Bo Schembechler named Fisher the new head coach. On a trip to the White House, Robinson was asked to recreate his free-throw heroics in the Rose Garden. He made the first and handed a surprised President George Bush the ball for the second shot. Bush's shot was a metal detector on the rim, but it fell through the net.

Everyone cheered.

They were the Good News Wolverines.

Wolverines high fives after scoring a goal.

The *Celebration*

(left) Celebrating the National Championship trophy.

Coach puts the finishing touches on a great job, clipping the nets.

THESE WOLVERINES HAD SHOCKED THE WORLD — MISSION ACCOMPLISHED

Hail! to the victors valiant...

Truly, it was a team victory.

Chaos reigned in the Seattle Kingdome where Michigan had just nipped Seton Hall in overtime for the National Basketball Championship. The Michigan Basketball Band was at its very best as a throng of Wolverine fans stood and joined in on a chorus of the "greatest fight song ever written," Following the official awards presentation to the Wolverines, the U-M players and staff grabbed one last precious souvenir of their visit — they cut down the nets.

By the time the Wolverines finally returned to their locker room, nearly 30 minutes had gone by since Rumeal Robinson sank the last of two very important free throws. Steve Fisher was the first to offer his praise to each and every player. University President James Duderstadt congratulated the Wolverines on one of the greatest achievements in Michigan athletic history. Athletic Director Bo Schembechler echoed those sentiments and reminded the team that he was equally proud of the manner in which the players had conducted themselves throughout the stormy tournament. Outgoing Big Ten Commissioner Wayne Duke was also on hand, and he expressed his personal thanks to the Michigan team for helping to make his last official appearance at the Final Four a special one.

The net comes down, the news goes up.

Printed-in-advance caps tell it all.

Hail! to the conquering heroes . . .

With the National Championship comes an obligation to face a seemingly endless stream of bright lights, microphones and cameras. The Wolverines took it all in stride, accommodating each and every reporter's request before returning to the Bellevue Hyatt. There, the players and staff gathered for a quiet buffet in a secluded wing, giving all the opportunity to relax and reflect — while watching a videotaped recording of the game.

Three flights below in the Hyatt ballroom, Michigan alumni and fans gathered to celebrate the school's first-ever national title. The sea of Maize and Blue faithful sang "The Victors", then chanted for an appearance by coach Steve Fisher.

One more team huddle.

Celebration and recognition back on the Ann Arbor campus.

Alumni Association Director Bob Forman wouldn't allow the group to be disappointed. Forman found Fisher exiting the buffet line and escorted the coach to the ballroom stage. Fisher was greeted with heart-felt cheers and applause, and the coach responded with words of gratitude for the loyalty and spirit of the Michigan supporters.

After Fisher's appearance, the night turned into a rollicking celebration. As the players finished dinner, they trickled downstairs to the ballroom where WJR's Larry Henry played emcee and introduced the Wolverines, urging each to grab the microphone and say a few words to the fans.

As it turned out, few of the players and coaches (and fans, for that matter) got any sleep at all before the team buses departed for Sea-Tac Airport at 8 a.m.

Hail! Hail to Michigan, the leaders and best . . .

From Bursley Hall and South Quad to Fraser's Pub and Dooley's, the students and fans in Ann Arbor began celebrating just moments after the Michigan victory. Thousands poured into the streets to share the single greatest achievement in Wolverine basketball history. For the most part, the party was orderly and peaceful, but a handful of fans — primarily unaffiliated with the university — vandalized a few area merchants. That black mark aside, the majority of U-M boosters represented Ann Arbor and the university well, and many planned to greet the Wolverines upon their arrival at Crisler Arena the following afternoon.

The team buses pulled into the Crisler Arena parking lot just before 6 p.m. An estimated 10 thousand fans filled the arena to pay tribute to the newly-crowned champions. After the Michigan pep band welcomed the crowd with its traditional U-M favorite, P.A. announcer Howard King introduced the players and coaches.

(left) Glen Rice gives No. 1 acclaim.

Loud and clear, celebration goes on and on.

Front and center, a big hand for everybody.

Each was greeted with a thunderous ovation. Terry Mills egged the masses on by shaking his fist; Sean Higgins strutted his stuff with arms upraised and sunglasses in place; Mike Griffin simply gave the crowd a nice, long look at his NCAA Championship ring.

The loudest applause was reserved for Rumeal Robinson, who sank those two crucial free throws in the waning moments of overtime. Or perhaps it was for Glen Rice, the All-American who broke every record in sight on his way to the Final Four Most Outstanding Player Award. Or, perhaps it was for Steve Fisher. the man who rose from the shadows to become the first rookie coach ever to win the NCAA crown.

Regardless, this Michigan team knew it took the efforts of every player and coach to win the title, and in this, their shining moment, they shared the limelight.

Coach and national champions take one final salute.

Hail! to the victor's valiant . . .

Exactly one week after winning the championship, Athletic Director Bo Schembechler announced that Steve Fisher would indeed be the man to guide the Michigan basketball program into the 1990's. To many observers, it was a forgone conclusion that Fisher would be offered the head coaching job. Schembechler, however, realized the significance of this appointment and wanted to be absolutely sure that Fisher was the right man for the job. And just as Bo had suspected, he was.

Later that same day, the annual Michigan basketball bust was held at Crisler Arena. The forum gave the Michigan coaches and seniors Glen Rice, Mark Hughes and J.P. Oosterbaan the opportunity to publicly express the importance of the university and its fans to their success. It was an emotional evening, to be sure, and one that few who attended will ever forget.

Fisher family, all smiles (and then some) in Seattle.

Hail! to the conquering heroes . . .

Within days, the Wolverines found themselves headed to Washington, D.C. for a congratulatory visit to the White House. President George Bush and Vice-President Dan Quayle welcomed the Michigan team with a tour of the White House. While in the Rose Garden, President Bush surprised the team with an authentic backboard and hoop, and the President challenged Rumeal Robinson to duplicate the late-game heroics that gave U-M the national title. Robinson removed his jacket and sank his first free throw, then tossed the ball to the President and returned the challenge. To the delight of the team, White House staff and media, Bush drained his toss as well.

Wolverines at the White House with President Bush.

Before returning to Ann Arbor, the Wolverines toured many of the city's national treasures and were treated to a reception in their honor on Capitol Hill.

To the Michigan players, coaches and staff, the mission was now complete.

Hail! Hail to Michigan, the Champions of the West!

The
Media

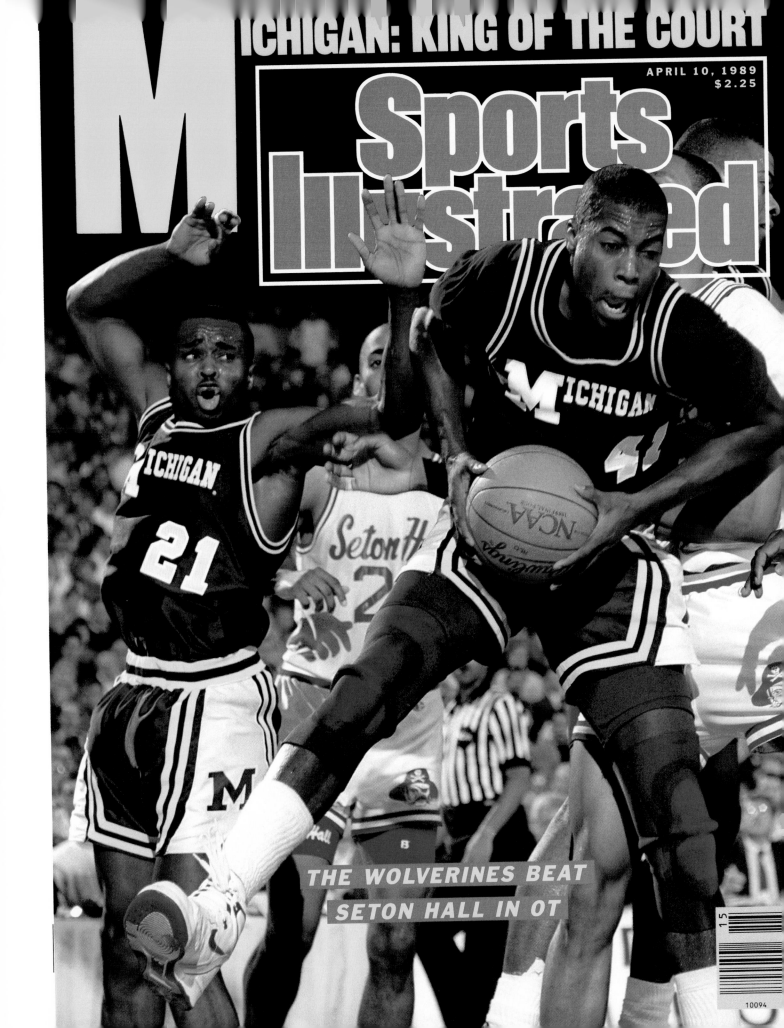

MICHIGAN: KING OF THE COURT

APRIL 10, 1989
$2.25

Sports Illustrated

THE WOLVERINES BEAT SETON HALL IN OT

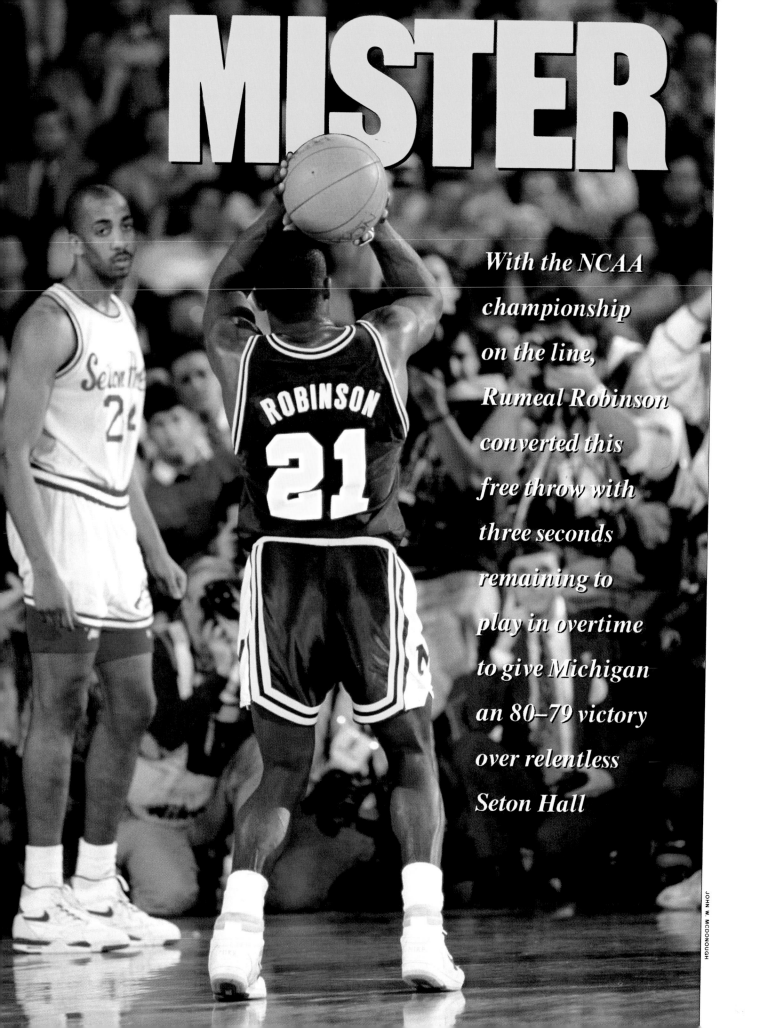

MISTER

With the NCAA championship on the line, Rumeal Robinson converted this free throw with three seconds remaining to play in overtime to give Michigan an 80–79 victory over relentless Seton Hall

CLUTCH

Sports Illustrated

APRIL 10, 1989

WORLD OF NINTENDO
Its empire knows no bounds
THE WAY WE LIVE, 1B

PLAY BALL! TIGERS AND RANGERS OPEN '89 SEASON
Detroit sports several new faces tonight — but not quite as many as Texas
SPORTS, 1D

Detroit Free Press

METRO FINAL

Partly cloudy. High 57, low 36
Wednesday: Partly cloudy.
Details, Page 2A ■■■

TUESDAY

April 4, 1989
For home delivery call 222-6500
20 cents

MICHIGAN	80
SETON HALL	79

HAIL TO THE VICTORS!

STEVEN R. NICKERSON/Detroit Free Press

From left, from Angie, Mark, U-M interim basketball coach Steve and Jonathan Fisher celebrate the Wolverines' national championship Monday night in Seattle.

In Michigan, New Jersey, the fans hang on every shot

INSIDE

SPECIAL SECTION

■ A special section looking back at the Wolverines' championship in Wednesday's Free Press.

IN SPORTS

■ Robinson's free throws in OT give U-M its first NCAA title. Page 1D.
■ U-M's incredible turnaround. Page 8D.
■ Dream slips away in South Orange. Page 9D.
■ Seton Hall's Morton was spectacular. Page 10D.

WELCOME HOME

■ The University of Michigan's basketball team will be greeted with a rally at 5:30 p.m. today at Crisler Arena in Ann Arbor. The Wolverines are to arrive at Metro Airport by charter flight about 4:30 to 5 p.m. The team will take a bus to Crisler, where they will be met by a pep band, cheerleaders and fans.

Free Press Staff

The night they won the championship.

Three Hours to Tipoff: Ken Hunt parked himself at a table just a lay-up away from the 20-by-20-foot TV screen at Mr. Sports bar in Farmington Hills.

"Michigan has been my life," said Hunt, 27, of Auburn Hills. "They have to win."

Ninety Minutes to Tipoff: 500 students scrambled for 150 seats in front of a 9-by-12-foot TV in the main lounge of the student center at Seton Hall University in South Orange, N.J.

A disc jockey announced "a message to Michigan" and cranked up "Get Ready" by the Temptations.

" 'Cuz here we come!" the students yelled as they jumped on the chairs to dance. The disc jockey asked them to please not do that. They got down.

One Hour to Tipoff: "For my dad's sake, I hope Seton Hall wins," said Susan Keels, 22, a bartender at Mr. Sports; 20 years ago, her father, John, now 48, played basketball for the Pirates.

Fifteen Minutes to Tipoff: At the University of Michigan Law Library, Robert Cardenas, a third-year law student from Houston, closed his books and headed for the exit.

"I'm not going to sit here," he said. "I'll get to a friend's house or go somewhere to watch the game."

Ten Minutes to Tipoff: Sophomore Anthony Rizzo watched Sister Pius Yavor of campus ministries, wearing her habit and a white Seton Hall sweatshirt, dance to the rock music at the student center.

"I thought you could go to hell for that," Rizzo said.

"I don't care right now," said the

See FANS, Page 6A

GARY STEWART/Associated Press

University of Michigan guard Rumeal Robinson leaps into the arms of teammate Glen Rice Monday night after the Wolverines captured the NCAA Division I basketball championship with an 80-79 overtime victory over Seton Hall University in the Seattle Kingdome.

A game with everything, a team with just enough

SEATTLE — He stood at the free throw line, the loneliest man in the world. All around him was the enemy, hooting and hollering, the demons in Seton Hall uniforms talking trash, the crowd suddenly an army of "MISS IT! MISS IT!" The referee bounced the ball twice, slowly, like an executioner, and tossed it to him. Life came to a standstill. A school and a nation and a glorious destiny held its breath.

MITCH ALBOM

Dribble. Shoot. Swish.
Tie game.
"All right baby!" yelled Glen Rice to Rumeal Robinson. "One more. One more."

Robinson licked his lips. What was riding on this shot? Only an entire season. Only a fairy tale ending. Only the championship of the world in college basketball. Pressure?
Dribble. Shoot. Swish.
Champions.

"WOOOOH! WOOOH! WOOH!" screamed Glen Rice, hugging Robinson three seconds later, crying in his arms, after Michigan had hung on to win the national championship in overtime, 80-79, in the most fantastic finish to a basketball season you could ever imagine. "WOOH! WOOH!"

Were there any other words? How else could you describe it? A game that had everything, classic theater, wonderful drama — the first overtime game in a tournament final since 1963. It had heroes and villains and magnificent plays and bonehead plays and moments when you could cut the pressure with a buzz saw, and moments when all the players, good and bad, succumbed to it.

It had Glen Rice, the tournament's MVP, keeping his team alive all game long with miracle shots, scoring from every angle, yet missing a jumper at the buzzer that could have sealed it. It had Sean Higgins, the young, free-spirited guard, who three weeks ago you wouldn't trust with his own sneakers, sinking two clutch free throws in the final moments of regulation. It had Steve Fisher, the interim coach, calming his team when

See ALBOM, Page 6A

Chrysler ups the ante in sales incentive war

BY GREG GARDNER
Free Press Automotive Writer

Chrysler Corp. hurled the latest weapon Monday in the Big Three's cutthroat war of sales incentives, saying it wouldn't charge a cent of interest on loans of two years or less.

"It's a jungle out there. If you have to play in it, you might as well go for defoliation," said Bennett Bidwell, the tart-tongued chairman of the Chrysler Motors Corp. unit. "Let's put an end to this one-upsmanship."

Chrysler's one-upmanship extends only to the two-year loans. On most other loans, it's merely keeping up with the Fords and GMs. Rates are 5.9

■ A rundown of buyer incentives offered by Big Three, Page 12A.

percent for loans up to 36 months, 6.9 percent to 48 months and 10.9 percent to 60 months. Ford and GM are at 9.9 percent for 60 months.

The zero financing deal will help only those who can afford to finance a car over so short a period; on a $12,000 loan, a monthly payment would be $500. Finance companies say less than 15 percent of new cars and trucks are financed over 24 months or

See CHRYSLER, Page 15A

INSIDE TODAY

Ann Landers	2B	Jumble	6C
Bridge	14D	Movie Guide	15D
Business	10A	Obituaries	8C
Classified Ads	6C, 12D	Science/Medicine	1C
Comics	14D	Stock Markets	11A
Crossword Puzzle	15D	Television	4B
Dateline Michigan	5C	50 plus	3B
Death Notices	6C		
Editorials	8A		
Entertainment	6B		
Feature Page	7B		
Greater Detroit	4A		
Horoscope	14D		

Volume 158, Number 326
© 1989, Detroit Free Press

Michigan		
Monday	680 and 2982	
Lotto jackpot	$6 million	
Ohio		
Monday	462 and 8770	
Lotto jackpot	$9 million	

■ Foreign debt, drug trafficking open talks in Cuba between Soviet President Mikhail Gorbachev and President Fidel Castro. Page 15A.

■ U.S. requires airline tests for plastic bombs. Page 15A.

■ City's own crews to join demolition effort. Page 3A.

Study: Toxic pollutants still plague 4 waterways

BY BOB CAMPBELL
Free Press Environment Writer

The connecting channels of the upper Great Lakes — the Detroit, St. Clair and St. Marys rivers and Lake St. Clair — remain plagued with toxic chemicals, despite two decades and hundreds of millions of dollars already spent on controlling water pollution, according to a bi-national study released Monday.

Until a major commitment is made by industry, government and the public to reduce continuing sources of pollution in the waterways, fish will remain contaminated and the rivers and lake will fall short of their full recreational

and economic potential, the study suggests.

"The good news is that conditions have improved dramatically in most areas and that nothing extraordinary was found in terms of large problems," said Rich Powers, a surface water quality specialist for the Michigan Department of Natural Resources. "The bad news is we've got a long ways to go yet."

The four-year, $20-million study found that the Detroit River, specifically its Michigan shoreline from Zug Island to Lake Erie, has the worst contamination of the four waterways.

See WATER, Page 15A

NBA/NHL

■ Blackhawks get their wish:
Wings, 6D; NBA Central
tough as they come, 7D.

Tuesday, April 4, 1989

SPORTS

Detroit Free Press

A-maizing Blue, 80-79

With the weight of the world on his shoulders,
Rumeal Robinson prepares to take the free throw that
would give Michigan a one-point lead with three
seconds left in the NCAA Championship game.

Rumeal Robinson raises his fist after his one-two punch from the free-throw line sent Seton Hall down for the count.

Rumeal Robinson: 'I could have easily missed those shots'

BY JOHNETTE HOWARD
Free Press Sports Writer

SEATTLE — The Michigan Wolverines started to think
the national title might be theirs when Glen Rice hit a
jumper, then saved the ball at the opposite end of the court
to start a relay-race fast break the other way — Robinson to
Mills to Vaught.

But when Rumeal Robinson screamed down the baseline, then rose with a suddenness you had never quite seen
before and threw in an implausible two-handed dunk over
his head, why, their hearts were screeching now.

Problem was, a fat 14:18 still remained in the game. And
for Michigan, it seemed like an eon. Each minute on the
clock seemed more like a year. The seconds ground by. And
the lead that had swollen to 51-39 with Robinson's net-
hissing jam was bleeding away like a watercolor in the rain.
Would tears follow?

Overtime did first. But Robinson — after wiping the
sweat off his hands onto his oversized shorts — dropped in
two of the smoothest free throws you've ever seen, giving
U-M its first national basketball championship Monday
night, 80-79, over Seton Hall.

And just as remarkable was the way Robinson set it up
with a length-of-the-court drive in which he weaved by four
Seton Hall players as if they were traffic pylons before
Gerald Greene, his old high school adversary, fouled him in
desperation with three seconds left.

That set up Robinson's one-and-one free throws and a
chance to make U-M history.

"Coach Fisher told me if I had the chance to get the ball
downcourt, take it downcourt real quick," Robinson said.
"They were a little slow getting back on defense, and I was
just going to take it on my shoulders, and they fouled me.
Thank God. I could have easily missed those shots. Thank
God it went in."

See **RUMEAL ROBINSON**, Page 9D

Robinson's OT free throws give U-M 1st NCAA title

BY STEVE KORNACKI
Free Press Sports Writer

SEATTLE — Rumeal Robinson had
it all before him. Win, lose or another
overtime — it depended on his free
throws with three seconds left.

The first tied the game at 79, and a
smiling Robinson thrust a fist high. The
second also hit nothing but net, 80-79
— and Michigan became college basketball's national champion Monday
night at the Kingdome.

Robinson had been fouled by Seton
Hall's Gerald Greene on a drive to the
basket.

"I made up my mind to put it on my
shoulders, and take that last shot,"
Robinson said. "I didn't want to pass
off. I got fouled, and thank God I made
those."

The Wolverines (30-7) beat the
Pirates (31-7) of the Big East in the
first overtime title game since 1963. It
is the first NCAA Tournament title for
Michigan, which lost its two previous
trips to the championship game. It was
the Big Ten's second title in three
years.

And the Wolverines did it for interim coach Steve Fisher.

"I feel like a ghost rider," Fisher
said. "I'm going to retire unbeaten,
untied. . . . No, good things will happen."

And who is to doubt Fisher when it
comes to fate? U-M won six tournament games under him.

After accepting their NCAA rings
on a podium, putting on pre-made
championship T-shirts and cutting
down the net, the Wolverines finally
made it to the locker room.

That's where they let out a group
cheer: "One, two, three — mission
accomplished!"

Glen Rice, the tournament's Most
Outstanding Player, placed them on
the "mission to shock the world" after

See **WOLVERINES**, Page 10D

BATTLE IN SEATTLE

More on the championship

■ Mitch Albom's column. Page 1A.
■ Team members speak out on
the championship. Page 8D.
■ Bo Schembechler avoids
questions about coach. Page 8D.
■ U-M star Glen Rice is his humble
self. Page 9D.
■ Joe Lapointe on TV coverage.
Page 9D.
■ Seton Hall's John Morton just
missed being a hero. Page 10D.
■ Tournament history. Page 10D.
■ Photostory. Page 16D.

Rose, Reds winners as baseball returns

BY GENE GUIDI
Free Press Sports Writer

CINCINNATI — Beleaguered Cincinnati Reds manager
Pete Rose arrived at Riverfront Stadium shortly after 9 a.m.
Monday for his 27th Opening Day as a major league player
and manager.

With game time still five hours away, Rose found the
Reds' clubhouse nearly deserted when he arrived. But on
this day, Rose didn't need much company to be happy.

"There's nothing like Opening Day — especially here in
Cincinnati," Rose said. "When I was a kid growing up here,
you could get out of school if you showed your teacher that
you had a ticket to the game.

"I never get more revved up than I do on Opening Day
— it's a great American tradition."

And the Reds, playing in their 103rd Opening Day in
Cincinnati, treated the home crowd to a 6-4 victory over the
Los Angeles Dodgers. Kirk Gibson, bothered all spring by
injuries, not only played for LA, he got the first hit of the season — a first-inning single — and homered.

Paul O'Neill powered the Reds, going 4-for-4 with a
three-run homer. Danny Jackson got the victory, the Reds'
fifth straight on Opening Day under Rose.

Earlier, Rose talked about another great American

See **REDS**, Page 5D

Dodgers catcher Mike Scioscia and the Reds' Paul
O'Neill look for the umpire's call in the second inning
Monday. O'Neill was safe.

For the Tigers, a quiet new look

Tonight's opener offers contrast with Rangers

BY JOHN LOWE
Free Press Sports Writer

ARLINGTON, Tex. — A billboard
near Arlington Stadium carries the
Texas Rangers' motto for this season:
"It's a whole new and improved ballgame."

The cover of the team's media
guide shows the backs of five jerseys.
They bear the names and numbers of
the quintet of new Rangers: pitchers
Nolan Ryan and Jamie Moyer, and
infielders Julio Franco, Rafael Palmeiro
and Buddy Bell. All but Bell were
acquired in a three-day span at last
December's winter meetings.

When the Tigers visit them for the
season opener tonight, the Rangers
will be starting over in search of their
first championship.

The Tigers wouldn't invoke many
of these Rangers techniques. They
wouldn't have a team slogan, or take
out a billboard to advertise improve-

ment. They would never herald new
players as franchise-turners.

The Tigers have always preferred
to stress continuity. Their conserva-
tive operation implies an unspoken
promise: Any year you visit the corner
of Michigan and Trumbull, you will see
a workmanlike team wearing the Olde
English D, backed by an organization
intent on winning.

Manager Sparky Anderson and
general manager Bill Lajoie have completed a major adjustment of their
attack.

The Tigers will not rely on age and
power nearly as much as in the last few
seasons. Speed and youth better describe them now.

The need for a change became clear
when the power — then the runs, and
finally the victories — disappeared
after the All-Star break last season.

See **TIGERS**, Page 4D

THE OPENER

Tigers vs. Rangers, tonight, 8:30 at
Arlington Stadium, Channel 4,
WJR-AM (760).

TIGERS	POS.
Kenny Williams	cf
Torey Lovullo	1b
Lou Whitaker	2b
Alan Trammell	ss
Fred Lynn	lf
Matt Nokes	c
Chris Brown	3b
Chet Lemon	rf
Pat Sheridan	dh
Jack Morris (15-13)	p

RANGERS	POS.
Cecil Espy	cf
Scott Fletcher	ss
Rafael Palmeiro	1b
Ruben Sierra	rf
Julio Franco	2b
Pete Incaviglia	lf
Geno Petralli	c
Buddy Bell	dh
Steve Buechele	3b
Charlie Hough (15-16)	p

U-M's incredible turnaround

Players amazed by changes

BY JOHNETTE HOWARD
Free Press Sports Writer

SEATTLE — Plenty of drama already had been played out by the time the University of Michigan and Seton Hall University met in Monday night's NCAA championship basketball game.

But even if, a few days from now, the Wolverines' names have disappeared from the sports pages, the discoveries they made in the last few weeks about themselves, let alone about playing basketball, were evident before the title game was over.

And most of the revelations were things you never shake. The change that came over the U-M players after the departure of former coach Bill Frieder was "incredible even to us," said forward Loy Vaught.

To U-M interim coach Steve Fisher, the striking thing has been the intensity his players brought to the six tournament games, the way they suddenly listened, pulled together and admitted maybe they hadn't done as much as they could have before. Then they went out in the tournament and, Fisher said, got a "lesson that we could play harder than we probably knew we could."

Guard Rumeal Robinson was struck by the super-heated atmosphere of U-M's tournament run, the ever-present threat of being eliminated at every juncture and U-M's ability to shrug off the pressure every step of the way — acknowledging only the excitement and thrill of going farther than they ever had before.

"I feel that every game we've played in the NCAA has been a championship game," Robinson said before Monday's game. "But the feeling I have is still up in the air. Playing for the national championship, it's more than just a boyhood dream. It's more like looking forward to riding your first bike, but you can't ride it until morning comes."

For center Terry Mills, a phoenix in U-M's tournament story, the metamorphosis from a potential champion to a championship team was a lesson about what's really important. At times, Mills said, the question a player must ask himself is whether he wants to win games or assure himself that he stars in them.

Somewhere along the line in these last three weeks, winning began to obscure everything else. Then, suddenly, it didn't matter anymore if U-M players were asked to get 10 rebounds or 10 points or set 10 screens for star forward Glen Rice. When you win, everything feels good just the same.

"I feel it's been a mistake to judge me and Loy by how many points we're getting now because we're doing other things that we need to win," Mills said. "When you've got a man shooting the ball like Glen Rice or Sean Higgins or Rumeal Robinson, you'll just about give up your body for them — do anything to set a screen, whatever, to get them open."

Before each tournament game, Fisher and assistants Mike Boyd and Brian Dutcher talked to each U-M player individually to outline what his role would be. For Higgins, the sixth man who won the semifinal game over Illinois with a last-second follow shot, the orders for that game were to play a hard, all-around game whether his shot was falling or not. It paid off with the basket Higgins called "a dream come true."

"Coach Fisher had told me all year that shots like that come off the weak side, so I just put myself in position to get the rebound," Higgins said. "I finally listened."

For Vaught, who owned the second-best field-goal percentage in the country, the job has been putting scoring aside in some games — like that Illinois showdown Saturday — and hording enough rebounds for U-M to win.

And Vaught responded with a career-high 16 — 12 in the first half.

"We knew rebounding would be the key to that game, and I just made a commitment to myself to get every rebound there was," Vaught said Sunday.

Along the way, there was something fortifying to the Wolverines about setting their minds to a goal and pulling it off. Soon — quickly — this U-M team began to feel as though it could do anything.

It began to feel powerful.

"Against Illinois, me, Terry and Glen knew we all had to play great games," said Mark Hughes, a 6-foot-8 senior reserve. "And we just said we were going to do it — we're not going to let them have alley-oop baskets; we're not going to let them have second shots; we're not going to let them beat us on dribbles and drives to the hoop. We just got together and said, 'We're going to do it.'"

For Rice, who always visualizes that his shots will fall in without fail anyway, that also meant feeling so invincible that even a twanging hamstring wouldn't slow him down. Not now. "I just feel like I can't be physically hurt right now," Rice said after the victory over Illinois. "I just feel so much strength."

And if, heading into Monday's game, Rice was justly proud of what Michigan had done to come that far, he said: "No, I'm not impressed yet. As soon as we win the national championship, I'd be impressed then."

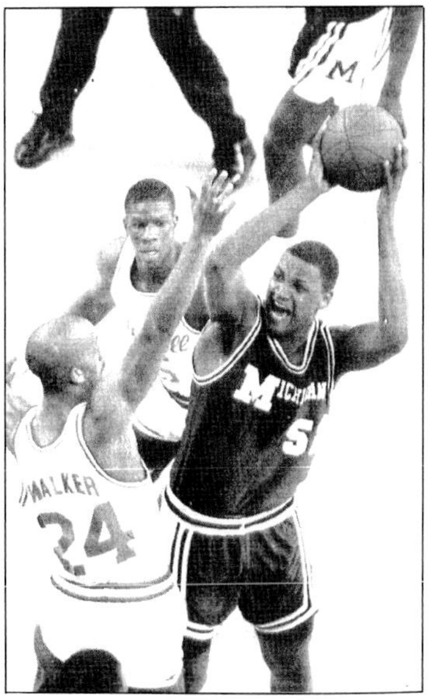

UPI

Terry Mills shoots over Darryl Walker; Mills finished with eight points and six rebounds.

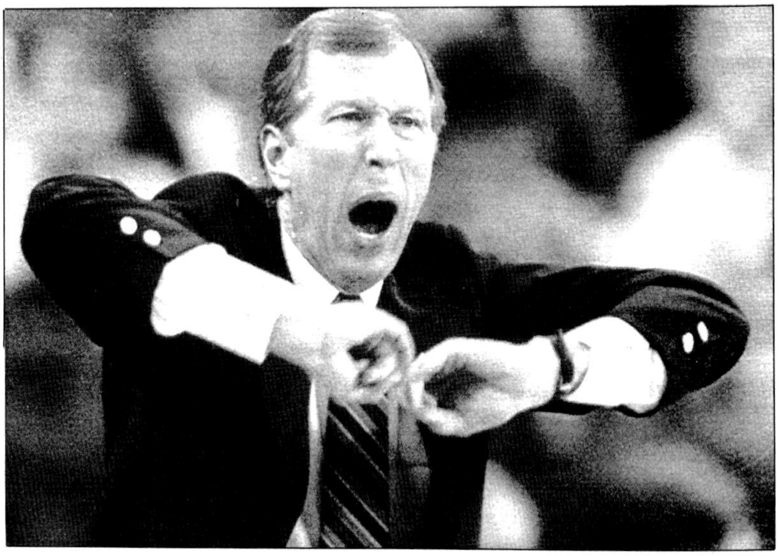

Interim coach Steve Fisher encourages his Wolverines as they battle toward the NCAA Championship Monday night.

LISTEN TO THE CHAMPS

The Wolverines talk about their victory over Seton Hall in the NCAA final:

Guard Rumeal Robinson

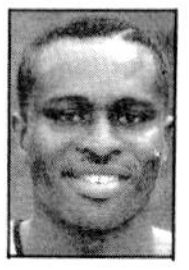

"I felt like I was going to hit it either way — whether it was a free throw or not."

Guard Rob Pelinka

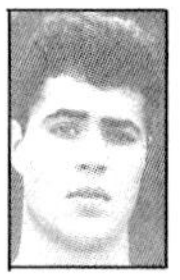

"This is great. It spoiled us freshmen. We want to do it three more times. It'll make us work that much harder because we want to contend again next year."

Forward Loy Vaught

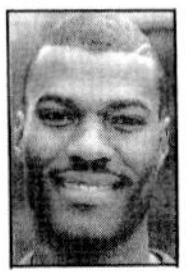

"All this seems fake. Bo said it would sink in later. But I'm looking at this ring, and it sure looks real right now. We started talking mission late in the Big Ten season, and it's accomplished."

Guard Sean Higgins

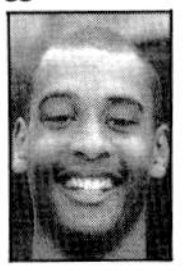

"Now we know how to win. We've got two years left to do it again. We know what a mission is like."

Center Mark Hughes

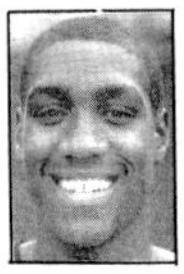

"It means a great deal because nobody thought we could do it. We set the goal of a national championship like most teams. But we got it."

Guard Demetrius Calip

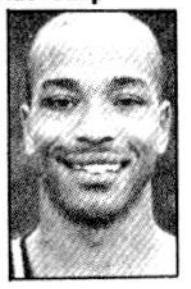

"It feels great, unbelievable."

Forward Glen Rice

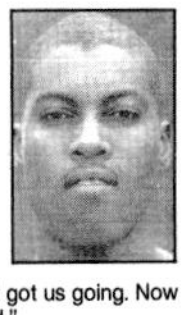

"It has not hit me right now in the way it is going to hit me. It's a great moment. Coach Fisher told us we had an open spot for the championship banner, and that got us going. Now we've got it filled."

Senior J.P. Oosterbaan

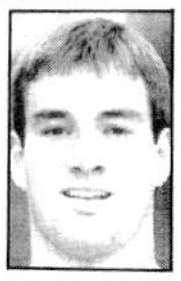

"This is why I came back for a fifth season. At the start of the year I had the feeling we could win it all."

Guard Mike Griffin

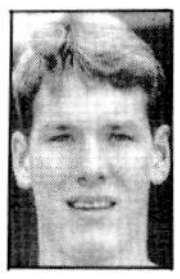

"On that last drive I thought Rumeal was going to kick it back. I wasn't sure the ref was going to call it. Whoever calls something like that with three seconds left? The whole time, I was just saying, 'Rumeal's gonna redeem himself (for missing two game-winning free throws against Wisconsin in the regular season). But to stand behind him out there and see them both go in, it was just incredible."

Center Terry Mills

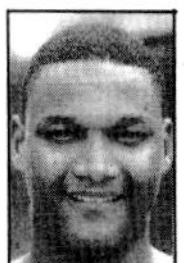

"I'm probably going to party for about a week, then get down to business all over again. It's been a long, long day. Putting in a little overtime in the end doesn't help any."

Guard Mark Koenig

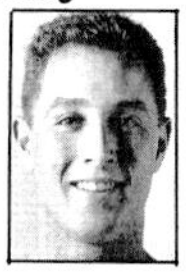

"My voice is going fast. I was screaming and yelling the whole game. I've sat at home in LA and watched people stand on that podium, put on the T-shirts and the hats and cut down the nets."

Guard Kirk Taylor

"I accepted having a knee injury, mostly because there was nothing I could do about it. But I was up there on the podium with them. And I was in the first row of the stands, waving my crutches when we won. It was a joy for me."

Assistant coach Mike Boyd

"I'm just going to sit back and relax tonight and when I pick up the newspapers tomorrow and see that Michigan won the national championship, it'll hit me then. I'm just going to take a couple of days and enjoy it."

Coach Steve Fisher

"I'm going to enjoy this now and relax with it. I'm going to go back, put on the VCR and watch it all again."

Does Fisher get the job? Bo keeps coach waiting

BY CORKY MEINECKE
Free Press Sports Writer

SEATTLE — As Michigan players and coaches celebrated the school's first NCAA basketball championship Monday at the Kingdome, Bo Schembechler again stiff-armed questions about hiring Steve Fisher as coach.

"When we get home we'll sit down, have a nice talk and see how things go," said Schembechler, U-M's athletic director and football coach, leaving everything to the imagination.

With that off his chest, Schembechler made his way to center court, where the Wolverines were receiving their just rewards. He walked up to the podium, stuck his hand into a sea of arms and grabbed sophomore guard Sean Higgins, whose last-second shot beat Illinois Saturday and put Michigan into the championship game against Seton Hall.

Then Schembechler found Fisher.

They shook hands, but no deal was made.

"I don't know what's going to happen, and I'm not going to worry about it," Fisher said. "All of us will be winners."

Fisher does plan on calling one of his friends, former Kalamazoo resident Dan Morse. Before each game, Morse would call with a prediction. Morse picked Michigan by five over Xavier (92-87 final) and by a bunch over Virginia (102-65). So, Fisher listened when Morse said the Wolverines would win in OT and that senior Mark Hughes would be the hero.

Hughes wasn't the star, but it didn't stop Fisher from saying, "I'd better call (Morse) and ask him about Bo. Maybe I'd better start getting my resumes ready."

If Schembechler chooses to look elsewhere for a coach, Fisher can join Bill Frieder at Arizona State or shop for one of several coaching jobs up for grabs. Illinois State has reportedly put off its search until the Fisher situation is resolved.

"Twenty-six openings," said Wolverines assistant Mike Boyd.

Boyd, too, could be in line for a Division I position — perhaps at Western Michigan, which needs to replace Vern Payne. Boyd has paid his dues at Michigan, putting in 10 years under Johnny Orr, now at Iowa State, then with Frieder.

Boyd's phone already has been ringing.

"Yeah, it has," Boyd said, "but the calls have been from people wanting tickets. Plus, I haven't been easy to find because I've been on the road for most of the last three weeks. I want to be a head coach, but I'm a Michigan man, too."

Like Fisher, Boyd would like for the decision to be made quickly — if not in the next couple of days, then at least before April 10 (the signing date for high school players) or April 12 (Michigan's basketball banquet).

"You always want it to be over and done with," Boyd said.

Fisher and Boyd made all the right moves Monday — especially in the final 17 seconds of regulation, with the game tied at 71. After a timeout, the Wolverines followed Fisher's directions to perfection, getting Glen Rice an open jumper from the key with about three seconds left.

"I thought it was going in," Fisher said later. "I expected it to go in, the way Glen was shooting in the tournament. We were all shocked when it didn't go in."

Fisher also played it mighty cool when the Wolverines were down, 79-78, with less than a minute to play. The Pirates had the ball, and were in position to work the game clock down to about eight seconds. Rather than order his team to foul quickly, Fisher gambled on his defense.

And it paid off big.

The Pirates put up an air ball, the Wolverines got the rebound and guard Rumeal Robinson headed upcourt. He was fouled with three seconds left, then sank the winning free throws. Fisher then designed a defense that allowed Seton Hall no more than a desperation heave as time expired.

"All those things worked because the kids worked," Fisher said proudly.

"Yep," Schembechler said, "Fisher did a good job."

U-M'S PAST TITLE TUSSLES

Michigan had played in two NCAA championship games before Monday night, losing both times, to UCLA (91-80) in 1965 and to Indiana (86-68) in 1976. A look at those games:

1965

Michigan led early, 20-13, but UCLA outscored the Wolverines, 21-1, in the first half's final minutes at Portland, Ore. The Bruins' zone press frustrated U-M.

"Basketball is a game of momentum, and they took it," said Michigan coach Dave Strack. "We aren't slow for our size, but we gave away quickness. We knew we had to dominate the boards . . . but they get up into the air quickly."

UCLA stretched a 47-34 halftime lead to 56-39 in the early minutes of the second half.

All-America guard Gail Goodrich scored a game-high 42 points and backup forward Kenny Washington 17 as the Bruins won their second straight national title. Cazzie Russell scored 28 for Michigan, followed by Oliver Darden with 17 and Bill Buntin with 14. Buntin, Darden and Larry Tregoning fouled out.

Michigan finished 25-4, UCLA 28-2.

1976

Unbeaten Indiana played nearly flawlessly in the second half, overcoming a six-point halftime deficit to win easily at Philadelphia.

"They were super, man," said Michigan coach Johnny Orr. "I don't think anybody in the country could have beaten them. We were super in the first half, but in the second half, they didn't make a mistake."

The Hoosiers committed only one turnover in the first 16½ minutes of the second half, when they increased their lead to 73-59.

Indiana guard Bobby Wilkerson suffered a slight concussion in the game's opening minutes and didn't play again, but that didn't stop the Hoosiers from winning their first national title for coach Bobby Knight.

Indiana's Scott May led all scorers with 26 points, made four assists and grabbed eight rebounds. Indiana center Kent Benson, the tournament most valuable player, scored 25.

Guard Rickey Green led four Wolverines in double figures with 18 points.

Indiana finished 32-0, Michigan 25-7.

"Indiana had the best team here," Orr said. "Hell's fire, anybody who believes anything else is a g------ imbecile."

By Scott Walton

HOOPLA

Pirates' fans sad, proud

By DUANE NORIYUKI
Free Press Staff Writer

SOUTH ORANGE, N.J. — After filling Seton Hall students with hope and high-pitched anticipation, The Dream slipped away Monday night like a heartfelt sigh.

The tiny school that had people pulling out their maps finally reached the end of the road, losing to Michigan, 80-79, in the championship. The overtime loss stunned a crowd of about 1,000 students who gathered in the school's student center to watch on a giant television.

"I'm still in shock," said Kevin McParlend, 20, a sophomore from Matawan, N.J., who sat quietly as the crowd streamed out of the student center. "It was a great comeback, but to lose like that, it hurts. I think it would have been easier if we would have been blown out."

Father Gene Koch, director of campus ministry, said he was exhausted.

"The emotions shifted back and forth so many times in the final seconds from hope to disappointment," he said. "It's sad, but I'm very proud of the team. We've been saying a lot of prayers, but at least the school got to be known through the efforts of the team."

Eddie Gonzales, 19, a sophomore from Newark, said all was not lost.

"They did a lot for the school and the entire state of New Jersey," he said. "They put us on the map. People didn't even know who we were, but they do now."

Monsignor Andrew Cusack, director of the National Institute for Clergy, said making the Final Four will have "lasting impact" on Seton Hall.

"Athletics and academics are hand in glove," Cusack said. "You can just look at the history of Notre Dame to understand that."

Cusack said the attention the game brought to the school will boost enrollment.

"It's very valuable to the school," he said. "Basketball is a million-dollar communication of our great university."

"The thing this has done — beyond all the talk about the money and respect it brings to the school — is that it has given students and the community a sense of pride and inner confidence," said Dr. Jerry Kaplan, a 17-year professor at the school.

"A lot of the students here are from lower economic backgrounds. Many of them are the first members of their families to go to college. They're the ones who are really gaining something from this."

At Bunny's Tavern, the undisputed home away from home of the Pirates basketball team, Mark Laner, 27, of River Vale, N.J., was among the people crying and hugging others after the game.

"We still did better than people predicted," he said. "You've got to look forward to the future. It's a real disappointment but, hey, what's going to happen next year?"

Job protection

College basketball coaches are taking steps to aid colleagues who have lost their jobs this season.

"We think this is so important that we are making available $2,000 for any coach to use for counseling, for self-rehabilitation, for career guidance or for family rehabilitation," said Michigan State coach **Jud Heathcote**, outgoing president of the National Association of Basketball Coaches.

The 3,000-member NABC is concerned that coaches are being fired before they can effectively turn a team around. Heathcote also criticized the dismissals of **Don Donoher** at Dayton and **Bob Donewald** at Illinois State, well-regarded coaches who experienced recent downturns. Donewald's first losing record was this season.

A coaches' union is a possibility, but Heathcote said, "We're not close to it now."

By Perry A. Farrell

Pep talk

Fisher received a pep talk from **Gov. James Blanchard** before Monday's championship game.

Blanchard's spokesman, **Tom Scott**, said the governor spoke by telephone with Fisher.

"He praised him (Fisher) and the team for their great efforts and said not only is all of the state rooting for them, but everybody is proud of their accomplishments as they approach this final challenge," Scott said.

Bernie narrates finish; who hears?

When Michigan beat Seton Hall in overtime for the NCAA basketball championship Monday, Detroit Channels 4 and 7 seemed cheated because the frantic finish — on CBS and Channel 2 — ran through their 11 p.m. newscasts.

JOE LAPOINTE
TV/Radio

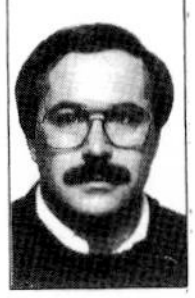

Sports anchor Bernie Smilovitz of Channel 4 noted at about 11:17: "Don't you feel like you're doing a show for yourself?"

Then he handled the problem nicely by watching Channel 2 on a TV set and giving a play-by-play.

"I'll bet CBS will be thrilled by this," he said, looking off camera as he narrated shots and time-outs. "I can't wait until the FCC sees this. . . . Michigan wins! That's it! Savor it! Enjoy it!"

Then he immediately began to show highlights of the game. What great presence of mind!

Channel 4 even showed the back of the TV set Smilovitz watched. Anchor Margie Reedy cheered.

The stunt was similar to that of ABC's Al Michaels, who announced "Monday Night Football" while digressing to a play-by-play of the Boston-New York Mets World Series in 1986.

On Channel 7, anchor Bill Bonds said: "I wish we could show it to you."

PACKER COMMENTS: CBS analyst **Billy Packer** didn't think much of Michigan athletic director **Bo Schembechler's** promise to give interim coach **Steve Fisher** the "first interview" as candidate for coach.

"If Bo would win the national championship in football, would he get the first interview to retain his job? Aw, give me a break!" Packer said.

Toward the end of the game, Packer kept insisting that U-M guard **Rumeal Robinson** should drive to the basket. When Robinson did it at the end of overtime, he was fouled, and made the two free throws that won the championship.

PICTURE PERFECT: CBS director **Bob Fishman** cut another near-perfect telecast, showing us just enough crowd and bench reaction while the ball was in play to add flavor without distracting. If CBS assigns him to the NBA Finals this year, the quality of its pro telecasts will improve considerably.

During time-outs in the last minutes, Fishman cut to shots of Schembechler, **Magic Johnson**, Robinson's mother, the coaches' wives, a little boy sleeping beneath a blaring tuba. The announcers kept quiet and let the band play and the crowd roar.

TELLING DETAILS: Two nice touches by CBS right before tip-off: candid, slow-motion tape of the wives of ex-coach **Bill Frieder** and Fisher hugging when they met in the stands; **James Brown's** report that Fisher had trouble getting into the arena because he didn't have the proper credentials.

THE NEXT DECADE: Instead of the soft and boring halftime features we usually see on CBS, Brown hosted a thoughtful report looking to college basketball in the 1990s. Among suggestions from coaches and rule makers: Move back the three-point line, raise the basket, play two halves of 22½ minutes each. **Dick Schultz**, the NCAA's executive director, urged discontinuation of athletic dorms and training tables, and limitations on practice time. Interesting to hear Georgetown coach **John Thompson** use the word "hypocritical" to describe college administrations that order coaches to win-or-else but complain when student athletes fall short in other areas.

SHINING 30 MINUTES: **Eli Zaret's** pregame show on Channel 2 — "One Shining Moment" — was a well-paced half-hour with a sharp point of view. The show gave credit to Frieder, who built the Wolverines but took a job at Arizona State right before the tournament. Although Frieder wanted to coach Michigan through the tournament, Schembechler said no.

"Bill Frieder is a friend of mine," Fisher said.

"We'd definitely like to win it for him," **Terry Mills** said.

Of Fisher, Frieder said: "I'll be astonished if he doesn't get the job. Even if Bo doesn't want to hire him, he has to, don't you think so?"

Zaret, wearing a necktie of Michigan maize, sat in front of a blue "M" banner, a team pennant and a backboard.

Among the best film and tape scenes: a young Frieder, sitting at **Johnny Orr's** side during the 1976 loss to Indiana in the title game; Schembechler and sidekick **Tom Monaghan**, the Tigers' owner, looking glum in the stands during the regular-season finale, a loss to Illinois; **Fred Heumann's** interview with Frieder, who said he maintains contact with Fisher and wants some credit for Michigan's success.

The only major flub came at the end, when cameras lingered on Zaret while theme music played. When directors finally got the closing video on screen, the theme music vanished for a few seconds.

NOTED QUOTE: Sometimes, TV announcers reach too far for pithy quips. But you had to chuckle at CBS studio host **Jim Nantz**, who said: "Steve Fisher becomes the most famous fill-in from the University of Michigan since **Gerald Ford**."

Robinson: 'I wanted it to be me'

RUMEAL ROBINSON, from Page 1D

Before the game, U-M athletic director Bo Schembechler had said his old heart — which already has had more bypasses than I-75 — couldn't take another one of these throat-constricting games. But U-M was lucky Robinson's could. Sean Higgins walked up to him and said: "I made my free throws (with 34 seconds left in regulation), now you make yours."

After Seton Hall called a time-out to ice Robinson, senior reserve J.P. Oosterbaan hauled him aside and said, "I love you, and our whole team loves you."

Oosterbaan said later: "I just wanted him to know, whether he made them or missed them, that we still loved him. After all he's been through, this couldn't have happened to a nicer guy."

Just in this 45-minute slab of his career, Robinson had to come back from a lot to finish with 21 points and 11 assists. Especially after he got off to a slightly shaky first-half start against Seton Hall's rugged defense.

In the opening five minutes alone, U-M made five turnovers and Robinson — lowering his shoulder and driving the lane again and again, like a runaway boulder — missed three point-blank shots and made only one.

But he slowly began to find his game, starting with a basket he scored near the 13-minute mark, after he rose in a crowd beneath the rim to snag an offensive rebound and muscle a shot up and in.

At first, Robinson found that getting passes inside to Terry Mills or Glen Rice or Loy Vaught was like trying to rifle the ball through a car wash without getting it wet.

When Seton Hall climbed back into the game in the second half, Robinson would not let U-M lose. From the opening tap he had his eyes on the rim, and he moved toward it whenever he had the opportunity — blazing by guard John Morton, squirting by Greene, going chest to chest with formidable Seton Hall center Ramon Ramos, even ending up like a piece of pressed meat in a sandwiching collision between Ramos and Gaze with 1:06 left in the first half.

If that hard foul was meant to discourage Robinson from venturing in among the big boys, it didn't work. In the second half he was at it again, shaking off a turnover here or a 3-on-1 break that Michigan failed to convert.

Then, when he stepped to the line with the national championship at stake, he forgot about that regular-season game against Wisconsin, too. The one he had a chance to win with seven seconds left. That time he failed.

"But the next day he was in the gym an hour early, and he shot a minimum of 100 free throws every day for weeks after that," said U-M interim coach Steve Fisher. "That's the type of resolve and commitment this kid has to becoming successful."

And when Seton Hall's Morton rose and tried an off-balance jumper with 10 seconds left, Robinson was there again, calling frantically for the ball with open palms even as Rice ripped down the air ball with both hands, sending Robinson off on his game-winning way.

"I didn't want to put it on anybody else's shoulders," Robinson said. "I didn't want to just come down and pass the ball and be hiding out there like you are a lot of times when there's a last-second shot. If anybody was going to take the last shot, I wanted it to be me."

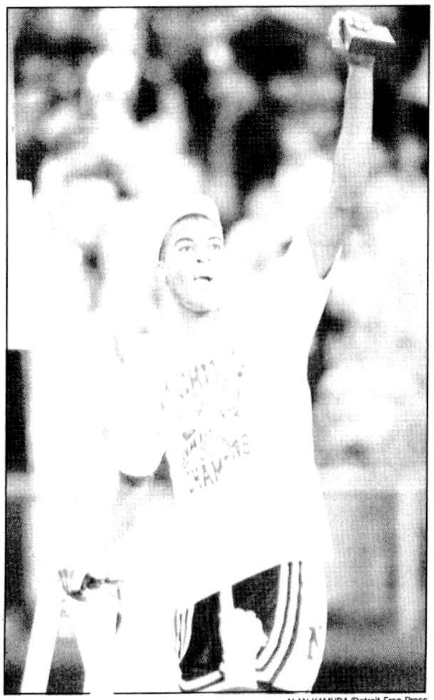

ALAN KAMUDA/Detroit Free Press

Glen Rice, who l… e Wolverines with 31 points, was named Most Outstanding Player in the NCAA Tournament.

Record-breaker Rice stays humble to end

By JOHNETTE HOWARD AND STEVE KORNACKI
Free Press Sports Writers

SEATTLE — Glen Rice wore a hat atop his head that said, "Just Did It! No. 1" and a nylon net was slung around his neck. Though it seemed a little unfitting when he missed the shot at the buzzer that could have lifted the University of Michigan to its first national championship in regulation, you couldn't miss that three-pointer he made with 1:03 left to keep U-M in the game.

Or that rebound he grabbed with 12 seconds left in overtime, sending Rumeal Robinson off on his game-winning jaunt to the free-throw line.

In the aftermath of U-M's 80-79 victory over Seton Hall Monday for the national championship, Rice was his typical understated self. He laughed and sighed when asked again and again to put his feelings into words. He's not anxious to do that even on an ordinary day. He shook his head from side to side when all of his new NCAA records were rattled off:

- He was named the tournament's most outstanding player.
- His 184 points broke the single-season tournament record of 177 that Bill Bradley set in 1965 for Princeton.
- His 75 field goals broke Houston's Elvin Hayes' record of 70, set in 1968.
- His 31 points against Seton Hall gave him 2,442 for his career, moving him ahead of U of M's Mike McGee (2,439) into No. 1 on the Big Ten scoring list.

So what did Rice have to say about all of that?

"I think overall it's a great individual achievement, but I feel I owe the most credit to my teammates, my coaches," Rice said. "Without them, I feel my accomplishments wouldn't have been possible."

Honest. That's what he said. And this: "I feel winning the national championship is great. But right now it really hasn't hit me. Each individual on this team played a great part in our success, including a lot of individuals who are back in the locker room, not up here (before the press)."

If you want fireworks, you'll have to watch him play.

NOTEBOOK

A DIG AT FRIEDER: Former U-M coach **Bill Frieder**, who resigned before the tournament to take the head-coaching job at Arizona State, is cropped out of the Michigan team picture in the official Final Four souvenir program. That seems a bit too cruel.

IT CAME TO THAT: The Seton Hall starters went into the game shooting 82.9 percent at the free throw line in the final four minutes of games. U-M's starters were shooting 78.8 in that same situation. But at the end, only one stat mattered: Robinson's two free throws.

THE DOTTED LINES: The Wolverines are 104-1 when scoring 90 points or more since 1975-76. . . . Seton Hall is 19-0 when it reaches 80 points; the Pirates fell one short Monday night. U-M is 28-2 when it hits 80. . . . Rice was 5-for-12 on three-pointers; he had 27 for the tournament, breaking the previous record of 26 set in 1987 by **Freddie Banks** of Las Vegas. . . . . . . Robinson had 11 assists; he needed 12 to tie U-M's single-season record of 234 set by **Gary Grant** last season.

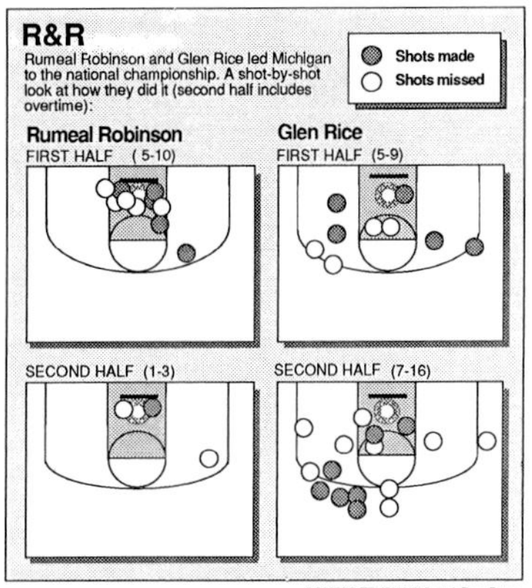
R&R
Rumeal Robinson and Glen Rice led Michigan to the national championship. A shot-by-shot look at how they did it (second half includes overtime):
Shots made
Shots missed
Rumeal Robinson
FIRST HALF (5-10)
Glen Rice
FIRST HALF (5-9)
SECOND HALF (1-3)
SECOND HALF (7-16)

DOMINIC TRUPIANO/Detroit Free Press

RICE'S TOURNAMENT HEROICS

Michigan senior forward Glen Rice, in six NCAA games this season, set a single tournament record for points with 184. He was selected the tournament's most outstanding player.

Game-by-game with Glen Rice in the NCAAs

YEAR	RESULT	FG	FT	REB	AST	PTS
1986	U-M 70, Akron 64	6-9	2-2	2	1	14
1986	Iowa State 72, U-M 69	1-3	0-0	4	0	2
1987	U-M 97, Navy 82	10-17	1-2	12	3	21
1987	No. Carolina 109, U-M 97	10-17	1-1	10	1	22
1988	U-M 63, Boise State 58	3-7	2-4	3	1	8
1988	U-M 108, Florida 85	16-24	4-4	5	5	39
1988	North Carolina 78, U-M 69	7-16	0-0	7	3	18
1989	U-M 91, Xavier (Ohio) 87	9-22	0-0	3	2	23
1989	U-M 91, South Alabama 82	16-25	1-1	8	5	36
1989	U-M 92, North Carolina 87	13-19	0-0	6	2	34
1989	U-M 102, Virginia 65	13-16	2-2	6	2	32
1989	U-M 80, Seton Hall 79	12-25	2-2	11	0	31
TOTALS	**U-M 1,029 FOES 948**	**.580**	**.833**	**6.4**	**2.1**	**23.3**

Glen Rice's NCAA scoring record

Michigan senior forward Glen Rice became the all-time leader for points scored in a single NCAA tournament.

PLAYER	SCHOOL	YEAR	FINISH	PTS
1. Glen Rice	Michigan	1989	First	184
2. Bill Bradley	Princeton	1965	Third	177
3. Elvin Hayes	Houston	1968	Second	167
4. Danny Manning	Kansas	1988	First	163
5. Hal Lear	Temple	1956	Third	160
5. Jerry West	West Virginia	1959	Second	160
7. Austin Carr *	Notre Dame	1970	None	158
7. Joe Barry Carroll	Purdue	1980	Third	158
9. Johnny Dawkins	Duke	1986	Second	153
10. Stacey King	Oklahoma	1988	Second	152

*** Notre Dame finished third in its regional.**

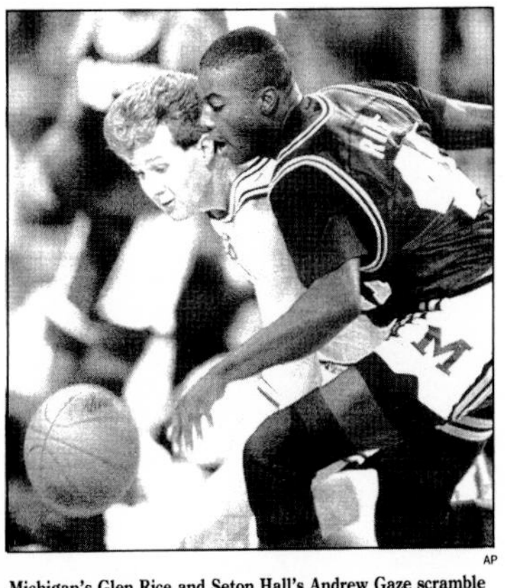

AP

Michigan's Glen Rice and Seton Hall's Andrew Gaze scramble after a loose ball in the first half Monday night.

The Road To The NCAA History Book

YEAR/SITE	FINAL	MVP
1989 Seattle	Michigan 80, Seton Hall 79	Glen Rice, Michigan
1988 Kansas City, Mo.	Kansas 83, Oklahoma 79	Danny Manning, Kansas
1987 New Orleans	Indiana 74 Syracuse 73	Keith Smart, Indiana
1986 Dallas	Louisville 72 Duke 69	Pervis Ellison Louisville
1985 Lexington, Ky.	Villanova 66, Georgetown 64	Ed Pinckney, Villanova
1984 Seattle	Georgetown 84, Houston 75	Patrick Ewing, Georgetown
1983 Albuquerque	N.C. State 54, Houston 52	Akeem Olajuwon, Houston
1982 New Orleans	North Carolina 63, Georgetown 62	James Worthy, North Carolina
1981 Philadelphia	Indiana 63, North Carolina 50	Isiah Thomas, Indiana
1980 Indianapolis	Louisville 59, UCLA 54	Darrell Griffith, Louisville
1979 Salt Lake City	Michigan St. 75, Indiana State 64	Magic Johnson, Michigan State
1978 St. Louis	Kentucky 94, Duke 88	Jack Givens, Kentucky
1977 Atlanta	Marquette 67, North Carolina 59	Butch Lee, Marquette
1976 Philadelphia	Indiana 86, Michigan 68	Kent Benson, Indiana
1975 San Diego	UCLA 92, Kentucky 85	R. Washington, UCLA
1974 Greensboro, N.C.	N.C. State 76, Marquette 64	David Thompson, N.C. State
1973 St. Louis	UCLA 87, Memphis State 66	Bill Walton, UCLA
1972 Los Angeles	UCLA 81, Florida State 76	Bill Walton, UCLA
1971 Houston	UCLA 68, Villanova 62	Howard Porter, Villanova
1970 College Park, Md.	UCLA 80, Jacksonville 69	Sidney Wicks, UCLA
1969 Louisville, Ky.	UCLA 92, Purdue 72	Lew Alcindor, UCLA
1968 Los Angeles	UCLA 78, North Carolina 55	Lew Alcindor, UCLA
1967 Louisville, Ky.	UCLA 79, Dayton 64	Lew Alcindor, UCLA
1966 College Park, Md.	Tex. Western 72, Kentucky 65	Jerry Chambers, Utah
1965 Portland, Ore.	UCLA 91, Michigan 80	Bill Bradley, Princeton
1964 Kansas City, Mo.	UCLA 98, Duke 83	Walt Hazzard, UCLA
1963 Louisville, Ky.	Loyola (Ill.) 60, Cin. 58 (OT)	Art Heyman, Duke
1962 Louisville, Ky.	Cincinnati 71, Ohio State 59	Paul Hogue, Cincinnati
1961 Kansas City, Mo.	Cincinnati 70, Ohio St. 65 (OT)	Jerry Lucas, Ohio State
1960 San Francisco	Ohio State 75, California 55	Jerry Lucas, Ohio State
1959 Louisville, Ky.	California 71, West Virginia 70	Jerry West, West Virginia
1958 Louisville, Ky.	Kentucky 84, Seattle 72	Elgin Baylor, Seattle
1957 Kansas City, Mo.	North Carolina 54, Kansas 53 (3 OT)	Wilt Chamberlain, Kansas
1956 Evanston, Ill.	San Francisco 83, Iowa 71	Hal Lear, Temple
1955 Kansas City, Mo.	San Francisco 77, LaSalle 63	Bill Russell, San Francisco
1954 Kansas City, Mo.	LaSalle 92, Bradley 76	Tom Gola, LaSalle
1953 Kansas City, Mo.	Indiana 69, Kansas 68	B.H. Born, Kansas
1952 Seattle	Kansas 80, St. John's 63	Clyde Lovellette, Kansas
1951 Minneapolis	Kentucky 68, Kansas State 58	None
1950 New York	CCNY 71, Bradley 68	Irwin Dambrot, CCNY
1949 Seattle	Kentucky 46, Okla. A&M 36	Alex Groza, Kentucky
1948 New York	Kentucky 58, Baylor 42	Alex Groza, Kentucky
1947 New York	Holy Cross 58, Oklahoma 47	George Kaftan, Holy Cross
1946 New York	Okla. A&M 43, North Carolina 40	Bob Kurland, Oklahoma A&M
1945 New York	Okla. A&M 49 New York 45	Bob Kurland, Oklahoma A&M
1944 New York	Utah 42, D'mouth 40 (OT)	Arnold Ferrin, Utah
1943 New York	Wyoming 46, Georgetown 34	Ken Sailors, Wyoming
1942 Kansas City, Mo.	Stanford 53 Dartmouth 38	Howard Dallmar, Stanford
1941 Kansas City, Mo.	Wisconsin 39, Washington St. 34	John Kotz, Wisconsin
1940 Kansas City, Mo.	Indiana 60, Kansas 42	Marvin Huffman, Indiana
1939 Evanston, Ill.	Oregon 46, Ohio State 33	None

NCAA champions by state

- **FOURTEEN: California:** Stanford, 1942; San Francisco, 1955-56; California, 1959; UCLA, 1964-65, 1967-73, 1975.
- **SEVEN: Kentucky:** Kentucky, 1948-49, 1951, 1958, 1978; Louisville, 1980, 1986.
- **FIVE: Indiana:** Indiana, 1940, 1953, 1976, 1981, 1987.
- **FOUR: North Carolina:** North Carolina, 1957, 1982; North Carolina State, 1974, 1983.
- **THREE: Ohio:** Ohio State, 1960; Cincinnati, 1961-62.
- **TWO: Kansas:** Kansas, 1952, 1988.
- **TWO: Michigan:** Michigan State, 1979; Michigan, 1989.
- **TWO: Oklahoma:** Oklahoma A&M (now Oklahoma State), 1945-46.
- **TWO: Pennsylvania:** La Salle, 1954; Villanova, 1985.
- **TWO: Wisconsin:** Wisconsin, 1941; Marquette, 1977.
- **ONE: Illinois:** Loyola (Ill.), 1963.
- **ONE: Massachusetts:** Holy Cross, 1947.
- **ONE: New York:** CCNY, 1950.
- **ONE: Oregon:** Oregon, 1939.
- **ONE: Texas:** Texas Western (now Texas-El Paso), 1966.
- **ONE: Utah:** Utah, 1944.
- **ONE: District of Columbia:** Georgetown, 1984.
- **ONE: Wyoming:** Wyoming, 1943.

Morton just misses being hero

By PERRY A. FARRELL
Free Press Sports Writer

SEATTLE — John Morton was spectacular.

Seton Hall's 6-foot-3 senior guard drove, twisted, shot, defended and rallied his Seton Hall teammates against Michigan in the final 11:16 to a 71-all tie after the Pirates had fallen behind, 53-43.

Morton finished with 35 points. He had 32 in regulation and 25 in the second half. He scored 17 of the Pirates' last 20 points on an assortment of acrobatic routines.

"We were running a lot of baseline isolations and I was penetrating and getting past my man," said Morton, who had been taken out of the game early in the second half after he attempted a three-pointer.

Glen Rice usually was the man trying to keep up with him.

When Morton's three-pointer in overtime put the Pirates (31-7) ahead, 79-76, it appeared as though he had etched his name in stone in this 51st national championship in the first overtime game since 1963.

Then Rice, his only challenger for most outstanding player honors, got the better of him.

Morton's last two shots came up empty. Morton drove the lane and banged the ball hard off the rim with the Pirates up by three. Rice then forced him to shoot an air ball as the shot clock ran to zero and 10 seconds remained in the game.

"That comes with the game," Morton said of his misses. "It's a disappointing loss, but we have to keep our heads on straight and go on with our lives and be proud. These are the two greatest teams in the nation playing for the championship and we lose by one point in overtime."

Rumeal Robinson would unseat Morton as the hero.

He pushed the ball up the court and drew a foul on Gerald Greene with three seconds left and the Pirates ahead by just one, 79-78.

Robinson's two free throws gave the Wolverines their first NCAA title, leaving Morton and Co. as bridesmaids when Daryll Walker's desperation shot as time ran out bounced off the backboard and into Rice's hands.

"I was supposed to catch it and get the ball to John Morton or Andrew Gaze," Walker said. "The ball was deflected so both me and Gerald went up for it. It was too late to give it to someone else, so I took the shot."

Seeing the outcome decided on a foul and two free throws seemed like a bad way to end this one, but Seton Hall coach P.J. Carlesimo was satisfied.

"We have no problems with (referee) John Clougherty; he's one of the best officials in the country," Carlesimo said. "In a situation like that, I want him making the call.

"It's all hard to put into perspective. In one sense you want to be tremendously proud because of what we've been able to accomplish, and in another sense you're disappointed because we came up short. Michigan's a great team and tonight they were one point better than we were."

All involved called it a classic.

"It was one of the greatest games in NCAA history," said Greene, whose 23rd birthday was Monday.

Did he foul Robinson?

"I thought the call could have gone either way," he said.

"I thought I had good enough defensive position to draw the charge, but the referee called me for the block. I just saw him penetrate to the hole and I just tried to cut him off at the angle. We both collided."

Seton Hall's defense had come to its rescue throughout the tournament, and it almost happened again. But Carlesimo said the Wolverines did a better job of rebounding (45-36), Greene missed a crucial free throw with 1:17 left in overtime and Michigan's defense outplayed Seton Hall's. Gaze was hounded and made just one of five three-point attempts for five points.

"Their defense really presented problems for me," Gaze said. "I had to work really hard on defense, also. It took a lot of work to fight through those screens."

Said Carlesimo: "Whenever we hold a team to a low shooting percentage or force them to take shots they don't want to take, we always credit our defense.

"So we have to credit Michigan's defense. You can talk about specific things we did or didn't do, and we had a lot of things we might do differently, but it's over."

OT Path To Victory

What happened in overtime in Michigan's 80-79 victory over Seton Hall:

TIME	PLAY	SCORE
4:53	Rice 9-footer in lane	73-71, U-M
4:43	Gaze 3-pointer on left side	74-73, SH
3:45	Higgins 12-footer left baseline	75-74, U-M
3:23	Walker 6-foot follow shot	76-75, SH
2:56	Higgins free throw	76-76
2:50	Morton 3-pointer on right	79-76, SH
0:56	Mills 11-footer on right	79-78, SH
0:03	Robinson two free throws	80-79, U-M

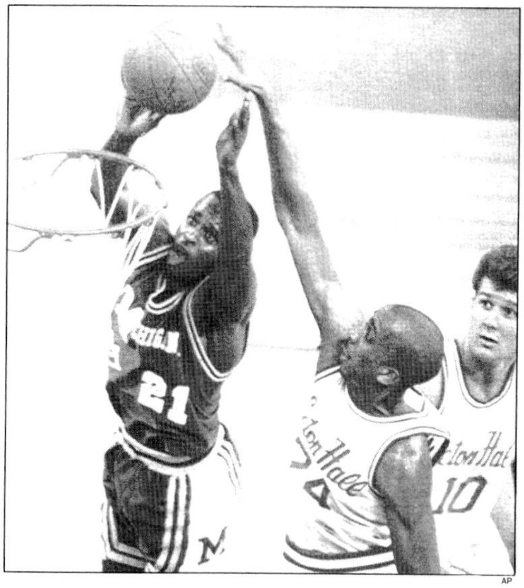

AP

Rumeal Robinson scores two of his 14 first-half points despite the efforts of Seton Hall's Daryll Walker. Robinson ended up with 21 points.

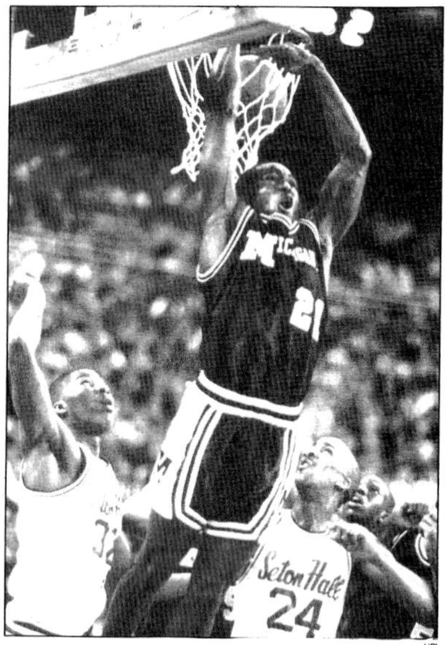

UPI

Rumeal Robinson slams for two in the second half.

U-M beats Pirates for NCAA title, 80-79

WOLVERINES, from Page 1D

U-M lost at Indiana, 76-75, Feb. 19. Michigan then won 11 of its last 12 games.

"I told them, 'Now we're on a mission,' " said Rice, the victory net around his neck. "That got them motivated. Everyone seems to like that word, mission."

Rice and Robinson were named to the all-tournament team with Greene and Seton Hall's John Morton and Danny Ferry of Duke.

Robinson's regimen of shooting 100 free throws after every practice paid off in a big way. His 9-for-10 free-throw shooting was instrumental in the win. He had become angry with himself after missing the free throws that cost Michigan a 71-68 loss at Wisconsin Jan. 21. The result was his 100-shots-a-day drill.

But the Pirates had one last chance to steal his glory. A chance was all, though.

Daryll Walker's 20-foot shot off the glass followed a three-quarter-court pass from Ramon Ramos. The shot never hit the rim, and Walker walked off the court, eyes welling in tears. Teammate Andrew Gaze patted him on the head.

At the same time, Sean Higgins was pounding the hardwood for joy in a prone position. Everyone was hugging everyone.

"I had tears in my eyes," Higgins said. "I had to drop down so not to let anyone see me. The emotion just took over."

Higgins scored 10 points and hit crucial free throws near the end of regulation to keep the hopes alive.

Robinson finished with 21 points. Rice scored 31, giving him 2,442 points and making him the Big Ten's career scoring leader.

Rice had a chance to fulfill his lifelong dream of hitting a winning shot at the buzzer in college. But his jumper from the top of the key swirled off the rim, and Walker rebounded for Seton Hall as the buzzer ended regulation.

"I was shocked I missed," Rice said.

Rice gave Michigan a 69-68 lead with 58 seconds left. It was a stunning shot from the left of the key, and silenced a Seton Hall run. He finished with a tournament-record 27 treys.

Rice set an NCAA Tournament record with 182 points and 75 field goals, breaking records set by Bill Bradley (177 points for Princeton in 1965) and Elvin Hayes (70 field goals for Houston in 1968).

Higgins put the Wolverines up, 71-68, with two free throws with 34 seconds to go in regulation.

Morton (35 points) answered with a no-hesitation three-pointer 10 seconds late to tie the score at 71.

It wasn't nip and tuck earlier in the half.

Seton Hall had the Wolverines right where they wanted them midway through the second half. U-M had a 51-39 lead, but quickly began playing not to lose. The Pirates have a way of doing that to teams.

Morton scored six straight in the Pirates' run of eight unanswered points. Two of the buckets came off fast breaks. Seton Hall cut it to two points twice.

Michigan pulled away again, 66-61, but Morton jerked them right back. He hit two fast-break baskets off turnovers to cut it to one, and penetrated for the short shot that gave the Pirates a 67-66 lead with 2:31 remaining.

The Wolverines opened the second half with a 14-6 run. Robinson's reverse, two-hand slam off a baseline buzz through the big trees dazzled the crowd of 39,187 at the Kingdome.

But the Wolverines did as much with highlight-film footage as with teamwork.

Early in the second half, Rice saved a ball going out of bounds along the Pirates' baseline with as backward flip. Robinson caught it and shouted, "Here we go, Lo!" He dribbled upcourt and fired to Loy Vaught near the lane. Vaught dropped it off to Terry Mills for an easy slam.

Michigan didn't have anyone with more than one foul in the first half. That limited Seton Hall to only four free throws; the Pirates never got into the bonus situation. And more important, U-M kept out of foul trouble against a physical, defensive team.

The Wolverines led, 37-32, at the half, as Robinson (14 points) and Rice (13) established themselves as the offensive thrusts. They took 19 of the team's 30 shots before intermission.

Rice also limited Andrew Gaze, who averages 13.8 points, to two points and sparked several fast breaks with defensive rebounds. Guard Mike Griffin limited him to three points in the second half.

Robinson scored most of his points on acrobatic moves to the hoop.

Seton Hall stayed with Michigan in the early going by penetrating and powering the ball inside to Ramos and Walker.

Guards Greene and Morton hit back-to-back three-pointers as exclamation points to a 12-point run that made it 26-20 for the Pirates. They combined for 18 first-half points.

The Wolverines also had a six-point lead, 20-14, as every starter contributed points early.

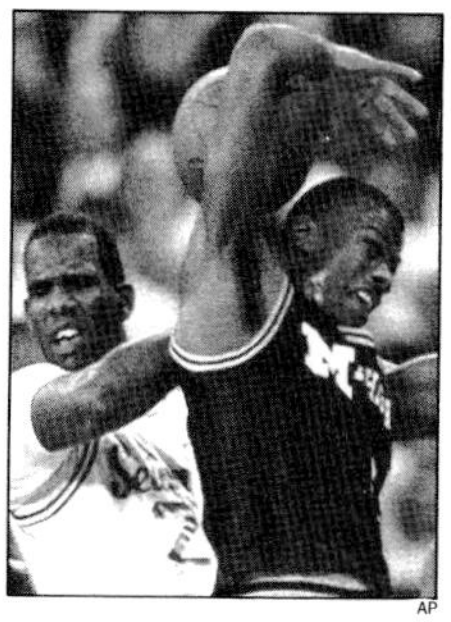

AP

Seton Hall's Ramon Ramos (left) comes down on the back of Michigan's Loy Vaught during the first half.

Fifth Title OT

Michigan's 80-79 victory over Seton Hall was the fifth NCAA championship game to go into overtime. The last was in 1963, when Vic Rouse hit a follow shot at the buzzer in Loyola of Chicago's 60-58 victory over Cincinnati, denying the Bearcats a third straight title.

One championship went into triple overtime — North Carolina's 54-53 victory over Kansas in 1957. Other overtime championships were Utah's 42-40 victory over Dartmouth in 1944, and Cincinnati's 70-65 victory over Ohio State in 1961.

Winning Wolverines

How Michigan defeated Seton Hall in the NCAA championship:

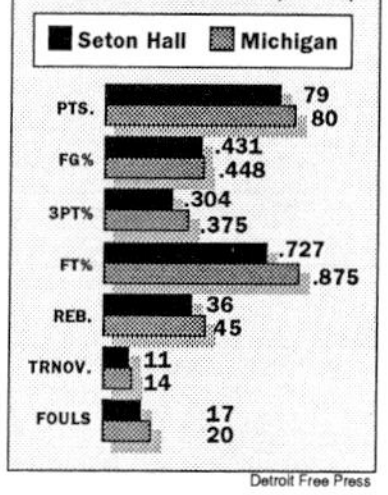
Seton Hall
Michigan
PTS.
79
80
FG%
.431
.448
3PT%
.304
.375
FT%
.727
.875
REB.
36
45
TRNOV.
11
14
FOULS
17
20

Detroit Free Press

U-M Summary

Michigan 80, Seton Hall 79

MICHIGAN WOLVERINES (80)

	MIN	FG	FT	R	A	PF	PTS
Rice	42	12-25	2-2	11	0	2	31
Mills	34	4-8	0-0	6	2	2	8
Vaught	26	4-8	0-0	7	0	2	8
Griffin	17	0-0	0-0	4	3	4	0
Robinson	43	6-13	9-10	3	11	2	21
Higgins	27	3-10	3-4	9	2	3	10
Hughes	25	1-1	0-0	2	0	2	2
Calip	11	0-2	0-0	0	1	3	0
Totals	225	30-67	14-16	45	19	20	80

Three-point goals: 6-16 (Rice 5-12, Higgins 1-4). Percentages: FG .448, FT .875. Team rebounds: 3. Blocked shots: 4 (Mills 3, Higgins). Turnovers: 14 (Robinson 5, Griffin 2, Mills 2, Rice 2, Vaught 2, Higgins). Steals: 3 (Mills 2, Vaught).

SETON HALL PIRATES (79)

	MIN	FG	FT	R	A	PF	PTS
Gaze	39	1-5	2-2	3	3	3	5
Walker	39	5-9	3-4	11	1	2	13
Ramos	33	4-9	1-1	5	1	2	9
Greene	43	5-13	1-3	5	5	3	13
Morton	37	11-26	9-10	4	3	3	35
Cooper	14	0-0	0-0	2	0	1	0
Avent	11	1-2	0-0	3	1	0	2
Volcy	7	0-0	0-2	1	0	2	0
Wigington	2	1-1	0-0	0	0	1	2
Totals	225	28-65	16-22	36	14	17	79

Three-point goals: 7-23 (Morton 4-12, Greene 2-5, Gaze 1-5, Walker 0-1). Percentages: FG .431, FT .727. Team rebounds: 2. Blocked shots: 2 (Cooper, Ramos). Turnovers: 11 (Morton 3, Gaze 2, Greene 2, Walker 2, Cooper, Ramos). Steals: 4 (Greene 2, Gaze, Ramos).

	1ST	2D	OT	FINAL
Michigan	37	34	9	— 80
Seton Hall	32	39	8	— 79

Attendance: 39,187.

NEAL SHINE

Old soldiers remember service in different ways

Bill Billet was on the phone from his home in Red Lion, Pa. Plans for the reunion trip were not going well, he said. Maybe there was something I could do in the paper to stir up a little interest.

I asked him to send me some material and I would see what I could do.

"But I just sent you all the details a couple of weeks ago," he said.

"I know, but I don't have it anymore."

"What happened to it?" he asked.

"I threw it out," I said, trying not to sound guilty. There was a moment of silence before he answered.

"Oh," he said quietly.

I don't know whether or not Billet would find it comforting to know I did not cavalierly consign his material to the wastebasket. In fact, I read it all carefully, the list of names of those who were going, the places they'd be visiting. The Vienna Woods, Schoenbrunn Palace, the Wachau Valley, Melk Abbey, down the Danube to Krems, Mozart's house, Berchtesgaden. And, of course, time set aside in Salzburg to "visit old bases."

Interest in trip wanes

A few years ago Billet formed an organization he called USFA (U.S. Forces in Austria) Veterans for those who had served in that country from 1945 until the Austrian peace treaty was signed in 1955 and the occupation troops departed.

The group had its first reunion last year, and plans were laid for the old soldiers' return to Austria to visit Vienna, Salzburg and Innsbruck. There was a lot of interest at the time, he said, but some of those who said they'd be going backed out.

Now Billet finds himself about 10 people short of getting 54 people to go, which is the capacity of the private railroad car the Austrian government is providing for the visit. The government is, in fact, making a big deal of the whole thing, which is why Billet is hoping at least to fill the railroad car.

If you are a USFA veteran, you can reach Billet through P.O. Box 206, Red Lion, Pa. 17356.

The list of those who are going contained no names I recognized, a circumstance not entirely unexpected.

It was probably a condition of our servitude, but I can't recall anyone in my unit ever mentioning anything about getting together someday and coming back to visit the old bases.

Occupying our time after war

The range of our barracks conversation, which could never be described as global, was generally limited to talk about going home and the collective idiocy of the American military establishment as demonstrated by the way it was being operated at the battalion level.

We were, to be sure, posted in a country with more than its share of natural beauty.

But, if the hills were alive with the sound of music, we must not have been paying attention, because even surrounded by them there was never a moment we did not wish we were someplace else. Places like Detroit; Plano, Texas; Ballengee, W.Va.; Silverton, Ore.; Newark; the Bronx, and Buffalo.

We became friends, took care of each other when that was called for, but with no bond of combat to bring us close to each other. We were peacetime soldiers who knew this was not really our life — that it was an interlude, an interruption, and when it ended it would be over forever.

We would go back to doing whatever it was we were doing before and the years would compress that long-ago adventure into a few bright memories reinforced by a box full of fuzzy snapshots.

So one day we threw our duffel bags on the back of a truck and said good-bye to each other, the closest thing to a promise to get together being phrases like, "If you ever get to New Albany, look me up. Just ask at the store. Everybody in town knows me."

Marshall Lowe and I bunked together and I went to his wedding in Long Island in 1955 and saw him once more, a dozen years later, in New York. John Larkin, the company clerk, drove up from Toledo one Sunday with his wife, but my daughter, Judy, bit his little girl, and they never came back.

Maybe that's why I have decided to deal with the memories of those years on my own terms.

The Champs

Glen Rice and other Michigan team members show off their NCAA Men's Division I Basketball Championship trophy Monday after their 80-79 overtime win at the Kingdome in Seattle.

Photo by Steven R. Nickerson

NAMES & FACES

Critic heats up N.Y., won't back down

The critic's lot, to paraphrase Gilbert & Sullivan, is not a happy one — to which laser-tongued theater critic **John Simon** of New York magazine can attest. Simon has enraged not only some denizens of the theater world but also New York NAACP officials for his review of a new production of Shakespeare's "The Winter's Tale" in which he suggested the actors are too Jewish and too black for the Bard. Simon scribbled that actor **Mandy Patinkin** looked like a "cartoon Jew" and actress **Alfre Woodard** resembled Topsy, a character in the novel "Uncle Tom's Cabin." "I've been accused of everything under the sun," Simon said. "I've been accused of being a seducer of 15-year-old girls. It doesn't bother me. There's nothing to apologize for."

YUSEF ISLAM (formerly pop star **Cat Stevens**) has come up with an in-your-face for several American radio stations who have blacklisted his old hits ("Moon Shadow," "Peace Train," etc.) because he advocated the death penalty for "The Satanic

Islam:
Radio blast

Simon:
Magazine blast

Verses" author **Salman Rushdie.** Sayeth Islam: "I've been trying to get record companies to stop selling my records for a long time. This is saving me the trouble."

WE INTERRUPT with a report on the sportin' life. Politicians, it seems, live for three things in this world: re-election, kissing babies and making symbolic bets on sports events. So Michigan's U.S. senators are taking their own piece of the Wolverine winning streak. **Sen. Carl Levin** already has won one round of bets, on Saturday night's Michigan vs. Illinois tilt, winning two cases of Illinois-made Orange Crush from **Sen. Paul**

Simon, D-Ill. And to rub it in, the two had a side bet that requires losing Simon briefly to replace his trademark bow tie with a U-M maize-'n'- blue model. Feeling confident, Levin and **Sen. Donald Riegle** wagered on Monday night's finals with the senators from Seton Hall, New Jersey Democrats **Bill Bradley** and **Frank Lautenberg.** Michigan's senators put up a case of hometown Vernor's ginger ale, a maize-and-blue U-M jacket and a baseball cap that declares: "American by birth, Wolverine by choice." Bradley and Lautenberg countered with two cases of a sweet Garden State product: M&Ms.

KITTY DUKAKIS said Monday she "went crazy" upon learning no women speakers were scheduled at a luncheon honoring the new Democratic National Committee chairman. The wife of Mass. Gov. **Michael Dukakis** arrived midway through a luncheon and felt compelled to urge the 200 or so attending to "be sensitive to the 10 million more of the female gender who are part of the voting public."

JIMMY & WILLIE

No, former President Jimmy Carter won't be providing hand-claps on Willie Nelson's next album. Carter was just applauding the country star's presence at an Austin, Tex., fund-raiser the other evening for Carter's pet charity, Habitat for Humanity.

BRIEFLY

■ **Expiring:** On Wednesday, the deadline for Ferrysburg, Mich., businessman **Richard Hemmelsbach** to raise $3 million to regain title to a baronial castle in West Germany. "If we go down for the count, we'll try to do it with dignity," Hemmelsbach said. "But my heart will personally be broken."

■ **Planned:** For pop star **Whitney Houston** to join gospel singers **BeBe** and **CeCe Winans** onstage, according to BeBe, during their concert Friday at the Royal Oak Music Theatre. Houston sings in one song, "Hold Up the Light," on the duo's new album, "Heaven."

■ **Alleged:** By retired Tiger pitcher **Milt Wilcox**, that his reputation as a sports personality was damaged in 1988 when Gibraltar Trade Center pulled the plug on plans to film his talk show at the Taylor market. Wilcox filed Friday in Wayne County Circuit Court, charging Gibraltar Trade Center operator **James Koester** with breaking a $12,000 contract to pay Wilcox for taping 12 shows and signing autographs at the center between last November and this April. The lawsuit seeks more than $10,000 in damages and a jury trial.

Edited by John Smyntek
from staff and wire reports

SPECIAL SECTION
New Tigers, new season/ 1C

BASEBALL '89
How big-time money is changing the big leagues

OPENING DAY
Reds **6** Dodgers **4**
Indians **2** Brewers **1**
Orioles **5** Red Sox **4**

Sunny
Low tonight
35°
High Wednesday
50°
Details, page **10F**

Tuesday
April 4, 1989

The Detroit News

15¢
20c outside metro Detroit area

GOOD DAY
BRIEFLY IN THE NEWS

Suit blames Exxon for gas price rise

SANTA ANA, Calif. — A federal suit was filed Monday against Exxon Corp. on behalf of Californians who buy gasoline, contending the Exxon Valdez oil spill in Alaska increased prices at the pump by more than 20 cents a gallon.

The class-action suit accused Exxon and Alyeska Pipeline Service of gross negligence over the spill on behalf of an estimated two million Californians.

Oil deliveries have been slowed by the spill, which covers more than 1,000 square miles. The shortages have jacked up gas prices.

Agnew asks tax break

SACRAMENTO, Calif. — Former Vice-President Spiro T. Agnew, claiming he is entitled to tax deductions for the $142,500 he paid Maryland as restitution for bribes he collected while governor, is asking the state Board of Equalization to refund $24,197 in California income taxes.

Agnew, now a resident of Rancho Mirage near Palm Springs, claimed the deduction on his 1982 California income tax return. The deduction was disallowed four years later by an auditor.

Wings' Kocur sentenced

Detroit Red Wings forward Joe Kocur was sentenced today to six months' probation plus $105 in court costs and ordered to make $165 in restitution to a Northville woman who said he struck her during a bar argument last summer.

Kocur, 23, pleaded guilty in January to disorderly conduct on a charge brought by Janet Maschke, 22.

Maschke had accused Kocur of punching her in the arm Aug. 23 at Mr. Sports One-of-a-Kind Bar in Farmington Hills.

Medicine from tobacco

IRVINE, Calif. — Cigarette companies soon might have unusual competitors for tobacco harvests.

Researchers from Biosource Genetics Corp. of Vacaville said Monday that they developed an artificial virus that can be sprayed on fully grown tobacco plants to convert them into "minifactories" producing immune system stimulants.

The plants can produce medicine such as interferon, an immune system protein used in certain cancer treatments, and an enzyme that makes melanin, which can be used to create a sunscreen for the skin.

Cons get cosmetic help

HOUSTON — Hundreds of Texas state prison inmates have been getting face-lifts, liposuction and other cosmetic repairs at taxpayers' expense for more than 20 years, according to the Houston Chronicle.

The operations have been performed at Galveston's John Sealy Hospital, which provides medical and surgical staff for state prisons and is a teaching hospital for the University of Texas Medical Branch in Galveston, the newspaper reported.

The hospital said the expenses are paid by taxes because the hospital is part of a state-funded college. The medical school said the practice helps surgeons perfect their skills.

From News staff and wire reports.

QUOTE OF THE DAY

❝I'm dazed. I knew Rumeal was going to make those free throws, but I didn't know it would ever feel this good.❞

Sean Higgins
on Robinson's game-winning free throws

INSIDE ...

Accent	1D	Horoscope	8F
Bridge	8F	Local news	1B
Business	1E	Movies	5D
Classified	5B	Obituaries	4B
Comics	8F	Sports	1F
Crossword	9F	TV	4D
Editorials	6A	Weather	10F

The Detroit News
Michigan's largest newspaper
A GANNETT Newspaper/115th Year No. 225
Copyright, 1989 The Detroit News, Inc.

Home Delivery/	Classified Ads/
222-NEWS	977-7500

THE NCAA CHAMPIONSHIP
MICHIGAN 80 · SETON HALL 79

HAIL, MICHIGAN

What a finish! What a feeling! U-M wins an overtime thriller

KIRTHMON DOZIER/The Detroit News
Proud Wolverines Rumeal Robinson (left) and Glen Rice show off the NCAA championship trophy.

What does someone see when he stands there, alone, naked but for the millions of eyes on him? What does it look like from the standpoint of 15 feet away and the entire college basketball season loaded upon your shoulders? Is it dark? Bright? Does the mind build a tunnel to that orange rim? Does the human spirit grow blinders that make everything else dissolve, out of sight, out of mind?

So many questions. But only one answer. Really only one way to express yourself.

Swish. What'd you say, Rumeal? Say it again. Say it even louder this time.

Swish.

Hail to the Victors.

Two free throws with three seconds left in overtime. Michigan beats Seton Hall by one point, 80-79. Three seconds left and alone at the line, where privacy is impossible. The rumbling sound of a powerful beating heart. Wolfen in nature. Body by Fisher. Twelve men — nobody is young ever again by this time — all piled into one muscled form.

"I wanted it to be me," Robinson said later. "I wanted the ball and the shot. In the past in games like this I passed the ball to someone else and tried to hide. But tonight I wanted it."

Got it, too. Then made the statement that explains the times of a lifetime. Swish. Swish. Blue Heaven. The Wild Blue Yonder. Blue skies, nothing but blue skies. These are the times of a lifetime.

Shelby Strother
in Seattle

Greet the champs

Michigan will celebrate its newest champions today at a 5:30 p.m. pep rally at Crisler Arena in Ann Arbor. The Wolverines are expected to arrive at Metro Airport between 4:30 and 5 p.m.

A souvenir to savor

The Detroit News will publish a souvenir section Wednesday to commemorate Michigan's NCAA championship.

The last picture show: Robinson's fist thrust high, a pulsating answer to the questions. Offered in body english. Bold print. Underlined in red. Self-addressed. Lick the stamp, mail it into history. The envelope, please. Your NCAA national champion for 1988-89 is Michigan.

A gremlin guard named John Morton constantly poured salt on an ever-widening gash Tuesday night. There easily could have been a hideous scar instead of a shiny trophy for a souvenir of this team's message to the world of college basketball. The three-point dagger Morton jammed into the heart of the Michigan Wolverines in overtime could easily have finished off a beast with a normal heart. But remember, there were 12 hearts inside.

Please see Strother/4A

Hearty fans scream till they're blue for Wolverines in final game

By Bonnie DeSimone and Dave Anderson
News Staff Writers

Michigan fans Monday erased any doubts about their heart. And their class. Amid deafening noise, they rooted for their heroes at both gamesite in Seattle and gatherings all over Ann Arbor.

Leather-lunged choruses cheered the team to its first national basketball championship ever.

Even Crisler Arena has never heard such noise.

It was exciting, even on television.

"I wanted it so badly for them," said Fred Kahler, an emeritus professor who was at the game.

"They've worked so hard, and (interim coach) Steve Fisher is such a positive person," he said.

"I wanted it for them, not for me." Interim Coach Steve Fisher got an 11th hour pep talk Monday from Gov. James Blanchard before the Wolverine basketball team faced Seton Hall in the NCAA championship game.

Please see Fans/4A

■ FALLS: ROBINSON WAS KEY TO THE VICTORY **1F**
■ OUTSTANDING PLAYER RICE SETS 4 RECORDS **5F**
■ COMPLETE COVERAGE OF THE TITLE GAME **1F, 4F, 5F**

Chrysler offers interest-free 2-year loans

By James V. Higgins
News Staff Writer

Chrysler Corp. joined the auto industry's latest price war Monday by offering interest-free two-year loans on a variety of new cars and trucks.

But automakers appear far from panicky over the apparently cooling national economy and rising interest rates. Car and truck production forecasts for the second quarter remained relatively strong, indicating the Big Three believe consumers are good for at least one more incentive-boosted car buying spree.

Negative economic news during the past month has caused only minor downward adjustments in sales expectations by automakers and independent experts.

The latest large-scale attempt to stimu-

Chrysler incentives

Chrysler Corp. joined the auto industry's latest price war Monday by offering interest-free two-year loans on a variety of new cars and trucks:
■ 0.0 percent financing for 24-month loans
■ 5.9 percent up to 36 months
■ 6.9 percent up to 48 months
■ 10.9 percent up to 60 months

Please see Chrysler/5A

U-M professors turn down plan for mandatory class in racism

By James Tobin
News Staff Writer

A proposal that would have required most University of Michigan undergraduates to study racism was narrowly voted down Monday by professors who said the idea smacked of political indoctrination.

The vote ends, at least temporarily, months of argument over the proposal, which arose after widely publicized student protests over racial problems at U-M in 1987 and 1988.

THE STUDENT GROUP that first demanded a required course on racism, the United Coalition Against Racism (UCAR), disowned the proposal last week after faculty sponsors made several concessions to critics.

Approval required the consent of a majority of professors in the College of Literature, Science and the Arts (LSA), U-M's biggest college with 15,000 students.

But at the end of a third faculty debate Monday, the proposal went down by 20 to 25

Please see U-M/2A

Bush urges end to Israeli occupation

AP and Reuter

WASHINGTON — President Bush on Monday urged an end to Israel's occupation of the West Bank and the Gaza Strip, endorsed the "achievement of Palestinian political rights" and said a "properly structured" international peace conference could play a useful role.

Opening a week of intensive talks on the Middle East, Bush met with Egyptian President Hosni Mubarak and said "a new atmosphere" must be created between Israel and Arab nations as the first step toward peace.

The tone of the president's remarks suggested United States may attempt to exert

Please see Israel/5A

IN WEDNESDAY'S FOOD SECTION : Superfastfood — meals you can make at home in less than 15 minutes

■ Inside
■ Baseball scoreboard

☐ Missouri recruiting linked to Detroit / 2F
☐ Watson's making no major threats / 2F
☐ Kocur takes hands-on approach / 6F
☐ Daly thinks Blazers may be trouble / 6F

SUPER Sports

☐ **American League**	☐ **National League**
☐ Baltimore 5, Boston 4, 11 inn.	☐ Cincinnati 6, Los Angeles 4
☐ Toronto 4, Kansas City 3	☐ New York 8, St. Louis 4
☐ Cleveland 2, Milwaukee 1	☐ San Francisco 5, San Diego 3
☐ Oakland 3, Seattle 2	See Baseball report/ 3F

Sports

The Detroit News
Tuesday, April 4, 1989 •••

☐ Sports scores/963-8424   ☐ Home delivery/222-NEWS   ☐ Classified ads/977-7500

NCAA CHAMPIONS

Joe Falls
in Seattle

Rumeal ticket to Michigan's dream victory

Rumeal Robinson, abandoned twice in his life . . . once living in a doorway for two weeks, finally found himself a home Monday night.

It was at the foul line of the biggest basketball game of the year.

He stood there, this game little guy with the deadpan expression, and calmly tossed in two free throws as if it was a summer league game back in his hometown of Cambridge, Mass.

But this was smack in the middle of the Kingdome, with only three seconds left in overtime and more than 40,000 fans and countless millions on TV looking in from every part of the country.

Swish.

Swish.

The sophomore guard put down both shots and that gave Michigan a pulsating 80-79 victory over Seton Hall for the NCAA championship.

It was a tremendous game, especially through the last 10 minutes — five in regulation when Seton Hall came roaring back to nearly pull it out. And five more in overtime, when Seton Hall seemed to have it won until these wondrous Wolverines came through in the biggest moment of their young lives.

Down by three points in the last minute, they scored the final four points and did it against a defense that is deemed among the best in the land.

And so this climaxed a whirlwind three weeks for Steve Fisher, the only interim coach to win a national championship. He is unbeaten, untied and, at the moment, unemployed. At least as a head coach.

When this stirring game ended, Bo Schembechler told a national TV audience that he "would definitely give Fisher an interview when the team returned to Ann Arbor."

It is obvious that Bo hasn't made up his mind, or that he is not sure Fisher is the man to lead his basketball program in the future, even though he brought it to this unprecedented pinnacle by sweeping through

*Please see **Falls/5F***

KIRTHMON DOZIER/The Detroit News

Michigan's Steve Fisher savors his shining moment as he becomes the first rookie coach to win an NCAA basketball championship.

Robinson sinks 2 at line in OT; U-M wins, 80-79

By Bob Wojnowski
News Staff Writer

SEATTLE — On another night in another arena in another last-second situation, Rumeal Robinson had missed two free throws. It had cost Michigan a midseason game against Wisconsin and began a slide that would cost U-M the Big Ten title.

Three months later, the stakes were higher, the job the same.

Two free throws for victory. Two free throws for the national title.

Against the Badgers on Jan. 21, Robinson had missed twice. Against Seton Hall Monday night before a Kingdome crowd of 39,187, he stood three seconds and 15 feet from victory and redemption.

Fittingly, Robinson, the gritty symbol of a comeback team, completed U-M's remarkable turnaround with a pair of free throws, giving the Wolverines a pulsating 80-79 overtime victory against Seton Hall and their first NCAA basketball title.

A 64-percent free-throw shooter, Robinson was fouled by Seton Hall guard Gerald Greene at the end of a full-court drive. He calmly swished both to cap one of the most thrilling games — and stunning seasons — in NCAA history.

"I'd just as soon have him as anybody at the line," said interim coach Steve Fisher, who led a 6-0 march to the national title after head Coach Bill Frieder left for Arizona State March 15. "He's a tough, tough kid who has fought through so much, just as we've fought through so much. My mind flashed back to the Wisconsin game, but I was comfortably confident he was going to make both of them."

Robinson, who finished with 21 points and 11 assists, was completely confident. After the first, he turned around and smiled. After the second, the celebration began.

U-M still had to weather Ramon Ramos' full-court pass to Daryll Walker, who missed a 20-foot jumper as time expired, but the victory was sealed by Robinson, who practiced 100 free throws a day for two weeks after the Wisconsin loss.

"You have to believe you're going to make them, because if you don't, you won't," he said. "The feeling was great."

"I knew Rumeal was going to make them," guard Sean Higgins said. "I told him what we had talked about all season, about winning the national championship. I told him it was in his hands now."

The free throws sealed U-M's first NCAA championship of any kind since 1970, when the men's gymnastics team captured a national title.

Robinson supplied the clinching points but senior forward Glen Rice again provided the clutch ones. He had 31 points, 11 rebounds and was named the tournament's most outstanding player.

He also moved past Mike McGee and into first place on U-M's, and the Big Ten's, all-time scoring list with 2,442 points.

The victory probably nudged Fisher closer to becoming U-M's permanent coach. Athletic Director Bo Schembechler attended the game but made no comments afterward on Fisher's future.

*Please see **U-M/4F***

Inside

■ Strother: Rumeal has the final say / 1A
■ 4 arrested during campus celebration / 1A
■ 3-pointers won't change, NCAA says / 4F
■ Finish leaves Musburger speechless / 4F
■ Rice: tourney's outstanding player / 5F
■ Seton's guards can't coax last victory / 5F
■ Bo bows before new national champs / 5F

Lions go from WJR to WWJ, sources say

By Beth Tuschak
News Staff Writer

The Lions are switching their main radio outlet to WWJ-AM (950) after more than a decade with WJR-AM (760), industry sources said Monday.

The deal is to last through the next three seasons.

Executives at both stations and Lions officials offered only "no comments" Monday, but some WWJ and WJR staffers weren't as closemouthed. The ink apparently isn't dry, but the deal is done, they said. An announcement is expected later this week.

According to one source, WJR actually dropped out of serious contention some time ago, although a last-minute effort to retain the rights

was discussed but failed.

An announcing team hasn't been set, but don't look for WJR sports director and longtime Lions play-by-play man Frank Beckmann to jump ship. Although approached by WWJ, Beckmann has been happy at his home station since the departure in January of program director Gary Berkowitz.

Figures haven't been revealed, but industry sources early in the bidding wars estimated the deal to be worth more than $1.2 million per year.

The switch further relaxes WJR's near stranglehold on major Detroit sports. WJR still has the Tigers and Red Wings, with WWJ handling the Pistons, and now the Lions. Both stations broadcast University of Michigan football and basketball games.

Opening Day at a glance

■ **Rose adored:** Reds Manager Pete Rose (left) and Dodgers Manager Tom Lasorda hug before Monday's game, which Cincinnati won 6-4. Rose, warmly received by Cincinnati fans, got a kiss on the cheek from owner Marge Schott.

■ **Going batty?:** Nope. Cardinals Manager Whitey Herzog didn't ask for Howard Johnson's bat to be checked, even though the Mets' Johnson homered and drove in three runs that led New York past St. Louis, 8-4. It was the Mets' 11th straight home-opening victory.

■ **Streaking Orioles:** It took the Orioles 11 innings to defeat the Red Sox, 5-4. Last year, it took Baltimore a record 22 games to win one. Stories / 3F

Lovullo's 'too solid' to fail, Sparky says

By Tom Gage
News Staff Writer

ARLINGTON, Texas — Now the real test begins.

When the Tigers take on the Texas Rangers tonight (8:30, Channel 4), Torey Lovullo will be only the second rookie to make one of Sparky Anderson's starting lineups on Opening Day in the last 10 years.

Chris Pittaro was the other, flaming out as Sparky's most ill-fated experiment since he's been in Detroit.

Anderson doesn't summon the same superlatives for Lovullo that he did for Pittaro. It's almost as if he doesn't feel the need to, since Lovullo

*Please see **Tigers/3F***

Tonight's lineups
How the Tigers and Rangers will start tonight:

Tigers		Rangers	
Williams	CF	Espy	CF
Lovullo	1B	Fletcher	SS
Whitaker	2B	Palmeiro	1B
Trammell	SS	Sierra	RF
Lynn	LF	Franco	2B
Nokes	C	Incaviglia	LF
Brown	3B	Petralli	C
Lemon	RF	Bell	DH
Sheridan	DH	Buechele	3B
Morris	P	Hough	P

SPORTS SPECIAL
News starts on A3

King beats Murdock
Lone Ypsilanti council Republican wins close race with incumbent, **A5**

Mayor Jernigan defeats Clevenger
Low voter turnout boosts margin as Ann Arbor mayor wins again, **A3**

Voters defeat Headlee waiver
Ann Arbor residents reject city's plea for more tax revenue, **A3**

INSIDE
Business A8,9
Classifed C6-11
Comics D9
Connection D1-4
Crossword D9
Deaths A2
Editorial A10,11
Entertainment D6,7
Horoscope D9
Metro A3-7
Nation/World C1-4
Sports B1-9
Television D8

WEATHER: Colder tonight. Chance of shower Wednesday. Details on A12.

THE ANN ARBOR NEWS

25¢
TUESDAY
APRIL 4, 1989

CHAMPIONS!

MICHIGAN 80, SETON HALL 79

Michigan's record-setting scoring leader Glen Rice cuts down the net after he led the Wolverines to the NCAA national championship.   AP PHOTO

Rice leads team to national crown

By JOHN BECKETT
NEWS SPORTS REPORTER

SEATTLE — Mission accomplished.

Six weeks ago, after losing a heartbreaking game at Indiana on a controversial 3-point buzzer-beater, Glen Rice and the Michigan Wolverines declared that they were on "a mission to shock the world."

They did just that Monday night, claiming the school's first-ever national basketball championship by edging Seton Hall 80-79 in overtime before 39,187 fans — the third largest crowd ever to watch a national championship game — in the Seattle Kingdome.

Junior guard Rumeal Robinson swished two free throws with three seconds left in overtime to lift Michigan to the win.

Rice, named the Most Outstanding Player of the Final Four, poured in 31 points to become not only the highest career scorer in Michigan history, but the Big Ten's all-time leading scorer and the highest scorer ever in a NCAA Tournament.

It was Rice, the senior co-captain from Flint, who pulled his teammates together after the Wolverines lost to Indiana for a second time, and told them to buckle down, work hard and not give up until they had won the national championship.

Monday night, it was Rice who caught the rebound of Seton Hall's last, desperate shot — and then caught Robinson in his arms, holding him aloft as they yelled at each other, "We did it! We did it!"

Indeed they did. And in the process, they wiped the slate clean once and for all of the talk that had dogged this team for years: that the Wolverines were a group of highly talented players who lacked the heart, togetherness and poise to win the big ones.

They don't come any bigger than Monday night's game, the first Final Four title game to go into overtime in 26 years, and only the fifth overtime title clash ever.

It was a gut-wrenching, back-and-forth clash, a war as much of wills as of basketball talent. And in the end, it proved to be redemption for the Wolverines and Robinson, the junior guard who had cost Michigan a victory when he missed two free throws at the end of a Big Ten game against Wisconsin.

"As soon as he got up to the line, I flashed back to the Wisconsin game," said junior guard Mike Griffin. "Rumeal's been talking about that all year, about how someday he was going to redeem himself.

"I thought he was going to knock it down. He seemed calm. I knew he wasn't panicking. Wisconsin can

INSIDE

■ **Campus disturbance:** Rowdy youths demolished parking meters (above), turned over a taxi and damaged a restaurant following Michigan's victory. **Page A3.**

■ **Robinson comes through:** A playground mentality helps a city kid keep his cool in the clutch. **Page B1.**

■ **Proud Pirates:** It was difficult to determine which was more gallant: Seton Hall's bid for a national championship or how the Pirates handled the defeat. **Page B4.**

■ **Key play:** Gerald Greene fouled Rumeal Robinson with seconds remaining in overtime, and Robinson calmly sank two free throws for the victory. **Page B4.**

■ **Winning formula:** Michigan threw a hot Glen Rice at Seton Hall, and the Pirates, like so many other opponents, couldn't help but wince. **Page B7.**

have that victory. We'll take this one."

They took it the hard way, scratching and clawing their way to a 12-point lead early in the second half, only to see Seton Hall storm right back behind its stifling defense and the nearly unstoppable penetration of guard John Morton, who finished with a game-high 35 points.

See CHAMPIONS, A2

Fisher's fate as coach still up in air

Pep rally today

The Michigan basketball team will be honored at a pep rally at 5:30 this afternoon at Crisler Arena. The public is welcome and admission is free. Crisler Arena will be open at 4:30. Interim coach Steve Fisher and Athletic Director Bo Schembechler will be among the speakers. Fans should enter through the regular entrances for games. There are no reserved seats. The pep band will attend.

By JOHN BECKETT
NEWS SPORTS REPORTER

SEATTLE — When Steve Fisher arrived at the Seattle Kingdome with his Michigan Wolverines basketball team Monday afternoon, he forgot one little thing: the pass that allowed him to get past security and onto the Kingdome court.

At first, security officials wouldn't allow Fisher inside. Then finally, an NCAA official intervened.

A few hours later, Fisher won his sixth game without a loss as Michigan's interim coach. He became the first, first-time coach to ever win a national basketball championship.

Now the question is whether Fisher, who nearly wasn't allowed inside the Kingdome, will be shut out of the Michigan head coaching job.

Strange as it may seem, as hard as it may

be to believe, that could happen.

Following Monday's historic victory, Athletic Director Bo Schembechler again refused to be pinned down about who he will name to succeed Bill Frieder.

Schembechler gave Fisher his due, saying he had done a "marvelous" job. But all that had earned him for the moment, Schembechler said, was a chance to interview for the job that opened when Frieder accepted the Arizona State University coaching job two days before the start of the NCAA Tournament.

Schembechler and Jack Weidenbach, associate athletic director, said they have no deadline for picking the new coach. Weidenbach said he and Schembechler haven't discussed the opening, but they probably would talk on the plane ride back to Ann Arbor today.

See FISHER, A2

Michigan interim coach Steve Fisher celebrates with his sons Mark and Jonathon after Monday night's victory. Fisher is the first, first-time coach to ever win a national basketball championship.
AP PHOTO

SPORTS

■ Red Wings start again in playoffs, **B2**
■ Adjustment time for Tiger Morris, **B3**
■ Orioles start fast, stop Red Sox, **B3**

B1

THE ANN ARBOR NEWS • TUESDAY, APRIL 4, 1989

U-M 80, SETON HALL 79

Victors valiant

JOHN BECKETT

Rumeal is truly for real

SEATTLE — You could call it redemption. You could call it vindication.

You could call it lots of things. I prefer justice. Sweet, sweet justice.

Rumeal Robinson squared the ledger with fate Monday night. With two free throws, two softly arching, sweetly swishing free throws, he took a giant step toward balancing the books of his life.

Maybe there is justice in the world, after all.

For much of his life, Rumeal Robinson has had a large burden to balance. He was abandoned by his natural mother, robbed of a year's playing time by Proposition 48, stigmatized as a student by the same rule, and then let down by the coach who had given him a college scholarship.

Since realizing as a boy that he could be a great basketball player, Robinson has sweated, strained, hoped, prayed and worked toward that goal.

All along, there have been roadblocks. One of the first major casualties of Prop 48, he was labeled as a poor student when he actually is a very good student who is on schedule to complete his degree early.

Even this year, when Robinson finally began to realize his awesome potential, he had to overcome adversity. He had to struggle to smooth out the rough edges of his game. He had to play over injuries.

And he had to live down that game at Madison, Wis. The one where he missed two free throws in the closing seconds with his team trailing by one point. The one that started Michigan's surprising skid out of the Big Ten race.

"All year long, Rumeal has talked about that Wisconsin game and how he was going to redeem himself," said teammate Mike Griffin.

Said Interim Coach Steve Fisher: "He came in the next day and for a solid two weeks straight, came in an hour early and shot a minimum of 100 free throws every day. That's the type of resolve and commitment this kid has to be successful. I think it showed tonight in his toughness, competitiveness, in his desire to make sure we won."

As most any coach will tell you, the key to making free throws is in the mind. It takes a certain kind of mental toughness to stand at that stripe, with the game — and in this case, a national championship — on the line, and put the ball in the net.

It also takes mental toughness to withstand what Robinson had to withstand Sunday.

That was the day the national media really discovered Robinson. That was the day that starters for both Michigan and Seton Hall were required by the NCAA to submit to 90 minutes of in-depth interviews.

There were over 800 reporters here for the Final Four. On Sunday, it must have seemed to Robinson that every one of them wanted to know about his childhood, about his thoughts on Proposition 48.

See BECKETT, B7

AP PHOTO
Michigan's 'mission to shock the world' ended with Mike Griffin and Sean Higgins celebrating the Wolverines' first NCAA title.

Michigan decks the Hall

By CHRIS McCOSKY
NEWS SPORTS REPORTER

SEATTLE — Sunday, Michigan's Rumeal Robinson told the national press:

"Basically, the only person that has stopped Rumeal Robinson this season is Rumeal Robinson."

Arrogance? Cocky? No way.

"You have to understand," said teammate Sean Higgins, "Rumeal is a city kid. He's like me. He has a playground mentality. You have to believe nobody is better than you. If you don't feel that way, the other guy has an edge on you."

Playground mentality.

Monday. National championship. Michigan vs. Seton Hall.

Michigan down a point, 79-78. The clock's ticking, less than 10 seconds left in the overtime.

More than 39,000 people are on their feet inside the Kingdome. Another 17 to 20 million watching on television.

In 10 seconds the national champion of college basketball will be crowned. Rumeal Robinson has the ball, and Michigan's fate, in his hands.

"I decided to take it on my own shoulders," he would say after. "I wasn't about to put it on anybody else's shoulders. I knew I wanted to take that last shot. So many times I've just passed off and hid in that situation. This time I wanted it to be me."

I wanted it to be me. Nobody's better. Playground mentality.

Robinson 'snakes his way past four Seton Hall defenders. The fifth defender — Gerald Greene, Robinson's old playground foe from New York — fouls him.

Three seconds left. His team down by a point. Robinson is at the free throw line shooting one-and-one.

I want it to be me. Nobody's better.

Nobody was. Both free throws dropped softly through the net.

Michigan 80, Seton Hall 79.

National champions. A first for the Michigan basketball program.

"I knew it, I knew it," said Higgins. "I told you it was going to be like that. Herky-jerky, one-on-one — just like on the playground."

Playground basketball. It's wild and it's rough. It's like a street fight. Only instead of sticks, knives and guns, your weapons are strength, speed, stamina, and a jump shot.

The final prize is the same. Survival.

That's the type of game it was Monday. Attack or be attacked. Deck the Hall before the Hall decks you.

Intimidate, don't be intimidated. Michigan's Terry Mills rejects a shot from Seton Hall's Daryll Walker. Next time down, Walker rejects Mills' shot.

Robinson drives past Greene and, back to the basket, throws down a spectacular over-the-head reverse dunk.

Greene counters with a coast-to-coast layup.

Nobody's better.

Greene and Robinson were the featured combatants in this playground battle. The two point guards, the two floor generals, who used to battle each other in summer camps back East.

"Gerald taught me a lot about how to control a game from the point-guard position," said Robinson, who grew up in Cambridge, Mass.

Robinson was giving the lessons on Monday. He scored 21 points and distributed 11 assists. Greene scored 13 points and dished out five assists.

"I felt like I was wearing him

See MICHIGAN, B7

On The Inside

■ **Proud Pirates:** It was difficult to determine which was more gallant Monday night: Seton Hall's bid for a national championship or how the Pirates handled the defeat. **Page B4.**

■ **The right words:** Your responsibility is to conjure just the right approach to help your players win the biggest basketball game they will ever play. Michigan interim coach Steve Fisher had the perfect story to tell. **Page B4.**

■ **Well-covered:** Monday night, the best defense against good defense was more good defense. Said Fisher: "We just told our kids, 'Hey, we are going to have to play better defense than they do.'" **Page B4.**

■ **Winning formula:** Michigan threw a hot Glen Rice at Seton Hall, and the Pirates, like so many other opponents, couldn't help but wince. **Page B7.**

■ **Remembering Frieder:** There was one man missing from Michigan's victory celebration — the man who built the team. But the Wolverines still feel loyalty to Bill Frieder, their former coach, who departed to Arizona State. 'This championship is for him,' said Sean Higgins. **Page B8.**

■ **Focus on TV:** For Michigan fans, there was a lot to like about CBS's broadcast of Monday's NCAA championship. Analyst Billy Packer was insightful, and announcer Brent Musberger kept the hype to a dull roar. **Page B9.**

Special section for Wednesday

Hail to the NCAA Victors! In the culmination to a dream season, in the NCAA Final in the Seattle Kingdome, Michigan played Seton Hall and simply wouldn't be beaten.

Interim coach Steve Fisher's Wolverines proved their mission was possible, and now The News will look back — and forward — Wednesday in a special section designed to help you savor the Wolverines' first NCAA championship in basketball.

What made Michigan the NCAA's best? Can the Wolverines reign again next year? The section will have answers for those questions and will replay Michigan's drive to Seattle and its triumphant return today to Ann Arbor.

SCORING AT A GLANCE

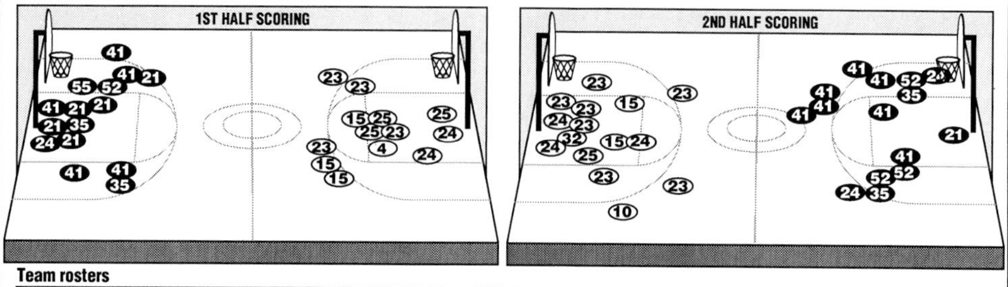

Team rosters

Michigan		Seton Hall	
13 - Demetrius Calip	41 - Glen Rice	10 - Andrew Gaze	23 - John Morton
21 - Rumeal Robinson	52 - Terry Mills	24 - Daryll Walker	32 - Anthony Avent
24 - Sean Higgins	55 - Mark Hughes	25 - Ramon Ramos	4 - Pookey Wigington
35 - Loy Vaught	54 - JP Oosterbaan	15 - Gerald Greene	

● - Michigan
○ - Seton Hall

Play-By-Play

First Half

Time	Play	U-M-SH
19:54	Rice 16-foot right angle jumper	2-0
19:26	Greene 22-foot 3-point right angle jumper	2-3
18:36	Mills 10-foot turnaround jumper	4-3
18:13	Vaught 18-foot jumper from left (assist Robinson)	6-3
17:39	Morton 22-foot 3-point right angle (assist Ramos)	6-6
15:45	Walker 6-foot turnaround by Walker (assist Morton)	6-8
15:32	Rice 13-foot jumper from left	8-8
14:55	Robinson 19-foot jumper from right	10-8
14:38	Rice dunk off break (assist Robinson)	12-8
14:16	MEDIA TIMEOUT	
13:50	Ramos dunk (assist Greene)	12-10
13:15	Robinson follow layup	14-10
13:01	Ramos 6-foot lane turnaround	14-12
12:13	Hughes 6-foot lane turnaround (assist Robinson)	16-12
10:31	Gaze 2 made free throws	16-14
10:07	Vaught reverse follow	18-14
9:33	Robinson bank flip (assist Griffin)	20-14
9:19	Walker layup (Avent assist)	20-16
8:34	Morton 6-foot lane jumper	20-18
8:19	Morton 14-foot jumper from left	20-20
8:19	MEDIA TIMEOUT	
7:11	Greene 21-foot 3-point jumper (assist Morton)	20-23
6:57	Morton 21-foot 3-point jumper from left (assist Gaze)	20-26
6:31	Rice 2 made free throws	22-26
6:03	Robinson 6-foot drive in lane	24-26
5:28	Wigington 7-foot lane jumper	24-28
5:05	Robinson driving layup	26-28
4:12	Rice 17-foot jumper (assist Robinson)	28-28
3:46	Ramos 8-foot bank (assist Walker)	28-30
3:46	MEDIA TIMEOUT	
3:16	Rice 22-foot 3-point jumper (assist Higgins)	31-30
2:47	Higgins driving layup	33-30
1:06	Robinson 2 made free throws	35-30
0:49	Greene 10-foot lane jumper	35-32
0:06	Robinson 2 made free throws	37-32

Second Half

Time	Play	U-M-SH
19:08	Mills 9-foot turnaround jumper	39-32
18:33	Ramos 4-foot bank from the lane	39-34
18:33	Ramos completes three-point play	39-35
18:20	Rice 18-foot jumper (assist Robinson)	41-35
18:04	Vaught 9-foot pullup jumper (assist Mills)	43-35
17:43	Robinson 1 made free throw	44-35
17:43	SETON HALL TIMEOUT	
17:34	Greene 10-foot jumper from the lane	44-37
17:19	Vaught 17-foot jumper (assist Griffin)	46-37
16:51	Rice 22-foot 3-point jumper (assist Robinson)	49-37
14:30	Morton 2 free throws made	49-39
14:17	Robinson driving dunk	51-39
13:07	Walker driving layup (Greene assist)	51-41
12:11	Greene 4-foot bank from the lane	51-43
11:59	MICHIGAN TIMEOUT	
11:40	Rice 7-foot bank from the lane	53-43
11:09	Avent follow flip	53-45
10:04	Morton 2 made free throws	53-47
9:45	Higgins 21-foot 3-pointer (assist Mills)	56-47
9:33	Morton 1 made free throw	56-48
9:01	Greene 1 made free throw	56-49
8:26	Rice 23-foot 3-pointer (Robinson assist)	59-49
8:13	Walker layup (Gaze assist)	59-51
7:47	Morton 2 made free throws	59-53
7:30	Morton layup on break	59-55
6:51	Morton 9-foot jumper	59-57
6:26	Robinson 2 made free throws	61-57
6:19	Morton 2 made free throws	61-59
6:05	Rice 23-foot 3-point jumper	64-59
4:07	Walker 2 made free throws	64-61
4:03	Mills 3-foot bank (Higgins assist)	66-61
4:03	MEDIA TIMEOUT	
2:57	Morton fast-break dunk (Greene assist)	66-63
2:38	Morton 14-foot base-line jumper (Greene assist)	66-65
2:13	Morton driving layup	66-67
2:01	MICHIGAN TIMEOUT	
1:12	Walker 1 made free throw	66-68
1:06	Rice 22-foot fallaway 3-point (Robinson assist)	69-68
0:34	Higgins 2 made free throws	71-68
0:34	SETON HALL TIMEOUT	
0:25	Morton 23-foot 3-pointer	71-71
0:17	MICHIGAN TIMEOUT	
0:17	MICHIGAN TIMEOUT	

Overtime

Time	Play	U-M-SH
4:53	Rice 9-foot jumper (Robinson assist)	73-71
4:43	Gaze 22-foot 3-point jumper (Morton assist)	73-74
3:45	Higgins 12-foot baseline jumper	75-74
3:23	Mills goaltending on Walker 6-footer	75-76
2:56	Higgins 1 made free throw	76-76
2:50	Morton 22-foot 3-pointer (Greene assist)	76-79
1:42	MEDIA TIMEOUT	
0:58	Mills 11-foot turnaround	78-79
0:03	SETON HALL TIMEOUT	
0:03	Robinson 2 made free throws	80-79
0:03	SETON HALL TIMEOUT	
0:03	MICHIGAN TIMEOUT	

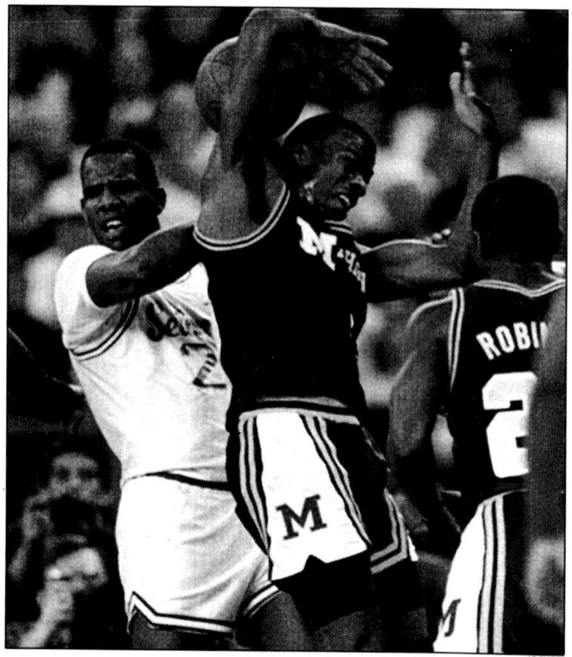

AP PHOTO

Ramon Ramos and Seton Hall didn't back off from Loy Vaught and Michigan in the final.

Game Boxscore

Michigan (80)

No Player	FG-Att 2-Pts	FG-Att 3-Pts	FT-Att	Reb O-D	PF	Pts	A	TO	Bk	S	Min
41 Glen Rice	12-25	5-12	2-2	1-10	2	31	0	2	0	0	42
52 Terry Mills	4-8	0-0	0-0	3-3	2	8	2	2	3	2	34
35 Loy Vaught	4-8	0-0	0-0	2-5	2	8	0	2	0	1	26
20 Mike Griffin	0-0	0-0	0-0	2-2	4	0	3	2	0	0	17
21 Rumeal Robinson	6-13	0-0	9-10	1-2	2	21	11	5	0	0	43
24 Sean Higgins	3-10	1-4	3-4	2-7	3	10	2	1	1	0	27
55 Mark Hughes	1-1	0-0	0-0	0-2	2	2	0	0	0	0	25
13 Demetrius Calip	0-2	0-0	0-0	0-0	3	0	1	0	0	0	11
Totals	30-67	6-16	14-16	12-33	20	80	19	14	4	3	225

Team rebounds included in totals.
Field-goal percentage: 50.0 first half (15-30), 40.5 second half and overtime (15-37), 44.8 game (30-67).
3-point percentage: 33.3 first half (1-3), 38.5 second half and overtime (5-13), 37.5 game (6-16).
Free-throw percentage: 100.0 first half (6-6), 80.0 second half and overtime (8-10), 87.5 game (14-16).

Seton Hall (79)

No Player	FG-Att 2-Pts	FG-Att 3-Pts	FT-Att	Reb O-D	PF	Pts	A	TO	Bk	S	Min
10 Andrew Gaze	1-5	1-5	2-2	2-1	3	5	3	2	0	1	39
24 Darryl Walker	5-9	0-1	3-4	3-8	2	13	1	2	0	0	39
24 Ramon Ramos	4-9	0-0	1-1	0-5	2	9	1	1	1	1	33
15 Gerald Greene	5-13	2-5	1-3	0-5	3	13	5	2	0	2	43
23 John Morton	11-26	4-12	9-10	1-3	3	35	3	3	0	0	37
31 Michael Cooper	0-0	0-0	0-0	0-2	1	0	0	1	1	0	14
32 Anthony Avent	1-2	0-0	0-0	1-2	0	2	1	0	0	0	11
30 Frantz Volcy	0-0	0-0	0-2	0-1	2	0	0	0	0	0	7
4 Pookie Wigington	1-1	0-0	0-0	0-0	1	2	0	0	0	0	2
Totals	28-65	7-23	16-22	9-27	17	79	14	11	2	4	225

Team rebounds included in totals.
Field-goal percentage: 40.6 first half (13-32), 45.5 second half and overtime (15-33), 43.1 game (28-65).
3-point percentage: 28.6 first half (4-14), 33.3 second half and overtime (3-9), 30.4 game (7-23).
Free-throw percentage: 50.0 first half (2-4), 77.8 second half and overtime (14-18), 72.7 game (16-22).

Score by halves: Michigan 37-34-9—80. Seton Hall 32-39-8—79. **Technicals:** none. **Officials:** Mickey Crowley, Tom Rucker, John Clougherty. **Attendance:** 39,187.

Scoring Leaders

Aggregate scoring leaders of the 1989 NCAA Tournament:

Player	Team	G	Pts	Avg
Glen Rice	Michigan	6	184	30.7
John Morton	Seton Hall	6	114	19.0
Danny Ferry	Duke	5	111	22.2
Richard Morgan	Virginia	4	106	26.5
Nick Anderson	Illinois	5	102	20.4
R. Robinson	Michigan	6	100	16.7
Phil Henderson	Duke	5	87	17.4
Rodney Monroe	N.C. State	3	86	28.7
Kenny Battle	Illinois	5	84	16.8
Andrew Gaze	Seton Hall	6	84	14.0
Bryant Stith	Virginia	4	82	20.5
Sean Higgins	Michigan	6	82	13.7

Rebound Leaders

Aggregate rebound leaders of the 1989 NCAA Tournament:

Player	Team	G	Reb	Avg
Daryll Walker	Seton Hall	6	58	9.7
Loy Vaught	Michigan	6	48	8.0
Nick Anderson	Illinois	5	46	9.2
Moses Scurry	UNLV	4	41	10.3
Ramon Ramos	Seton Hall	6	41	6.8
Glen Rice	Michigan	6	39	6.5
Terry Mills	Michigan	6	39	6.5
Danny Ferry	Duke	5	38	7.6
Brent Dabbs	Virginia	4	36	9.0
Billy Owens	Syracuse	4	35	8.8
Mark Hughes	Michigan	6	35	5.8

Assist Leaders

Aggregate assist leaders of the 1989 NCAA Tournament:

Player	Team	G	Ast	Avg
R. Robinson	Michigan	6	56	9.3
John Crotty	Virginia	4	39	9.8
S. Douglas	Syracuse	4	32	8.0
Steve Bucknall	NCarolina	3	28	9.3
Quin Snyder	Duke	5	28	5.6
Gerald Greene	Seton Hall	6	26	4.3
Greg Anthony	UNLV	4	25	6.3
Chris Corchiani	N.C. State	3	25	8.3
Steve Bardo	Ilinois	5	25	5.0
Kendall Gill	Illinois	5	22	4.4

Win

Stylish senior still U-M's hottest shot

By ALAN GREENBERG
HARTFORD COURANT

SEATTLE — When you get married, you throw rice. Old custom.

When you want to win a championship in 1989, you throw Rice at your opponent. New custom.

Notre Dame won the national championship when it threw Rice at West Virginia in the Fiesta Bowl. Quarterback Tony Rice was voted the game's outstanding player.

The 49ers won the Super Bowl when they threw Rice at the Cincinnati Bengals. Wide receiver Jerry Rice was voted the game's outstanding player.

Monday night at the Kingdome, the Michigan Wolverines threw Rice at Seton Hall. Forward Glen Rice was voted the game's outstanding player as Michigan beat Seton Hall in overtime, 80-79, to win its first NCAA basketball championship.

Rice's play?

"Almost indescribable," Michigan's interim coach, Steve Fisher, said.

We'll try anyway. Despite the fact Seton Hall's defense went after him like public enemy No. 1, the 6-7 senior forward led the Wolverines with 31 points and 11 rebounds. He also played the airtight defense that had a lot to do with the Pirates' John Morton — who scored a career-high 35 points — missing two key shots in the frantic final minute.

And when Morton's final shot, the would-be game-winner — a fadeaway 3-point jumper — turned out to be an airball, who slipped away from Morton and under the basket to haul it in as easily as Willie Mays making a basket catch?

Rice.

"My first move was to body (bump) him when he didn't have the ball," Rice said, "so when he did, he'd be off balance. I just wanted to make sure I had my hand in his face."

When Rice had the ball, about four different Seton Hall players took turns putting their hands in his face. That didn't keep Rice from making 12-of-25 field goal attempts, 5-of-12 from 3-point range.

Oh yeah. Monday night, Rice also broke Bill Bradley's NCAA Tournament scoring record and Mike McGee's Michigan career scoring record.

And afterward, he broke the NCAA Tournament's unofficial record for modesty, thanking his coach and teammates so many times you would have thought that his father had paid for his spot on the team.

"Overall, it's a great individual achievement," Rice admitted, when confronted with a litany of his accomplishments. "But, without my teammates and coaches, the accomplishments I made wouldn't be possible."

And without Rice, who won his

MICHIGAN

CONTINUED FROM B1

down, but he kept on coming," Greene said of Robinson. "I took some at him, he took some at me. He did some good for his club, I did some good for mine."

Nobody's better.

Michigan leads by 12 in the second half. Seton Hall fights back and takes a 68-66 lead with 1:12 left.

Michigan scores five unanswered points. Leads 71-68 with 34 seconds left.

Seton Hall's John Morton ties it with a 3-pointer. Overtime.

"We're never going to go down without a fight," Morton said. "You have to go out and beat us because we're not going to give up."

Talk may be cheap, but it's a way of life on the playground.

"Oh, the game wouldn't be any fun if there was no conversation out there," Robinson said.

There was Morton with the ball, isolated on Glen Rice.

"Come on, baby, come on," he'd say. Then, whoosh, he would scoot past the Rice for an easy basket.

Then there was Rice. He talks with his jump shot. As he releases his shot, he's knocked to the floor. Swish. The shot falls. Rice, picking himself up, smiles at the defender.

Nobody's better.

There was Robinson. At the line. three seconds left. Michigan down a point.

"Morton starts laughing at me, trying to throw me off," Robinson said. "I just start laughing back at him. I wasn't about to let him get at me."

ning recipe: Just add Rice

AP PHOTO

Glen Rice and U-M never gave Seton Hall sharpshooter Andrew Gaze a free moment, holding him to 5 points.

The Rice Breakdown

Game-by-game performances by Michigan's Glen Rice in the 1989 NCAA Tournament:

Game	Min	FG	FT	3-Pt	R	A	Pts
U-M 92, Xavier 87	40	9-22	0-0	5-9	3	2	23
U-M 91, South Alabama 82	37	16-25	1-1	3-7	8	5	36
U-M 92, North Carolina 87	37	13-19	0-0	8-12	6	2	34
U-M 102, Virginia 65	32	13-19	2-2	4-5	6	2	32
U-M 83, Illinois 81	37	12-24	2-2	2-4	8	1	28
U-M 80, Seton Hall 79	34	12-25	2-2	5-12	11	0	31
Totals	227	75-131	7-7	27-48	42	12	184

Scoring Leaders

All-time scoring leaders in the NCAA Tournament:

Pts	Player	School	Year	G
184	Glen Rice	Michigan	1989	6
177	Bill Bradley	Princeton	1965	5
167	Elvin Hayes	Houston	1968	5
163	Danny Manning	Kansas	1988	6
160	Hal Leer	Temple	1956	5
160	Jerry West	W. Virginia	1959	5
158	Austin Carr	Notre Dame	1970	3
158	Joe Barry Carroll	Purdue	1980	6
153	Johnny Dawkins	Duke	1986	6
152	Stacey King	Oklahoma	1988	6
147	Jim McDaniels	W. Kentucky	1971	5

Big Ten's Best

All-time scoring leaders in the Big Ten:

Player	School	Points	Seasons
Glen Rice	Michigan	2,442	1985-89
Mike McGee	Michigan	2,439	1977-81
Steve Alford	Indiana	2,438	1983-87
Rick Mount	Purdue	2,323	1968-70
Gary Grant	Michigan	2,222	1984-88
Don Schlundt	Indiana	2,192	1952-55
Cazzie Russell	Michigan	2,164	1964-66
Joe Barry Carroll	Purdue	2,147	1977-80
Scott Skiles	Michigan State	2,145	1983-86
Dennis Hopson	Ohio State	2,096	1983-87
Dave Schellhase	Purdue	2,074	1964-66

Michigan's Best

All-time scoring leaders at Michigan:

Player	Points	Seasons
Glen Rice	2,442	1985-89
Mike McGee	2,439	1977-81
Gary Grant	2,222	1984-88
Cazzie Russell	2,164	1964-66
Rudy Tomjanovich	1,808	1968-70
Bill Buntin	1,725	1963-65
Henry Wilmore	1,652	1971-73
Roy Tarpley	1,601	1982-86
Antoine Joubert	1,594	1983-87
Phil Hubbard	1,455	1976-79
John Tidwell	1,386	1959-61

second consecutive Big Ten scoring championship this season and entered Monday night's game averaging 25.5 points, the Wolverines probably wouldn't have even been included in the 64-team tournament field, let alone standing atop it.

"He has been as good as there is," Fisher said. "Nobody has done more for Michigan basketball than Glen Rice, not just over a six-game tournament, but over a career. It's the way he plays, with the all-out effort all the time, in practice as well as in a game."

Rice shoots like he's in practice, his form as fluid in the final seconds of a championship game as it is shooting jumpers in an empty gym. Rice made 58 percent of his field-goal attempts this season, an incredible percentage when you consider that most of his shots are jumpers from the perimeter.

Against Virginia in the Southeast Regional final, Rice made 13-of-16 field-goal attempts, 4-of-5 from 3-point range, and virtually blew the Cavaliers halfway back to Charlottesville all by his lonesome. If Rice isn't a sure-fire NBA forward next season, it'll be because they closed down the league.

Watching Rice this season and in this tournament, you would think that he had been everyone's All-Everything his entire basketball life. Not quite true. Growing up in Flint, he was Michigan's Mr. Basketball as a high school senior, but unlike three of his Wolverine teammates, was not a McDonald's All-American. What's more, he was among John Thompson's first cuts at the Olympic Trials. Makes you wonder what was going through the coach's mind.

Monday night, the main thing going through Seton Hall's mind was stop Rice. For that, the main responsibility went to Australian import Andrew Gaze, who got so worn out chasing Rice that he never got his own offensive game together. Gaze, a key factor in Seton Hall's comeback against Duke in Saturday's semifinal, made only 1 of 5 field goal attempts Monday night and finished with five points.

It was Gaze who was guarding Rice when Rice's would-be game winner with one second left in regulation, an 19-foot jumper, hit the rim twice and fell away, necessitating overtime.

"I was shocked (that he missed) because I was very much open," Rice said. "It (the shot) took a couple of bad bounces. Their defensive pressure was at times very good. They were very aggressive. They weren't letting me make the moves I wanted to make.

Missing that shot at the buzzer left Rice with one college fantasy unfulfilled.

But after a night like this, he wasn't about to complain.

AP PHOTOS

Rumeal Robinson signals making 1st free throw, then KOs Seton Hall with game-winner in OT.

You don't show fear. Playground mentality.

You hope people have forgotten that night in Wisconsin last January — that night you missed two free throws with seven seconds left and the team lost 71-68. You don't want them to know that for the next two weeks you came early to practice and shot 100 extra free throws every day.

"I felt I let the team down," Robinson said. "I wasn't going to do it again."

Swish. Swish. Michigan 80, Seton Hall 79. National champions.

Nobody's better.

"I was so happy I started to cry," said Higgins. "I had to run off by myself. I have a big ego, I can't let people see me cry."

Win or lose, you don't cry. Playground mentality.

Losers walk off the court with their heads high.

"We showed people a lot," said Seton Hall's Ramon Ramos. "No one expected us to get this far. Really, this was quite an accomplishment."

Winners stay and celebrate.

"I was sitting in my room last night watching the highlights of all the championship games from years past," Robinson said. "I can see myself 20 years from today sitting in my livingroom and watching us win the championship all over again. This moment will be with me the rest of my life."

Nobody's better.

BECKETT

CONTINUED FROM B1

It must have seemed that every one wanted to ask about how a benefactor had bought a plane ticket for Robinson's adopted father, Louis Ford, so he could fly from Cambridge, Mass. to Seattle for Saturday's semifinal game against Illinois.

Over and over, Robinson had to discuss how his mother had abandoned him when he was 10. He had to tell how Louis Ford had arrived in Seattle too late to see him play. He had to bare his soul, open old wounds.

It had to be hard, every bit as hard as standing at that free throw stripe with the fate of his team hanging on his shoulders. But he persevered, he hung in there, and he succeeded.

"I had all the confidence in the world," said Helen Ford, Robinson's adopted mother, as she awaited him outside the lockerroom. "He's the type of kid who gets the job done."

A few feet away, Robinson's six-year-old brother Louie, whom Robinson calls his good luck charm, rode atop a friend's shoulders and beamed brightly. "I was a little scared," he admitted, "but I thought he'd make it. I loved it."

So did Griffin, who wrapped an arm around Robinson and whispered in his ear between his two free throws.

"In our huddle before every game this year, Rumeal has said, 'God helps those who help themselves,'" Griffin said. "I just reminded him of that."

Then Robinson stepped forward and proved the truth of those words. He proved the value of hanging in there, of working hard, of never giving up, of keeping the faith.

It was justice. Sweet, sweet justice.

Final Four Notes _____

Among the more unusual figures were the following:

- Steve Fisher is the first rookie coach ever to win the NCAA basketball championship. He is also the first-ever interim coach to advance to the Final Four.

- Glen Rice finished the 1989 NCAA tournament with 184 points, breaking Bill Bradley's (Princeton, 1965) record. Rice also eclipsed tourney records for total field goals with 75 (old record: 70 by Elvin Hayes of Houston in 1968) and three point FG's with 27 (old record: 26 by Freddie Banks of UNLV in 1987).

- In the process, Rice also shattered the Michigan and Big Ten all-time scoring marks formerly held by Mike McGee. Rice finishes his career with 2,442 points, just three ahead of McGee's 2,439.

- Rice was selected Most Outstanding Player of both the Southeast Regional as well as the Final Four. He joins notable Rices Jerry (Super Bowl MVP - 49ers) and Tony (Fiesta Bowl MVP - Notre Dame) in 1989.

- Joining Rice on the Final Four All-Tournament team were teammate Rumeal Robinson, John Morton and Gerald Greene of Seton Hall and Duke forward Danny Ferry.

- Michigan is the first school in NCAA history to win the NCAA Basketball Championship and the Rose Bowl in the same year. The Wolverines defeated USC, 22-14, on January 2 in Pasadena.

- Michigan's overtime victory was the first in a title game since 1963 when Loyola (IL) edged Cincinnati, 60-58, in OT at Freedom Hall in Louisville, KY.

- Rumeal Robinson's 11 assists established a new championship game record (old record: 9 by Alvin Franklin in 1984). Robinson's two-game total of 23 also set a new Final Four assist mark (old record: 20 by Michael Jackson of Georgetown in 1985).

- The crowd of 39,187 was the third-largest to witness a championship game.

- There were 12 lead changes and six ties in the title contest. Michigan's largest lead was 12 (49-37 & 51-39) while Seton Hall's biggest bulge was six (26-20).

- Incidental stats from the title game: Michigan made 30 substitutions while Seton Hall made just 19, and Michigan had a firm advantage in bench scoring, 12-4.

- Real Incidental Stat: The Michigan Basketball Band played "The Victors" 14 times during the final game.

- Michigan set a school record for wins in a season in 1988-89, ended the year with a 30-7 mark. The Wolverines were 27-2 when leading at halftime, 29-1 when leading with five minutes left in regulation, and 2-0 in overtime contests.

- Michigan's final shooting percentage of 56.6 led the nation in 1988-89. It marked the second consecutive year that the Wolverines have accomplished that feat.

- Michigan became the fifth Big Ten school to win the NCAA Basketball Championship. The others are Indiana (5 titles), Michigan State, Ohio State and Wisconsin (one title each).

- Michigan led the Big Ten to a 15-4 record during the NCAA Tournament. The cumulative 78.9 winning percentage for those five teams (U-M, Illinois, Indiana, Minnesota, and Iowa) topped all other conferences.

After Title Game Quotes_____

STEVE FISHER . . .

"I have to think for an observer who didn't care who won, it had to be a terrific, terrific game to watch. It was emotionally draining for the players and coaches I'm sure for both teams. We got a couple of lucky bounces down the stretch. It looked at times we had a 12-point lead and I kept saying to myself 'one more basket, one more basket, and we are going to be able to maintain that double-figure lead,' but Seton Hall would not allow that to happen. Just as they have done all season, and in particular in this tournament, they turned up the defensive pressure a notch. I couldn't be prouder to be a part of this Michigan team that just won the national championship, a moment and an event that we will all have with us forever."

COACH FISHER . . .

(Last Moments): "We said we wanted to try to get it and go down quickly with it to try to get something out of the flow in hopes Rumeal could take it all the way; someway we would find Glen popping open for a screen. I think our first thought was find Glen, as it has been all season, all tournament. Rumeal is so good in the open court. He's very, very difficult to handle. He's so strong he can take it in and get bumped and shoved and still get his shot off. We were hopeful that would happen, and fortunately for all of us, it did."

RUMEAL ROBINSON . . .

"Coach Fisher told me if I had the chance to get the ball down the court, get it down real quick. I saw they were getting back on defense kind of slow so I was going to take it on my shoulders and get the last shot. They fouled me and thank God — I could have missed those shots that went in. Thank God they went in for me and that we are national champions."

LOY VAUGHT . . .

(On Last Three Seconds): "I was just praying he [Rumeal] would make them. He's our crunch man down the stretch. We knew it would be a game for 40 minutes no matter what happened. That helped us down the stretch. They didn't fold but this team has great character. We rebound in the crunch, hit free throws down the stretch."

SEAN HIGGINS . . .

(His Feelings After Game) "It's too much to say right now. I'm amazed I can talk right now." "Well, Glen is a great player. Whatever team in the NBA gets him, he'll be a force for them. He's a great guy, and I wish him the best."

MIKE GRIFFIN . . .

(Said Initially In Locker Room) "The university president talked and told us how proud he was of us and how proud the university, the state and the nation was of this team. He said he has been real proud of the football team on many occasions but this was a special kind of pride for this basketball team."

MARK HUGHES . . .

"Those were some anxious moments, but we knew when they were 12 down, they wouldn't die or quit. They came back from 18 down the other day. I'm just real happy but it hasn't hit me yet that we are national champs."

COACH P. J. CARLESIMO (Seton Hall) . . .

"Michigan is a great basketball team. They played a little bit better than we did and deserve to be the national champion. When it came down to it, they made a couple of big shots, and they made some enormous free throws, and we missed a couple. They shot 87 percent from the free throw line and I think when two good teams play, a lot of times that can be the difference."

ANDREW GAZE (Seton Hall) . . .

"Defensively they [Michigan] presented a lot of problems for me, and I had my hands full with Rice at the other end. He's just an incredible individual, with such a quick release. They send him through a lot of screens. It didn't seem as though he was missing. I was there most of the time, but it wasn't good enough."

Michigan Wolverines Statistics

NAME	G	ST	TOTAL FG FG	FGA	PCT	3-PT FG FG	FGA	PCT	FREE THROWS FT	FTA	PCT	REBOUNDS OFF	DEF	TOT	AVG	PF	DIS	AST	TO	BLK	STL	AVG MIN	PTS	AVG
Rice	37	37	363	629	57.7	99	192	51.6	124	149	83.2	77	155	232	6.3	75	1	85	81	11	39	34	949	25.6
Robinson	37	36	199	357	55.7	30	64	46.9	122	186	65.6	31	94	125	3.4	105	5	233	131	4	70	30	550	14.9
Vaught	37	21	201	304	66.1	2	5	40.0	63	81	77.8	94	202	296	8.0	94	3	36	50	11	19	23	467	12.6
Mills	37	37	180	319	56.4	0	2	.0	70	91	76.9	74	144	218	5.9	95	3	104	77	49	20	27	430	11.6
Higgins	34	16	158	312	50.6	51	110	46.4	54	70	77.1	31	76	107	3.1	76	2	51	60	11	10	23	421	12.4
Hughes	35	4	104	171	60.8	1	2	50.0	29	48	60.4	41	101	142	4.1	58	0	40	26	7	12	20	238	6.8
Griffin	37	31	33	65	50.8	0	2	.0	33	43	76.7	24	65	89	2.4	104	3	103	56	9	24	23	99	2.7
Taylor	21	2	33	69	47.8	7	18	38.9	22	36	61.1	12	34	46	2.2	30	1	46	23	6	20	17	95	4.5
Calip	30	0	22	50	44.0	2	9	22.2	14	17	82.4	5	14	19	.6	19	0	25	23	0	7	7	60	2.0
Oosterbaan	22	0	22	39	56.4	0	1	.0	9	13	69.2	9	17	26	1.2	15	0	11	9	3	0	5	53	2.4
Pelinka	26	1	9	25	36.0	4	14	28.6	7	10	70.0	5	10	15	.6	7	0	10	12	2	3	4	29	1.1
Koenig	7	0	1	1	100.0	0	0	.0	0	0	.0	0	1	1	.1	1	0	1	3	0	2	1	2	.3

Rice — HIGHS: PTS 38 vs Wisconsin | RBS 11 vs Western Michigan | AST 8 vs. Youngstown State

Robinson — HIGHS: PTS 24 vs Minnesota | RBS 8 vs Western Michigan | AST 13 vs North Carolina

Vaught — HIGHS: PTS 26 vs Youngstown State | RBS 16 vs Illinois | AST 3 vs Grambling State

Mills — HIGHS: PTS 24 vs South Alabama | RBS 13 vs. Northern Michigan | AST 7 vs Youngstown State

Higgins — HIGHS: PTS 31 vs Virginia | RBS 13 vs Seton Hall | AST 5 vs Ohio State

Hughes — HIGHS: PTS 21 vs Holy Cross | RBS 12 vs Western Michigan | AST 5 vs Indiana

Griffin — HIGHS PTS 8 vs Grambling State | RBS 8 vs Northern Michigan | AST 8 vs Northern Michigan

Taylor — HIGHS: PTS 12 vs Oklahoma | RBS 6 vs Tampa | AST 6 vs Oklahoma

Calip — HIGHS: PTS 9 vs Xavier | RBS 5 vs Virginia | AST 5 vs South Alabama

Oosterbaan — HIGHS: PTS 10 vs Northern Michigan | RBS 4 vs Tampa | AST 3 vs Western Michigan

Pelinka — HIGHS: PTS 8 vs Holy Cross | RBS 5 vs Holy Cross | AST 2 vs Northern Michigan

Koenig — HIGHS: PTS 2 vs Youngstown State | RBS 1 vs Northern Michigan | AST 1 vs Central Michigan

														TOT	AVG				TO					
TEAM														79	2.1				6					

NAME	G		FG	FGA	PCT	FG	FGA	PCT	FT	FTA	PCT	OFF	DEF	TOT	AVG	PF	DIS	AST	TO	BLK	STL		PTS	AVG
TOTAL	37		1325	2341	56.6	196	419	46.8	547	744	73.5	403	992	1395	37.7	679	18	745	557	113	226		3393	91.7
OPPONENTS	37		1055	2322	45.4	164	466	35.2	493	710	69.4	395	726	1121	30.3	705	15	514	578	36	237		2767	74.8

TOTAL — HIGHS: PTS 125 vs Northern Michigan | RBS 56 vs Iowa | AST 29 vs Holy Cross

OPPONENTS — HIGHS PTS 107 vs Iowa | RBS 54 vs Iowa | AST 24 vs North Carolina

	MICHIGAN	OPPONENTS
DEADBALL REBOUNDS	81	100

Play-by-Play

51st Annual National College Basketball Championship
The Kingdome — Seattle, Washington   *Championship Game — April 3, 1989*
The University of Michigan Wolverines vs. Seton Hall University Pirates

First Half

Time	Play	UM-SH Score (*lead change)
19:54	Rice right jumper	2- 0
19:26	Greene 3 pointer	2- 3*
18:36	Mills 10 ft	* 4- 3
18:13	Vaught left jumper	6- 3
17:39	Morton right jumper	6- 6
15:45	Walker 6 ft	6- 8*
15:32	Rice left jumper	8- 8
14:55	Robinson right jumper	*10- 8
14:38	Rice fast break	12- 8
13:50	Ramos dunk	12-10
13:15	Robinson layup	14-10
13:01	Ramos 6 ft	14-12
12:13	Hughes 6 ft	16-12
10:31	Gaze 2 FTs	16-14
10:07	Vaught followup	18-14
9:33	Robinson flip	20-14
9:19	Walker layup	20-16
8:34	Morton jumper	20-18
8:19	Morton left jumper	20-20
7:11	Greene 3 pt	20-23*
6:57	Greene 3 pt	20-26
6:31	Rice 2 free throws	22-26
6:03	Robinson 6 ft	24-26
5:20	Wigington 7 ft	24-28
5:05	Robinson driving	26-28
4:12	Rice left jumper	28-28
3:46	Ramos 8 ft	28-30
3:16	Rice 3 pt	*31-30
2:47	Higgins layup	33-30
1:06	Robinson 2 FTs	35-30
:49	Greene 10 ft	35-32
:06	Robinson 2 FTs	37-32

Second Half

Time	Play	UM-SH Score (*lead change)
19:08	Mills 9 ft.	39-32
18:33	Ramos 4 ft.	39-34
18:33	Ramos 1 FT	39-35
18:20	Rice left jumper	41-35
18:04	Vaught fast break	43-35
17:43	Robinson 1 FT	44-35
17:34	Green 10 ft	44-37
17:19	Vaught 17 ft	46-37
16:51	Rice 3 pt	49-37
14:30	Morton 2 FT	49-39
14:17	Robinson driving	51-39
13:07	Walker driving	51-41
12:11	Greene 4 ft	51-43
11:40	Rice 7 ft	53-43
11:09	Avent followup	53-45
10:04	Morton 2 FT	53-47
9:54	Higgins 3 pt	56-47
9:33	Morton 2 FT	56-48
9:01	Greene 1 FT	56-49
8:26	Rice 3 pt	59-49
8:13	Walker layup	59-51
7:47	Morton 2 FT	59-53
7:30	Morton fast break	59-55
6:51	Morton 9 ft	59-57
6:26	Robinson 2 FT	61-57
6:19	Morton 2 FT	61-59
6:05	Rice 3 pt	64-59
4:07	Walker 2 FT	64-61
4:07	Walker 2 FT	66-61
2:57	Morton dunk	66-63
2:38	Morton 14 ft	66-65
2:13	Morton layup	66-67*
1:12	Walker 1 FT	66-68
1:06	Rice 3 pt	*69-68
:34	Higgins 2 FT	71-68
:25	Morton 3 pt	71-71

Overtime

Time	Play	UM-SH Score (*lead change)
4:53	Rice 9 ft	73-71
4:43	Gaze 3 pt	73-74*
3:45	Higgins left jumper	*75-74
3:23	Walker 6 ft	75-76*
2:56	Higgins 1 FT	76-76
2:50	Morton 3 pt	76-79
:56	Mills 11 ft	78-79
:03	Robinson 2 FT	*80-79

Final
Michigan 80   Seton Hall 79

Official Box Score

SEMIFINAL #2 — University of Michigan vs. Illinois

No.	Name	Pos	Total FG FG	FGA	3-point FG	FGA	FT	FTA	REB	PF	TP	A	TO	BLK	S	MIN
41	Rice, Glen	f	12	24	2	4	2	2	5	1	28	1	0	0	3	37
52	Mills, Terry	f	4	8	0	0	0	0	9	4	8	5	2	1	0	31
35	Vaught, Loy	c	5	13	0	0	0	0	16	2	10	0	0	0	0	29
20	Griffin, Mike	g	0	1	0	0	0	0	1	2	0	3	1	0	2	17
21	Robinson, Rumeal	g	6	13	0	1	2	5	1	4	14	12	5	0	1	40
55	Hughes, Mark		4	5	0	0	1	1	6	3	9	1	2	0	0	19
24	Higgins, Sean		5	12	1	3	3	3	3	2	14	1	2	2	0	24
13	Calip, Demetrius		0	1	0	0	0	0	0	2	0	0	0	0	0	3
	TOTALS		36	77	3	8	8	11	45	20	83	23	12	3	6	200

Deadball Rebounds — 1

Illinois

No.	Name	Pos	Total FG FG	FGA	3-point FG	FGA	FT	FTA	REB	PF	TP	A	TO	BLK	S	MIN
25	Anderson, Nick	f	6	14	0	1	5	6	7	1	17	2	2	0	2	35
33	Battle, Kenny	f	10	17	1	1	8	10	7	2	29	1	1	1	0	40
45	Hamilton, Lowell	c	5	14	0	0	1	2	9	5	11	0	1	0	1	34
13	Gill, Kendall	g	5	9	0	2	1	1	4	1	11	2	1	0	3	40
35	Bardo, Steve	g	1	7	1	3	4	4	6	3	7	8	5	1	0	32
23	Smith, Larry		3	5	0	1	0	0	2	2	6	1	1	0	0	18
24	Small, Ervin		0	0	0	0	0	0	0	2	0	0	0	0	0	6
30	Liberty, Marcus		0	1	0	0	0	0	0	0	0	0	0	0	0	5
	TOTALS		30	67	2	8	19	23	39	16	81	14	11	2	6	200

Deadball Rebounds — 0

NCAA CHAMPIONSHIP GAME (FINAL) — University of Michigan vs. Seton Hall

No.	Name	Pos	Total FG FG	FGA	3-point FG	FGA	FT	FTA	REB	PF	TP	A	TO	BLK	S	MIN
41	Rice, Glen	f	12	25	5	12	2	2	11	2	31	0	2	0	0	42
52	Mills, Terry	f	4	8	0	0	0	0	6	2	8	2	2	3	2	34
35	Vaught, Loy	c	4	8	0	0	0	0	7	2	8	0	2	0	1	26
20	Griffin, Mike	g	0	0	0	0	0	0	4	4	0	3	2	0	0	17
21	Robinson, Rumeal	g	6	13	0	0	9	10	3	2	21	11	5	0	0	43
24	Higgins, Sean		3	10	1	4	3	4	9	3	10	2	1	1	0	27
55	Hughes, Mark		1	1	0	0	0	0	2	2	2	0	0	0	0	25
13	Calip, Demetrius		0	2	0	0	0	0	0	3	0	1	0	0	0	11
	TOTALS		30	67	6	16	14	16	45	20	80	19	14	4	3	225

Deadball Rebounds — 0

Seton Hall

No.	Name	Pos	Total FG FG	FGA	3-point FG	FGA	FT	FTA	REB	PF	TP	A	TO	BLK	S	MIN
10	Gaze, Andrew	f	1	5	1	5	2	2	3	3	5	3	2	0	1	39
24	Walker, Darryll	f	5	9	0	1	3	4	11	2	13	1	2	0	0	39
25	Ramos, Ramon	c	4	9	0	0	1	1	5	2	9	1	1	1	1	33
15	Greene, Gerald	g	5	13	2	5	1	3	5	3	13	5	2	0	2	43
23	Morton, John	g	11	26	4	12	9	10	4	3	35	3	3	0	0	37
31	Cooper, Michael		0	0	0	0	0	0	2	1	0	0	1	1	0	14
32	Avent, Anthony		1	2	0	0	0	0	3	0	2	1	0	0	0	11
30	Volcy, Frantz		0	0	0	0	0	2	1	2	0	0	0	0	0	7
04	Wigington, Pookey		1	1	0	0	0	0	0	1	2	0	0	0	0	2
	TOTALS		28	65	7	23	16	22	36	17	79	14	11	2	4	225

Deadball Rebounds — 1

ROAD TO SEATTLE: NCAA Div. I Men's Basketball Championship

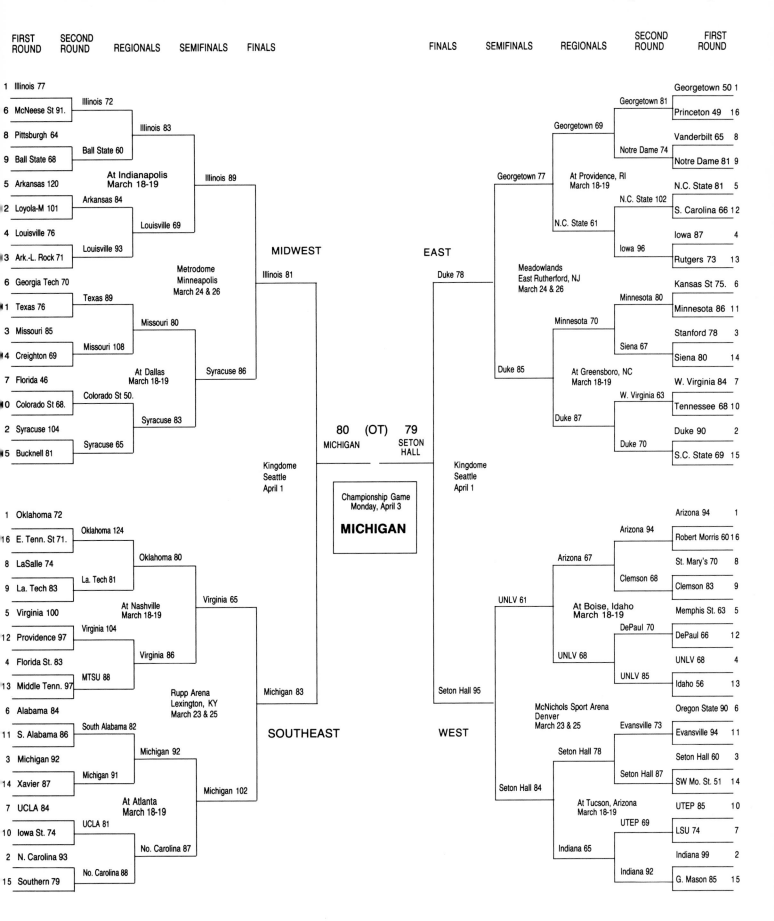

FIRST ROUND · SECOND ROUND · REGIONALS · SEMIFINALS · FINALS · FINALS · SEMIFINALS · REGIONALS · SECOND ROUND · FIRST ROUND

MIDWEST

1 Illinois 77
6 McNeese St 91.
  Illinois 72
8 Pittsburgh 64
9 Ball State 68
  Ball State 60
  Illinois 83
5 Arkansas 120
2 Loyola-M 101
  Arkansas 84
4 Louisville 76
3 Ark.-L. Rock 71
  Louisville 93
  Louisville 69
  Illinois 89
At Indianapolis March 18-19

6 Georgia Tech 70
1 Texas 76
  Texas 89
3 Missouri 85
4 Creighton 69
  Missouri 108
  Missouri 80
7 Florida 46
0 Colorado St 68.
  Colorado St 50.
2 Syracuse 104
5 Bucknell 81
  Syracuse 65
  Syracuse 83
  Syracuse 86
At Dallas March 18-19

Metrodome Minneapolis March 24 & 26

Illinois 81

EAST

Georgetown 50 1
Princeton 49 16
  Georgetown 81
Vanderbilt 65 8
Notre Dame 81 9
  Notre Dame 74
  Georgetown 69
N.C. State 81 5
S. Carolina 66 12
  N.C. State 102
Iowa 87 4
Rutgers 73 13
  Iowa 96
  N.C. State 61
  Georgetown 77
At Providence, RI March 18-19

Kansas St 75. 6
Minnesota 86 11
  Minnesota 80
Stanford 78 3
Siena 80 14
  Siena 67
  Minnesota 70
W. Virginia 84 7
Tennessee 68 10
  W. Virginia 63
Duke 90 2
S.C. State 69 15
  Duke 70
  Duke 87
  Duke 85
At Greensboro, NC March 18-19

Meadowlands East Rutherford, NJ March 24 & 26

Duke 78

Kingdome Seattle April 1

80 (OT) 79
MICHIGAN   SETON HALL

Championship Game Monday, April 3
MICHIGAN

Kingdome Seattle April 1

SOUTHEAST

1 Oklahoma 72
16 E. Tenn. St 71.
  Oklahoma 124
8 LaSalle 74
9 La. Tech 83
  La. Tech 81
  Oklahoma 80
5 Virginia 100
12 Providence 97
  Virginia 104
4 Florida St. 83
13 Middle Tenn. 97
  MTSU 88
  Virginia 86
  Virginia 65
At Nashville March 18-19

6 Alabama 84
11 S. Alabama 86
  South Alabama 82
3 Michigan 92
14 Xavier 87
  Michigan 91
  Michigan 92
7 UCLA 84
10 Iowa St. 74
  UCLA 81
2 N. Carolina 93
15 Southern 79
  No. Carolina 88
  No. Carolina 87
  Michigan 102
At Atlanta March 18-19

Rupp Arena Lexington, KY March 23 & 25

Michigan 83

WEST

Arizona 94 1
Robert Morris 60 16
  Arizona 94
St. Mary's 70 8
Clemson 83 9
  Clemson 68
  Arizona 67
Memphis St. 63 5
DePaul 66 12
  DePaul 70
UNLV 68 4
Idaho 56 13
  UNLV 85
  UNLV 68
  UNLV 61
At Boise, Idaho March 18-19

Oregon State 90 6
Evansville 94 11
  Evansville 73
Seton Hall 60 3
SW Mo. St. 51 14
  Seton Hall 87
  Seton Hall 78
UTEP 85 10
LSU 74 7
  UTEP 69
Indiana 99 2
G. Mason 85 15
  Indiana 92
  Indiana 65
  Seton Hall 84
At Tucson, Arizona March 18-19

McNichols Sport Arena Denver March 23 & 25

Seton Hall 95

UMI Publications publishes the ACC Basketball Handbook Magazine and The Southeastern Basketball Handbook Magazine. For subscription information, phone 704-374-0420.